BLUE TROUT
AND BLACK TRUFFLES

The Peregrinations of an Epicure

BOOKS BY

Joseph Wechsberg

BLUE TROUT
AND BLACK TRUFFLES
1953

THE
CONTINENTAL TOUCH
1948

SWEET AND SOUR
1948

HOMECOMING
1946

LOOKING
FOR A BLUEBIRD
1945

BLUE TROUT AND BLACK TRUFFLES

*The Peregrinations
of an Epicure
by Joseph Wechsberg*

Academy
Chicago
Publishers

Published by
Academy Chicago Publishers
363 West Erie Street
Chicago, Illinois 60610

First printing 1985
Second printing 2001

Library of Congress Cataloging-in-Publication Data

Wechsberg, Joseph, 1907–
    Blue trout and black truffles.
    Reprint: Originally published: New York: Knopf, 1954.
    1. Restaurants, lunch rooms, etc.—France.
2. Wine and wine making—France. I. Title.
TX910.F8W37   1985   647'.9544   85-3847
ISBN 0-89733-134-6

TO ANN,

MY LADY CHEF

THE AUTHOR'S THANKS are hereby made to the following magazines in which several of the chapters of this book originally appeared in somewhat different form: To *The Atlantic* for "Provence without Garlic"; to *Cosmopolitan* for "The Ladies from Maxim's"; to *Gourmet* for "Tafelspitz for the Hofrat" and "A Dish for Lucullus"; to *Holiday* for "Black Truffles," "The Mysterious Fish Soup," and "Worth a Special Journey"; and to *The New Yorker* for "A Balatoni Fogas to Start With," "Connoisseurs and Patriots," and "The Finest Butter and Lots of Time."

CONTENTS

BLUE TROUT
AND BLACK TRUFFLES

The Peregrinations of an Epicure

tra - la   tra - la   tra - la - la - la   la - la,

tra - la - lah,   tra - la - lah,   trah - lah - lah

SEVENTEENTH-CENTURY BURGUNDY WINE SONG

"Someday he'll want to eat
more than he's going to get."
DR. HIMMELBLAU

MY DELICATE CHILDHOOD,

OR: THE EDUCATION

OF A GOURMET

Nowadays I travel hundreds of miles and don't mind crossing international boundaries to lunch at one of my favorite restaurants, but I wasn't always like that.

As a child, I used to run away from food. I would chew on a bite of meat and refuse to swallow until my mother promised to let me go to the cinema. When I was a first-grader in Ostrava, my home town in Moravia, I would get sick every morning at the sight of my breakfast.

The grown-ups said I was a delicate, nervous child, over-sensitive and afraid of school. They were wrong. I didn't mind school—until the ten o'clock recess. Then the boys and girls would unpack their sandwiches and hard-boiled eggs, and I would turn green in the face and get sick again. I couldn't stand the smell of food.

In these years I was kept alive on a diet of frankfurters and cocoa. I had to be tricked into swallowing frankfurters and cocoa in odd moments of mental bemusement. Other foods had to be camouflaged to look and taste like frankfurters or cocoa before I would touch them. It might have been easier to feed me intravenously. I was a spoiled brat, but that's hindsight, of course.

People on the street would stop my mother and inquire about my sallow face. They said I must be quite ill, poor boy. My mother would start to cry. She had the ability to laugh and cry in the same breath, but in those days I rarely made her laugh.

Marie, our old cook, and Fräulein Gertrud, the governess, proffered various suggestions to break the deadlock of my stomach. They thought I should take long walks in the fresh air, or go to the mountains or to the sea. Sometimes they said I needed a good spanking.

Luckily, my father had no confidence in such amateurish suggestions. He knew that there was nothing wrong with me; the women just didn't handle me intelligently. To prove his point, he would take me out on Sunday mornings. We would get on the streetcar for Svinov, a dreary factory suburb, and for two hours we would ride back and forth. My father bribed the motorman to let me push my foot down on the bell; sometimes I was permitted to turn the wheel of the mechanical brake. The streetcar began to jolt and the people

(4)

inside would berate the motorman; once there was a fight and a policeman had to be summoned. In wintertime it was cold on the motorman's platform, but my father would stand next to me, and he didn't mind the cold. He seemed to enjoy the ride.

Afterward we would walk over to the Konditorei Wollgart, the best confectionery in town. I was still elated from driving the streetcar, and the sight of chocolate-coated *Indianer,* cakes, patisserie, *Sachertorte* with whipped cream wasn't repulsive at all. I would eat a couple of *Indianer* dreaming of a bright future when I was going to drive a streetcar all by myself.

When we came home, the air was filled with the aroma of the Sunday dinner. My face would turn green.

My father told my mother about the *Indianer.* "The boy would eat everything if you women would only treat him right," he would say.

The soup was served. I got sick. Small wonder, my mother said, acidly. After all that stuff I'd eaten at the *Konditorei.*

When I had one of my fits of prolonged starvation, refusing even frankfurters and cocoa, my father would call up Dr. Himmelblau, the family physician.

"Anything serious?" Dr. Himmelblau would ask. "I'll be right over."

"We-ll," my father would say, cautiously. He was a man of quiet dignity and he couldn't tell a lie. "He—he doesn't want to eat."

"Oh," Dr. Himmelblau would say. "I—I have to see a few patients. But I'll drop in tonight." He didn't consider me a patient.

Dr. Himmelblau's polished bald head was like a much-used billiard ball from any angle you looked at it. Throughout all the years his appearance never changed. Even in his sixties he had the timeless appearance of a slightly underfed Chinese Buddha.

He professed no concern whatsoever at my lack of appetite. Sometimes he would glance perfunctorily at my outstretched tongue, perhaps to please my anxious parents, but later on he wouldn't even do that. Fortunately, Dr. Himmelblau was thoroughly impervious to the theories of Professor Doctor Sigmund Freud, though Vienna, and Dr. Freud, were only a few hours by train from my home town. I hate to think what some of Dr. Freud's disciples would do to me today if I refused to eat anything but frankfurters and cocoa.

Once Dr. Himmelblau gave me a thoughtful look and said to my parents: "He will be all right. Someday he'll want to eat more than he's going to get." It was a remarkable blend of accurate diagnosis and correct prognosis.

A few months afterward I caught a cold, undernourished and transparent as I was, and came down with pneumonia and pleurisy. "He almost died," my mother later said. She would break into tears at the very memory of my sickness.

When I felt better, Dr. Himmelblau advised my parents to take me to a famous professor in Vienna for a checkup.

The professor, an internist, lived in the ninth district, practically within stethoscope range from Dr. Freud. He knocked all over my frail body, listened to the windpipes inside my chest, and pronounced that only the "southern sun" would heal me.

The nearest exposure to southern sun was in the South Tyrolian town of Merano. It then belonged to the Austro-Hungarian monarchy; today it is part of Italy. Merano is a lovely oasis of vineyards, orchards, palm trees, and flowers, surrounded by the jagged, snow-capped peaks of the Alps. In late summer, at sunset, the peaks reflect the reddish glow of the sun; the natives call it *Alpenglühen,* Alpine glow. The air tastes of Calville apples, which, like all apples, grow in summertime and are stored in many cellars in winter.

Merano is the home of the Merano Grape Cure, doubtless the most insignificant medical discovery of the century. It consists of walking in the balmy sunshine and eating four pounds of grapes every twenty-four hours, and is said to speed up recovery after any disease. The cure was a great success, particularly with hotel-owners, doctors, and the proprietors of the vineyards, who were the doctors' friends.

My mother and I stayed at a nice villa whose owners, the Lambergs, specialized in the care and upkeep of juvenile hypochondriacs. "Aunt" Lamberg thought I would be no problem. It was just a matter of finding the right diet for me, she said. She hopefully offered me eggs, coffee, butter, gorgonzola, *pasta asciutta* (spaghetti), white chicken meat, dark chicken meat, veal cutlets, ravioli, goulash, York ham, cooked Prague ham, uncooked Westphalian ham, *prosciutto,* sweet pickles, oatmeal, Swiss fondue, blinis, *Wiener Schnitzel, pizza,* chocolate pudding. I turned down everything and asked for grapes.

The local doctor was delighted. He said here was living proof that the Merano Grape Cure was effective not only for diseases of the digestive tract but also as "a palliative for a nervous strain in delicate children." The doctor brought two colleagues along. They examined me and said they were going to write about me in the local *Kurblatt.* I was still getting sick at the sight of a juicy steak.

The following year—it was 1914, and I was getting to be seven—the First World War broke out. It was late in August, and my parents, my two-year-old brother Max, and I were spending the summer vacation on the Semmering, a beautiful mountain resort near Vienna. There was no radio, but bad news traveled as quickly as today. Long before the Viennese newspapers had arrived, everybody knew that Kaiser Franz Josef I had ordered general mobilization.

My father, a reserve officer in the Austrian Army, said we must take the first train home, where he would report for duty. My mother cried and said the evening train was slow, couldn't we wait until the next morning and take the express? My father said it was his duty to go right away. He'd always been like that.

When we got home, my father settled his personal affairs, put on his uniform, took his saber, kissed us good-by, and left. I shall never forget that moment. I stood by the window of our fifth-floor apartment. Downstairs, in front of the

(8)

house, waited a horse-drawn landau that was to take my father and my mother to the railroad station.

My mother got in first. She seemed drawn and smaller than usual. She always looked small next to my father; at parties, I remember, she would walk under his outstretched arm without bending her head. Her performance always got a big laugh.

She slumped down in the rear of the coach, her shoulders trembling with sobs. Fräulein Gertrud, the governess, who stood next to me, holding my brother, and Marie, the cook, were crying too. I didn't understand why they were all crying. I was very proud of my father. To me he looked like a *Generalfeldmarschall* in his *Oberleutnant*'s uniform, with his light-blue blouse, dark-blue pants, high shako, and his saber.

He got up on the step of the landau, and then he turned around and waved up to us. From where I stood I could see the strange, tense expression on his face as if he, too, were crying—crying without tears. Then he quickly turned away, sat down, put his arm around my mother's shoulder, and told the coachman to hurry off.

I never saw him again. Less than three months later my mother was notified by the Austrian War Ministry that my father had been killed in action on the eastern front, after leading his infantry company "in a heroic assault against the overwhelming fire power of ten Russian machine guns." The entire company was wiped out.

My father and his men were buried in a mass grave deep inside the Polish woods, right there where they had died. A few months later a general from the War Ministry brought my mother a small velvet case with the *Verdienstkreuz,* Distinguished Service Cross, one of the highest Austrian Army medals, and a long-winded citation. My mother put the velvet case away and never looked at it.

℘ I didn't understand what was happening. A world had collapsed around me, but I wasn't aware of any change. We were still living in the large, pleasant apartment on the fifth floor of the stately family house. The premises of the family bank were on the second and ground floor. We still had Marie, the cook, and Fräulein Gertrud, the governess. Every summer we went to Tyrol for two months. There was little to eat and everybody complained about the lack of food, but that suited me just fine. The less to eat, the better.

Then the front collapsed and there were rumors in our town that "the Russians were coming." Many people left in a panic, shops closed, and food supplies ran out. The Russians didn't come, but the shops remained closed and there was nothing to eat.

My mother and my father had often spent their Sundays hiking in the near-by Beskid Mountains. Now my mother would take her rucksack and visit the peasants, to trade in some of her beloved Meissen cups and Bohemian crystal vases for half a dozen eggs or a pound of butter.

I wondered what the peasants were doing with the Meissen cups, and once I accompanied my mother on her errand. The houses of the peasants were crammed with *objets d'art* and bric-a-brac like the back room of an antique shop. In a stable I saw a large Bechstein piano, half buried under straw and manure. When I opened the cover, a pair of dirty shoes were lying inside.

In those months my mother began to suffer from insomnia. The war was lost, and the *Kriegsanleihe*—war bonds —which we'd been forced to buy had become worthless. Then the family bank folded. My mother said she would have to let Fräulein Gertrud go. We couldn't afford her any more.

Even frozen potatoes were hard to get now, and when there was bread, it looked and tasted like clay bricks. Sometimes we had only polenta with gravy for our noon meal. Polenta is ground maize. Before the war Marie had used it to feed the geese.

It was in these days, I think, that I began to show interest in food. Years afterward my mother would often describe the "wonderful and terrible" day when I first asked for a *Wiener Schnitzel*. It was wonderful, she would say, because I was hungry, like other people; and terrible because it was as easy to get a slice of veal in Ostrava in May 1919 as it would be today to get a pound of plutonium.

In the early 'twenties food became more plentiful. The more there was, the choosier I got. I would turn down ordinary things—meats, vegetables, soups, and desserts, and exasperated my mother by displaying a craze for hard-to-get delicacies at unexpected moments. Once I woke up in the middle of the night and asked for "blood" oranges. In those days only the children of black-marketeers and the mistresses of cabinet members got oranges. I also asked for smoked eel, Rhein salmon, *pain de faisan aux truffes,* saddle of venison, and sliced pineapple, though I had never tasted any of these things and knew them only from hearsay. I read surreptitiously the memoirs of Casanova, but I skipped the bedroom scenes, which bored me, and dwelt upon the author's mouth-watering descriptions of the magnificent meals with which he'd regaled his ladies, prior to their seduction.

I would come home from Gymnasium at one p.m. and go directly into the kitchen without so much as taking off my hat. I lifted the covers from the pots and began to sniff at the contents. Marie would get angry and throw me out. She had the irascible temper that comes from spending the best years of one's life near a hot range. Marie had learned her trade in an era that knew no Mixmaster and refrigerator. I don't think she would use a Mixmaster now if she were still alive. She used to say that to mix a dough well, you have to turn the wooden spoon counterclockwise. She needed no refrigerator; she could make wilted parsley look fresh again by dipping it into warm water, and she would put a drop of peroxide into the milk to keep it from getting sour. On hot days when the *Schlagobers*—whipped cream—melted, she would add a little fresh, uncooked milk and whip it again. Her kuchen was never dry; she would put a few drops of glycerin into the dough. Her kuchen was excellent.

Sometimes I'm asked where my enthusiasm for good food originates. I don't know. Neither the theory of environment nor that of heredity seems to apply to my particular case. There was always plain, healthy, nutritious food in our home—"nutritious" was one of my mother's favorite expressions—but it would hardly have qualified for the palates of jaded epicures. There were no epicures in our family; there were bankers, engineers, doctors, civil servants, businessmen, scholars—but not one gourmet among the whole lot. They were contemporaries of Carême and Escoffier, but they didn't know it, or didn't care. (I missed Escoffier by a few years and I also missed Gustav Mahler and Caruso. I'll never cease to regret it.)

The food in our home was distinguished only for its monotony. The menu of the noon meal was planned for weeks ahead. Every Monday, Tuesday, Wednesday, and Thursday we had consommé and boiled beef with vegetables (Monday: carrots; Tuesday: spinach; Wednesday: cabbage; Thursday: peas), followed by a dessert. Friday we had fish and on Saturday a roast.

Marie was a competent vegetable and dessert cook. But her delicious *gâteaux,* soufflés, puddings, and other frivolities were served only for guests. When we were alone, the dessert had to be a nutritious, cooked dish.

Today I know that the cooked *Mehlspeisen* of my delicate childhood are gastronomic delights. I can think of nothing better than *povidla-tascherln,* hoop-cheese dumplings, Bohemian *Dalken, Palatschinken* (pancakes), *Kaiserschmarren, Äpfel im Schlafrock* ("apples in dressing-gown," fried apple slices), *Schusterbuben* ("shoemaker's boys," a sort of potato noodles). But at home I hated them. I would have hated Sevluga caviar and Château Margaux 1899 if I'd had them five times a week.

On Fridays we had fish and I was afraid of fish. When I was five, I'd almost choked to death on a carp bone, an episode known in our house as the-day-he-got-blue-in-his-face. On Sundays the main dish was *Wiener Schnitzel.* The religious split in town ran straight through the populace's Sunday menu: the Jews had *Wiener Schnitzel,* the Gentiles had roast pork with sauerkraut and dumplings.

It was customary to have five meals a day. Breakfast was at half past seven in the morning. At ten o'clock, children had their *déjeuner à la fourchette,* sandwiches, sausages, hard-boiled eggs, fruit. Many men would go for half an hour to a beerhouse for a goulash or a dish of calf's lungs, and a glass of beer. Between ten and ten thirty little work was done in offices and shops; everybody was out eating. Two hours later, people were having lunch—at home, since eating lunch in a restaurant was unknown—and afterward they had a nap. Then to the coffeehouse for a demitasse and a game of whist or bridge, and back to the salt mines for an hour's work.

It was a strenuous life and around four thirty in the afternoon most people were hungry again and had to have their *Jause.* A genuine, central-European *Jause* consists of several large cups of coffee, topped off with whipped cream, of bread and butter, *Torte* or *Guglhupf* (the bizarre Viennese variation of a pound cake shaped like a derby on which several people have been sitting), and assorted patisserie. It is a feminine institution; my mother didn't mind skipping lunch and dinner but she had to have her *Jause*. She would often complain that she gained weight "practically from nothing," but it couldn't be the *Jause,* she said; you didn't gain weight from the *Jause*.

What with appetizers and hors-d'œuvres and a sumptuous dinner, many people had to go to Karlsbad once a year to take the cure, lose fifteen pounds, and get in shape again for another year of arduous eating.

It was a great day for me when my mother and I were invited for lunch by Uncle Alfred, the richest man in our family. He was an older brother of my father's and occasionally advised my mother in matters of financial investments. Uncle Alfred looked and acted like a better-class Wall Street millionaire of the postwar era. He was a tall, dapper man, clean-shaven and silver-haired, impeccably groomed in discreet shades of gray. He walked slowly, his head slightly bent forward, presumably under the burden of his financial responsibilities. He was the only member of our family who had salvaged and increased his personal fortune through the hectic postwar years, and his speculative investments were said to be daring and unorthodox. He was a virtuoso of the winning charm and the irresistible smile. When he condescended to pat people's backs, they were swept off their feet and would lend him money, buy his shares, or appoint him a member of the board of directors. He had gone to Vienna at the end of the First World War when our family bank in Ostrava was swept away by the tide of disaster along with other private banks and many corporations.

Everybody went broke, but Uncle Alfred prospered. He had the Midas touch and became a power in Viennese banking circles. On his engraved letterheads it said: "Managing Director of the Lombard-and-Escompte Bank." He built a modern villa in the exclusive Döbling district and moved among the right people. His wife had always aspired to become a social success. Now she was having her literary, artistic salon.

I didn't know what a salon was; I imagined darkly that it might be something I'd read about in the memoirs of Casanova. When their daughter got married—to an Austrian aristocrat who was long on debts and titles, and short on money and reputation—the Votiv Church was decorated with thousands of white roses. Yes, Uncle Alfred was a Success.

He took us for lunch to the Palace Hotel, the best place in town. I was thirteen, and I'd never been to a restaurant before. My head was swimming as we entered the magnificent dining-room and were taken in tow by an oily, impeccable headwaiter, past rows of tables that were gleaming with white linen, crystal glasses, and silverware. The waiter bowed deeply to my uncle and handed each of us a menu. My menu had a fat stain in the upper left corner.

My uncle pointed at the menu and said: "Go ahead, my boy. Order anything you like."

"Anything?" I said.

There were six different soups on the menu, three kinds of

boiled beef, at least a dozen entrées, and a profusion of hors-d'œuvres, vegetables, sweets. It was a terrifying and wonderful dilemma.

"Certainly, my boy," my uncle said, with his winning smile. "Just order."

He turned to my mother and told her that it had been proved scientifically that delicate children should do their own choosing. He quoted one of his friends, an eminent Viennese psychologist who believed in "young people's right of self-determination," whatever that meant.

I discarded the soups and boiled beef, which I had at home, but the next three plates attracted my fancy: *filet de bœuf gastronome, paupiettes de veau,* chicken breasts with mushrooms in white sauce. Those were the dishes I thought that Casanova would have ordered had he been lunching here. I couldn't make up my mind which one of the three I liked best, so I ordered them all.

The oily, impeccable headwaiter wrote down the order before anybody could stop him. "A nice consommé, to start with, sir?" he asked.

I hated consommé, but I felt a sudden affection for the headwaiter. No one had ever called me "sir."

I said: "Yes, a consommé, please."

Uncle Alfred gave my mother an ironical stare. "I thought he didn't like to eat," he said.

My mother woke up from her daydream—a dream in which I was eating huge meals several times a day—and told the headwaiter to bring me potato soup and a veal goulash with noodles.

(17)

I enjoyed the goulash. This seemed to displease my mother, oddly enough.

"At home he wouldn't even touch it," she said to my uncle.

It was a good lunch, but expensive for my mother. Uncle Alfred talked her into one of his financial investments. That one didn't pay off.

To soften the blow, Uncle Alfred invited me to Vienna to spend the Easter holiday at his modern villa.

The villa made me uncomfortable. It was a glass house; I never found out where the walls ended and where the roof began, but perhaps there was no roof. My aunt's salon was disappointing too. It consisted of a noisy gathering of actors, littérateurs, psychiatrists, artists, and other people who came only because they liked my uncle's wines and liquors. They were sitting on floors and stairways—there were few chairs, but dozens of stairways all over the house—drinking cognac and carrying on interminable discussions. It was a dismal crowd; Casanova would have been bored stiff among them. I specifically remember a famous actor who refused to sit on a chair because, he said, he despised mediocrity. He would sit on top of the Bechstein piano, cleaning his fingernails with a small pocket knife.

I enjoyed Vienna until my aunt insisted on taking me to Humhal, a tailor of renown, where she ordered for me a tuxedo and riding clothes, which, she said, "a young man of your background and class ought to have." I had never identified my background and class, whatever they were, with riding breeches. Besides, I was terrified of horses ever since I'd been bitten by one in Ostrava. I told my aunt I would never ride a horse.

"You don't have to ride a horse," she said, "but you have to have the clothes."

The clothes were very elegant, though much too expensive, my mother thought, when she got the bill from the Viennese tailor.

The climax of my trip was the night we had dinner at the Hotel Sacher. Back home in Ostrava everybody had talked about that famous Viennese restaurant where Austrian archdukes had entertained their lady friends from the Opera ballet. I'd been fascinated by one member of the Imperial family who one night had walked down the stairway dressed only in his military cap and saber and carrying an empty champagne bottle under each arm.

My uncle and aunt took me to the Volkstheater, where their friend the famous actor appeared as Marquis Posa in Schiller's *Don Carlos*. The actor consented to join us for supper at Sacher's. When we entered the dining-room, the waiters bowed deeply to the actor, and somewhat less deeply to my uncle. The actor surprised me by sitting down on a chair like everybody else, and the hell with mediocrity. While we waited for the food, the actor cleaned his fingernails with his small pocket knife.

The dining-rooms were sumptuous, crowded with beautiful women and elegant men. There was almost as much bowing from the waist, hand-kissing, and Old World kow-towing as in the Hollywood version of a Viennese operetta. I felt right at home among them in my brand-new tuxedo, which I had on for the first time. Unfortunately, one of the black imitation pearls jumped out of my starched shirt-front when I sat down and I was terrified the shirt might open, revealing my hairy chest. To avoid such a calamity, I sat up stiffly and straight all evening long. I must have looked like a character in Mme Tussaud's.

This time I didn't bother with plebeian goulash. I looked at the right side of the menu and ordered the most expensive item, which happened to be pheasant *à la Sainte-Alliance.* I don't remember much about the dish except that I was bothered by the fine bones, which got constantly between my teeth. I became embarrassed spitting them out in such distinguished company, and finally I gave up and swallowed them. I envied my uncle, who had ordered a wonderful-looking beef goulash, with no bones whatsoever.

When I came home from Vienna, I talked a lot about the good things I'd eaten there. Marie got angry and offered her resignation, and my mother had to give her a raise to make her stay. Strange things began to happen. On my way from school I would stand in front of the food shops, casting greedy glances at the displays of smoked eel, caviar, *Rheinlachs,* and goose livers. The pretty girls whom I escorted to dancing lessons or to a movie began to complain that I would drop them in the middle of sweet talk to stare in fascination at a wheel of (genuine) Emmental cheese in a delicatessen window. I began to lose girls when, on my way to a date, I stepped into a food shop for a *Rollmops* or a Jockey Club salad—asparagus, raw truffles, and mayonnaise. Delicious. I would forget all about my date.

In order to indulge in my expensive tastes, I began to tutor small boys who had failed their examinations. I was almost an accomplished scholar in Latin, Greek, history, physics, practically everything except mathematics. Unfortunately most of my pupils had troubles in math. I found myself in the embarrassing though perhaps not uncommon position of having to teach something of which I knew less than my pupils. I had to study a lot before I went to teach them. The lessons would drag on interminably. Only the thought of a good snack afterward kept me awake.

On the fifteenth and on the last day of each month, when I got paid, I would surprise my mother by bringing home a fancy assortment of exotic cheeses, canned sea food, weird spices, imported meats, and other frivolous delicacies which my mother wouldn't buy because they offended her principles of sound budgeting. Marie said if her cooking wasn't good enough, she might as well go, and there was another minor crisis in the kitchen.

Then I began to criticize the food at home and to suggest "improvements." I wanted to know why the boiled beef was tough, dry, and stringy. Maybe it was undercooked or over-cooked, had been too long on the hoof or too short in the butcher's icebox? I thoroughly disrupted our household. Sometimes I would sneak over to Martha, my mother's cousin, whose husband had spent his younger years as a musician in Spain and France, and was considered something of a connoisseur. They often had boiled beef—delicious, juicy, tender cuts.

One day my mother surprised me there at noontime. I had told her I was giving a math lesson and wouldn't be home for lunch. When she came in, I was at the table, eating boiled beef and spinach.

"I hope he didn't bother you too much," my mother said to my cousin. "We had boiled beef and spinach yesterday. You should have heard him!"

My cousin said I hadn't bothered them. "He asked for more meat," she said.

"And at home he makes a long face and drives all of us crazy," my mother said, with an undertone of bitterness.

"At home the meat isn't so good!" I said.

For a second I thought my mother would break into tears, but she didn't. Now that she had real worries, she cried much less than in her happy days. She walked out in silence. I'm still ashamed when I think of that day.

In the fall of 1925 I left Ostrava to study law at Prague University Law School. I had passed my *matura* examination with honors, except in math, which I'd passed only because of the teacher's kindness of heart. Family tradition demanded that the oldest son obtain an academic degree. I chose law, which was the easiest way of getting one. A law student didn't have to attend lectures and seminars. For a suitable gratuity, certain clerks would affix the stamps of the professors' signatures in the student's attendance book, which was proof that he had attended the lectures.

I went to Prague, enrolled, and paid my fees, but I didn't like the academic life with its petty intrigues, political fights, and students' fraternities. I left and went to Vienna, where they had good music.

My family took a dim view of music. Musicians were one notch above pickpockets and two below people cheating in card games. I surreptitiously went to the violin class of the Vienna Conservatory, but in order to neutralize the family's suspicions I enrolled at the *Hochschule für Welthandel*—College for World Trade. The dues were low and the exams were said to be a cinch.

But economics was even more boring than law, and the activities of the dueling *Burschenschaftler* created a serious threat to my survival. The *Burschenschaftler* were ardent followers of a former Austrian paper-hanger named Hitler who had been involved in a beerhouse putsch in Munich and was now serving time in Landsberg prison. No one in my circles had ever heard of him, but the *Burschenschaftler* carried his pictures and, by way of paying homage to their leader, beat up the Jewish students, who happened to be a tiny minority. We were beaten up an average of twice a week, either inside the *Hochschule,* where the Viennese police were not permitted to enter, or outside on the street, where the police looked benevolently the other way.

I attended the lectures, and beatings, for four or five months, until I discovered a better way of spending the best years of my life: I went to the State Opera, which was then one of the leading opera companies in the world. The singing was wonderful and all the beating took place on the stage.

Admission was expensive, even to the standing room way up in the fourth gallery, and I had no extra money to spare. I looked for prospects whom I might tutor in math, but there was no response; besides, most small boys in Vienna knew more about math than I did. There was only one way of keeping my budget balanced: to spend less on food.

I began to eat at the WÖK—*Wiener Öffentliche Küchenbetriebsgesellschaft*—a chain of inexpensive restaurants. Today the WÖK is respected and popular in Vienna, a sort of bargain-basement Childs, but in its early days the restaurants were located in cellars, abandoned salesrooms, and other unlikely places where the rental was low. The lights were dim —not to create "atmosphere," as in expensive night clubs, but to save electricity. No fuss was made about snow-white tablecloths; there were no tablecloths at all. The waitresses looked, and acted, like guards in a reform school. They operated on the take-it-or-leave-it principle. You entered past the cashier's table, paid for the meal, and were issued a ticket. (It was a wise precaution to ask advance payment; people might have refused to pay afterward.) You handed your ticket to the waitress and hoped for the best.

There were two menus, with no substitutions. The WÖK's cooks knew little about cooking, but they were accomplished camouflage experts. They would take a slice of beef as thin as heavy wrapping paper, pound it into leathery consistency, dip it into a concoction of glue and stale bread crumbs, fry it in used-over lard, surround it with a heap of sliced potatoes that had been soaked overnight in vinegar, and call the resulting horror *"Wiener Schnitzel* with potato salad." That was the more expensive menu. The cheaper one featured the loose ends of ox tail and was called "boiled beef." Every time I chewed on it, I atoned for my early sins in our home.

During the Christmas and Easter holidays I went back to Ostrava to gain new strength for more beatings and opera nights. The food in our house was wonderful. My mother cried happily and Marie outdid herself in fancy dishes.

Once Dr. Himmelblau came over for dinner. He was still the family physician, in his seventies now, but still looking timeless and healthy. He said nothing, as he watched me eat. I thought there was an amused smile around his lips.

There is an inverse, diabolic ration between riches and appetite. People start out hungry and poor; they work hard to overcome both handicaps, but when at last they have amassed enough money to eat well, they also have the ulcers that go with the making of too much money and don't enjoy their food. Twenty-five years ago I would spend my hungry evenings in the fourth gallery of Vienna's State Opera, looking enviously down at the opulent people in the parquet who could afford to have supper at Sacher's. Today I sit in the parquet, but I'm barred from Sacher's by my doctor's advice. Sometimes I find myself wistfully looking up at the gallery and the young people with their healthy appetites who don't yet know the meaning of "diet."

ℰℬ𝒳 I was always hungry on those nights. Sometimes my stomach started to make rumbling noises just as the tenor sang a pianissimo, and everybody looked at me. Some well-fed people made "shsh-t!" It was very embarrassing. My fellow standees in the fourth gallery were as hungry as I, and we began to experiment with low-priced cheeses and sausages, trying to determine which would be the cheapest, most nutritious food. We finally decided on raw bacon. It wasn't an original discovery, to be sure; Swiss mountain guides and Arctic explorers have subsisted for long periods of time on raw bacon.

We bought the bacon at wholesale prices with the help of a fourth-gallery opera enthusiast who carried on with the wife of a butcher in the Ottakring, a Viennese district with more thugs than street lamps. The butcher's wife was blonde, very blonde, and old, very old: almost thirty-eight. She would cut fresh rolls in the middle, place two slices of raw bacon between the halves, and sprinkle them with Hungarian paprika. During the first act of *Walküre,* while Siegmund and Sieglinde were singing their beautiful duet about sweet Love and Spring, the sweet scent of paprika seemed to descend, like light fog, all over the fourth gallery.

ℰℬ𝒳 It was a wonderful time. It would have been even more wonderful if Uncle Alfred had been in Vienna to take me to Sacher's, but he had left town. His unorthodox financial schemes and daring investments had collapsed. Inflation, repeated devaluation, and currency reforms had proved stronger than Uncle Alfred's Midas touch. He had gone back to our home town, where he lived in a modest three-room apartment. The modern villa in Döbling was for sale, but no one wanted it. I walked by there one afternoon. The glass walls were broken and dirty, and the roof seemed to sag down. The villa didn't look modern any longer, just shabby. Once I ran into the famous actor, my uncle's friend. I greeted him, but he failed to recognize me. He seemed aloof, more contemptuous of mediocrity than ever. I heard that he had become the friend of an industrialist who owned a baroque castle in Hietzing and a fine wine cellar.

Luckily, my cousin Steffi was living in town. There are certain drawbacks in having too many uncles and cousins, but there are advantages too. Uncle Bernard in Poland had a trout stream and an Opel car, and my cousin Dolfi taught me to drive and introduced me to the prettiest girls; Uncle Bruno let me play chamber music with his quartet; my cousin Martha who, by some quirk of relationship, was of my mother's age, was a wonderful woman always willing to help me with my troubles; Cousin Fritz introduced me to night clubs and French brandies; and Cousin Tilde who lived in Prague with her husband, an industrialist, was truly a perfect hostess who made you feel at home in her house, kept a book of her dinners and guests to make sure that no one would be subjected to the indignity of eating the same excellent dish twice in her house, and chose her table flowers in harmony with the eyes and hair color of her women guests.

Cousin Steffi in Vienna had a fine cook, an old woman belonging to the almost gone tradition of great Viennese cooking. Vienna's cuisine at its best was a happy blend of Czech, Hungarian, Serb, Polish, Italian, and Bavarian cooking, with a certain quality all of its own.

Steffi lived in a beautiful apartment in Schönbrunn, overlooking the Kaiser's castle. Her husband was a prominent women's tailor. They enjoyed life and people; their house was always warm with laughter and hospitality. It was always with a feeling of elation that I would arrive in Schönbrunn at one o'clock on Sunday and ring the bell. When the door was opened, a wave of delicious aromas would flow toward me, the promise of great things to come.

I had lived all week long on raw bacon, and under the sudden impact of the appetizing scent my taste buds would react violently and I would begin to swallow. The chambermaid, a sturdy, well-fed woman, gave me a knowing, ironical glance as she took my overcoat.

We first had brook trout—the finest fish of all—and afterward there was *Backhendl,* the Viennese variety of fried young chicken, or *Wiener Schnitzel,* tender and so dry that you could sit on it without having a fat stain on your pants—which in Vienna is the test of a perfect *Schnitzel.* Afterward came one of the great Viennese desserts, *Linzerschnitten, Milchrahmstrudel, Kaiserschmarren, Spritzkrapfen, Schaumrollen.*

The Sunday dinners in Steffi's house never lasted less than two hours. Sometimes it was four o'clock when we got up from the table—time for me to queue up at the Opera. On Sundays they gave Wagner operas, which started early.

I remember one dreary, cold Sunday in February when I

had to leave before the coffee was served. The performance of *Götterdämmerung* was to start at five and there would be a run for tickets.

"Why don't you stay here?" Steffi's husband said, pointing at the window. Outside a blizzard was raging. "Have supper with us."

"We'll have a saddle of venison with *Preiselbeeren* (cranberries)," Steffi was saying. "Don't leave now. It's awful out there." She shivered.

The temptation was overwhelming. The warmth of the room, the soft cushions on the couch, the smell of good food, the thought of venison and good wine . . .

I got up. I guess I was very young and the ideals of the soul were stronger than the wants of the palate. I braved the snowstorm, queued up for two hours to get a ticket, and stood in the fourth gallery from five to eleven o'clock. During Brünhilde's Immolation, I ate a roll with paprika bacon.

I don't think I would do it today—not for *Götterdämmerung*. I must be getting old.

Paris, reine du monde,
Paris, jeune et blonde . . .
SONG OF PARIS

THE FIRST TIME I
SAW PARIS

I saw Paris for the first time on a crisp, sunny morning in the autumn of 1926. I had gone there to study at the Sorbonne. My family was dissatisfied with the progress of my education in Vienna, where I had neglected to acquire an extensive knowledge in economics though I had become an expert at grand opera. They said that a semester or two at the Sorbonne would "round out" my education. They were worried because I had shown too much interest in music, writing, and other "breadless" arts.

"You must study law, finance, and economics," an old aunt

said to me. "Think of the future of our bank!" The poor woman was bedridden with a chronic heart ailment, and her children didn't dare tell her that the family bank existed no longer.

I created a crisis when I declared, at my grandmother's seventieth birthday party, that I was going to play the violin —for money. The family was shocked. A nineteen-year-old boy doesn't know what he wants to do, they were saying; he is told by his uncles and aunts, who know best. My mother started to cry. Then Uncle Siegfried, my brother's and my legal guardian, came up with the idea of the Sorbonne.

"Let him go to Paris," he said. "A few months there will make him forget all that nonsense about playing the fiddle."

Uncle Siegfried owned a prosperous general store in Přívoz, a suburb of Ostrava on the banks of the Oder. The store was crammed with textiles, sauerkraut, stockings, pickles in large barrels, hardware, spices, open canvas bags filled with coffee, rice, barley, dried peas, dried lentils, fishing gear, smoked herring, meats, mouse traps, cheeses, sticks of sausages hanging from the walls, candles and holy pictures, chocolate and flypaper. A wave of naphthalin, cinnamon, and bay leaf fused with the fragrance of toilet water and smoked herring, the smell of Pilsen beer, imported Jamaica rum, and the slivovitz that Uncle Siegfried and his clerks produced in the back room.

Uncle Siegfried was widely respected in the neighborhood for the quality of his slivovitz and for his generous credit policy. "If you wait long enough, you don't have to pay him back," his customers used to say. He was a powerful man with a large, black mustache and no hair on his head, which was always covered. In winter he wore a cap, in summer a Panama hat. Like the management of the State Railroads, Uncle Siegfried recognized only two seasons, winter and summer, irrespective of temperatures. Winter began on November 1, summer on May 1.

He ran his retailing empire from behind an old-fashioned cash register, where he received visitors, extended credit, handed candy to small boys, and made phone calls to the Odéon Cinema, which he ran as a profitable sideline. Uncle Siegfried looked upon himself as a patron of the arts. Playing the fiddle was all right, he used to say—*after* working hours.

I arrived in Paris at the Gare de l'Est and told the taxi-driver to take me to Montparnasse, on the Left Bank, where the Sorbonne and other institutions of higher learning are located, but he misunderstood my pronunciation of "Montparnasse" and took me to Montmartre instead. I knew nothing about Montmartre. I watched the meter click ahead with alarming speed, and when it jumped to nine francs I told the driver to stop, gave him ten francs, took my bag, and got out.

I found myself in the middle of a large square. The blue-white signs said Place Pigalle. It seemed a nice, quiet neighborhood. I knew nothing of Paris, but to me, that autumn morning at half past eight, Place Pigalle looked like a typical Paris square.

Yes, I decided, this was the place to live. In a dark, narrow side street I found a small, dreary hotel, with broken windowpanes and a shield: Régence Hôtel. The place appealed to me: it seemed run down and would probably be inexpensive. My funds were small and inelastic. Uncle Siegfried, mindful of the temptations that might beset a young man in Paris, had decided that I would be given a fixed amount of money for the entire trip. The length of my stay would depend on the strength of my moral principles. If I threw my money away on loose women and wine, I would be back soon. If I stretched my money, through thrift and asceticism, I could stay longer. Thus, Uncle Siegfried reasoned, Paris would teach me a lesson in morality and in the virtue of thrift.

The tiny, narrow entrance smelled of cheap perfume and of absinthe. There was no lobby. Behind a ramshackle desk sat a fat, middle-aged lady wearing a stained silk dressing-gown that was bursting along the seams. So was the lady. She was reading a paper-bound novel and dunking a *croissant* into a glass of red wine. She didn't look at me when I came in.

I said I wanted a room. Without interrupting her reading, she reached over her shoulder and took a key from one of the nails on the key-board behind her.

"*C'est pour un moment?*" she asked.

I said no, for a whole month.

She looked up, for the first time, and stared fixedly behind me as though she expected to see someone else.

"*Mais vous êtes seul!*" she said. Her mouth fell open, revealing a depressing job of French dentistry.

Her behavior was odd, but I'd read odd stories about the French. "Of course I'm alone," I said. "Now, how about the room?"

She lifted her fat forearms to heaven in a gesture of bewilderment, sighed deeply, took the key, and came out from behind the desk. The Régence Hôtel seemed to dispense with such luxuries as bellboys, receptionists, porters, elevators, telephones, palm trees, or room service. The *patronne* (I soon found out that she was the owner) ran the hotel herself with the help of François and Madeleine, a decrepit couple.

We walked up on the winding stairway. Halfway between two floors the *patronne* showed me the *cabinet,* which was built into the round wall, like a secret chamber. It was very quiet in the hotel, just what I wanted. I've always been a light sleeper. The *patronne* walked down a corridor and opened a room. On the floor was a heap of stockings, high-heeled shoes, dainty underthings, a dress, a hat, and the handbag of a lady who seemed to have shed her things on the spot, and in a hurry.

Then I saw the lady. She was in bed. Asleep. Her dark locks covered one side of her face, but the other was not unattractive. She wore no nightshirt.

The *patronne* gave an angry shrug, saying: *"Ça, alors!"* closed the door, and went on. The next room presented a Toulouse-Lautrec sort of still life of overturned bottles, filled ashtrays, half-filled glasses, and an empty, unmade bed.

"Excusez," the *patronne* said, to no one in particular, since the room was empty. She hastily closed the door and mum-

bled something. French people were certainly peculiar. The *patronne* didn't speak the academic French that I had learned in school. She would swallow the endings of most words. I decided that the French didn't speak good French.

The next room was unoccupied. It contained a washbasin behind a Japanese screen, a clothes-hanger by the door, a light-bulb dangling from a piece of string, and a very large bed. There was no closet. I asked how much the room was by the month. After much silent counting and lip-moving, the *patronne* quoted a price that was well within the limits of my budget. I was delighted. At the door she turned around and gave me what seemed to be a last glance of motherly affection.

"Listen, *mon petit*," she said, "are you sure you really want to stay in here?"

I nodded. She gave a sigh. She said this room had no key, but that I could bolt it from the inside.

"I'm always downstairs," she said. "When I have my dinner, François will be at the desk."

She went out, shaking her head and muttering in despair. I thought she was a character straight out of Balzac. My acquaintance with Frenchwomen was based solely on the works of Flaubert and Balzac.

I was tired after sitting up all night on the train. I hung up my suit, washed—the water was ice-cold—and went to bed. The bed was very comfortable.

When I woke up, it was dark outside. Every six seconds there was lightning, followed by no thunder. I got up and looked out. The lightning was caused by a neon sign across the street saying: LE PARADIS. From the street came the distorted sounds of voices, cars, whistles, shouts, and two hurdy-gurdies playing simultaneously *Auprès de ma blonde* and *Ain't She Sweet?* A drunk's voice shouted: *"Ta gueule!"*

Inside the hotel there seemed to be a lot of animation. People were laughing in the corridors, and I heard the clinking of glasses. Twice somebody tried to get into my room. I shaved—the water was piping hot now—dressed, and left the room. Downstairs two girls stood in front of the *patronne*'s desk. The *patronne* was still reading her paper-bound book, which, I saw, was the memoirs of the Marquis de Sade.

"Bonsoir, chéri," said the older of the two girls. She had curls all over and wore a very tight skirt of a shiny material. She was spreading clouds of the cheap perfume that I'd smelled here in the morning. I said *bonsoir*.

"Qu'il est mignon!" said the other girl. She was from Bordeaux. She must have been around when they discovered that 1899 would be an exceptional vintage in the Médoc.

"So you're the fellow who took the room for the whole month?" the curled girl said. Both exploded into coloratura laughter.

"Girls, *alors, alors!*" said the *patronne*.

"We're going to have fun with him," said Miss Vintage Bordeaux.

"Yes, *the whole month!*" the other one cried. That killed them. The curled one laughed so hard that she dropped her purse. I bent down and picked it up for her.

The door was opened and a girl and a man came in. The

girl greeted everybody like an old friend, and the *patronne* said: "The twenty-three, Yvonne, as usual." The man behind her seemed embarrassed.

"That's *him*!" Miss Vintage Bordeaux said to the new girl, pointing at me.

"Oh!" she said, and gave me a respectful glance. Then she turned toward her escort and said: "Come on, *chéri*," and they went upstairs.

I left the hotel. I knew the facts of life in Paris; I had been told by my worldly-wise friends that almost every Parisian hotel would let you have a room for a few hours, or a fraction thereof. In fact, a number of rooms on the lower floors were set aside for the pursuit of sinful happiness, I'd been told, but from the third floor up the guests were eminently respectable. My room was on the third floor.

At the corner I stood still and gasped. The blue-white signs still said "PLACE PIGALLE," but the square didn't seem to be the one I had seen in the morning. It was past ten p.m. All the shops were open and brightly lighted. On the sidewalk in front of the Café Le Paradis, an all-girl orchestra on a platform was playing *Singing in the Rain*. In the middle of the boulevard de Clichy several painters had put up their oils and watercolors under the trees. Near the Moulin Rouge a merry-go-round made shrieking noises. There was a cacophony of jazz music, organ-grinders, automobiles tooting their horns, policemen using their whistles, sightseeing Cook's buses ("Paris by Night") using *their* horns, and passers-by using their lungs. It was worse than Times Square on New Year's Eve. Men in need of a shave edged up to me, speaking

French and Arabic, offering "genuine Tabriz rugs," dirty postcards, Moroccan leather goods, their younger sisters, and a whitish powder that looked like, but wasn't, sugar. The peddlers hastily departed when two policemen approached. The police, I noticed, walked in pairs here.

I became aware of the persistent gnawing in my stomach. I hadn't eaten for over twenty-four hours. There was a restaurant next to Le Paradis, but the prices on the menu, which was displayed in a picture frame next to the entrance, ruled the place out for my budget. There were other restaurants, equally expensive. Most of them had dim lights. As you entered, the first thing you saw was a table with an arrangement of expensive fruit in a basket. The entrance was guarded by a couple of middleweights, wearing tuxedos. Once in a while a few dazed foreigners would stop to look at the fruit arrangement on the table, and before they could say "Crêpes Suzette," the middleweight tuxedos had bounced them in.

After a while I discovered a delicatessen that seemed to be a hangout of taxi-drivers, night-club musicians, girls of small if any virtue, and artists from the near-by Cirque Médrano. I ordered a *bock*—a wineglass filled with beer—and a French sandwich, a paper-thin slice of ham between two large slices of French bread.

It was almost two a.m. when I got back to the Place Pigalle. The noise was worse than before. A second merry-go-round on the boulevard was doing good business. Below the window of my room a street trio—violin, accordion, and drums—was playing *Mon Paris*. A thin, transparent-looking girl with big, haunting eyes and deep-red, heart-shaped lips sang the chorus in a shrill, somewhat guttural voice. After each chorus she would step among the listeners who formed a circle around the band to sell the sheet music of *Mon Paris*, for one franc a copy. Afterward the audience would join her and the orchestra in another chorus.

There was cheerful confusion in the narrow street crowded with cops, drunks, girls, flower-venders, tourists, more girls, peddlers, and *maqueraux*—"mackerels," as the French call their gigolos. In front of the Régence Hôtel, Miss Vintage Bordeaux stood with a silky-haired *maquereau*. He had polished fingernails and a tight-fitting jacket. She wanted to introduce me to him, but I escaped into the hotel and ran up the stairway. In my room I bolted the door from the inside.

I went to bed but I couldn't sleep. In the room next to me a man and a woman argued about the lousy sum of twenty francs. Downstairs the band was playing *Les Fraises et les Framboises,* and the girl's voice sang the chorus with a haunting ring. All night long doors were banged and people kept coming and going; glasses were broken and bells rang; once there seemed to be a fight among the girls in front of the hotel, and I heard police whistles. Dawn came reluctantly to the Place Pigalle, the neon sign LE PARADIS stopped blinking, and I fell into exhausted sleep.

I woke up at noon, tired and miserable. I went down and told the *patronne* I couldn't sleep in her hotel and would have to leave. She understood my reasons but refused to refund my money. She talked darkly about laws and the *règlement,* and about two *brigadiers* who were her good friends.

As I didn't know then that in Paris a *brigadier* is not a general officer, but a cop on the beat, I dropped the subject of money. I was stuck. The next night I slept a little better, and the following week I slept like a log. The trick was to stay up with the local populace and go to sleep with them, at dawn. Once in a while everybody would be roused when the cops raided Le Paradis and arrested the dope-peddlers, but thereafter all would be quiet for a few days.

After a few weeks I became acquainted in the *quartier.* I found a *prix-fixe* restaurant in a quiet side street less than a hundred yards and more than a hundred years from Place Pigalle. The restaurant had a tiled floor, sprinkled with saw-dust. There were small tables for four, covered with large sheets of white paper. When a guest had finished his meal, the waiter would write the *addition* on the paper, roll the paper with the bread crumbs together, and take it away. The next guest was given a fresh sheet of paper. The place was always crowded with little girls from the near-by department stores, pale clerks, and minor officials from the *Mairie* of the 18th Arrondissement whose faces had taken on the dusty, parchment-colored hue of their files.

There were no tourists with guidebooks, not even French-men from the *provinces.* The guests of the restaurants never went to Place Pigalle after nightfall. One man lived right behind the Moulin Rouge music hall, but he had never been inside. They discussed Place Pigalle with clinical detachment, the way brokers discuss shares, and actors their make-up. "Pigalle," they agreed, was a *formidable affair,* a sound business venture. If the silly foreigners wouldn't spend their money here, all the *Montmartrois* would have to pay higher taxes. "Pigalle," was all right as long as it created prosperity.

There was no fancy fruit arrangement on a table inside the entrance of the Prix-Fixe, no tuxedoed middleweight waiting to bounce you in. The proprietor himself would stand there, and after you'd come to his place twice, he would shake hands with you, and you belonged. It was customary to shake hands with the waiter, too—but not with the guests at your table, no matter how well you knew them.

My waiter was Gaston, an old, asthmatic man who suffered from rheumatism. On days when the weather was about to change, he was ill-tempered and disinclined to listen to the guest's order. Instead he would bring the guest what he himself liked to eat. But his taste was excellent and usually he made a better choice than I should have done.

The Prix-Fixe was a good place to round out one's education. I learned that it was all right to read *L'Intransigeant* while you ate the hors-d'œuvre, but not afterward. The hors-d'œuvre—*thon à l'huile, œuf dur mayonnaise,* or a slice of *pâté Maison* served on a lonely salad leaf—could be handled with the right hand while the left held the newspaper. After the hors-d'œuvre, you would place the paper under your seat and were supposed to converse with the neighbors at your table about local problems of the *arrondissement*. Listening to the quiet voices, you wouldn't have known that there existed Paris, or France, or Europe, or the rest of the world.

It was a nice place. I didn't know then that there existed restaurants in Paris like Lapérouse, L'Escargot, or La Tour d'Argent, where the *couvert* cost as much as the entire menu here. I'm sure that my Prix-Fixe never made the Club des Cent or *Parmi les Meilleures Tables de France,* but at the age of nineteen the enthusiasm of the heart is stronger than the fastidiousness of the palate. The omelet was light and fluffy, the *bœuf à la bourguignonne* delicious and aromatic, and the tender, small *bifteck* garnished with a heap of fresh watercress.

There were two menus, at 7.50 and at 10 francs, including the *couvert,* a small bottle of wine or a big bottle of *bière de Strasbourg,* and bread *à discretion.* (Four pieces of bread were permissible, I learned; to take more was considered indiscreet.) The smaller menu offered hors-d'œuvre, entrée, one vegetable, dessert, or cheese. On holidays I threw my money away recklessly and feasted on the ten-franc menu, which included a fish course.

The menu was written in violet ink and was as difficult to read as a French railroad schedule. The specialties of the day, like de-luxe trains, were marked in red ink. The specialties were "homely" dishes, *cassoulet toulousain, haricot de mouton, blanquette de veau à l'ancienne,* or a *petite marmite.* Since Gaston liked those dishes, I had them frequently. Gaston said that the best thing one can say about a restaurant is that it's "almost like home." There were no *suprêmes d'écrevisses au champagne* on the menu, no *escalopes de foie gras à la Talleyrand,* or *crêpes Suzette.* But the *tripes* were marvelous.

I learned many things at the Prix-Fixe. You would place one end of the napkin inside your shirt collar. You would wipe your plate with a piece of bread until it was clean. Each course, even potatoes and vegetables, was served on a special plate, but you always used the same fork and knife. If you forgot and accidentally left your fork and knife on the used plate, Gaston would gently lift them up and place fork and knife on the paper sheet.

I often admired Gaston's virtuosity. He could carry three small wine bottles by their necks between forefinger and middle finger of his right hand, while his forearm was loaded with three plates; his left hand would swing a filled bread basket. When he wasn't carrying plates, he would cut long sticks of French bread into small pieces with the cutting machine. He always kept the baskets well filled.

Young couples would hold hands while they ate a delicious *raie au beurre noir* or a *vol-au-vent.* Between bites of food they would exchange passionate kisses. No one sitting near pretended to notice, but everybody looked pleased, and there was a glow of happiness about the place. Gaston beamed. He used to say that love enhanced digestion. Sometimes a girl who had exchanged kisses with a man one day would come with another man the next day and kiss him just as passionately. Infatuations were short-lived, but they were violent. It was a very romantic Prix-Fixe.

Most of the customers lived in the small, steep side streets off the boulevard de Clichy, or up on the Butte Montmartre, the hill district north of Place Pigalle, which is crowned by Sacré-Cœur church and *les lieux ou souffle l'ésprit,* as Barrès once said. They had savings books with the nearest branch of the Crédit Lyonnais; their idea of a wild Saturday night spree was to go to a neighborhood cinema to see the latest exploits of Arsène Lupin, Master Detective, and afterward to sip a *chocolat* at Dupont (*"Chez Dupont Tout Est Bon"*). On Sunday afternoon they would venture out as far as the Grands Boulevards or the Champs-Élysées to take a look at the shop windows and have a *bock* on a café terrace. The Champs-Élysées, being actually located on the Right Bank, was considered neutral territory. Beyond, there was no man's land.

The inhabitants of the Butte Montmartre didn't recognize the rest of Paris, or of France. The Left Bank was like an unknown foreign country for which you needed visas and special permits. You had no business going there except on legitimate errands, such as to borrow money or to visit the grave of Baudelaire at Montparnasse Cemetery. The inhabitants of Montmartre were enthusiastic cemetery-goers. I spent many an afternoon at Montmartre Cemetery, visiting the graves of Heinrich Heine, Henri Murger, and Hector Berlioz. Several times in the course of my conversations at the Prix-Fixe I told my table companions that I had come to Paris to study at the Sorbonne. They thought I was joking and burst out laughing. I stopped talking about the Sorbonne and decided to round out my education, informally and alfresco, on the streets and squares of Montmartre.

The faculty had prominent experts in specialized fields of knowledge. My art instructors were the sidewalk painters. Some of them had been drinking-and-arguing companions of Utrillo, Utter, Suzanne Valadon, Friesz, and Raoul Dufy in the days when no one wanted their paintings. Now they were arguing *about* Utrillo and Dufy, and they would never agree. Often such arguments would last all night long. In the early dawn we would walk up to Montmartre Cemetery. At the grave of Mme Récamier we would stop and one member of the faculty, a leading anti-Utrilloist, would impersonate a grief-stricken Chateaubriand delivering the funeral sermon for Mme Récamier. He was a moving speaker, and at the end of his sermon everybody was crying. To refresh ourselves, we would proceed to the Moulin de la Galette for a couple of *bocks* before going to bed, between seven and eight in the morning.

My economics teachers were the sidewalk peddlers from North Africa. I learned a great many things from them that had never been taught at Vienna's College for World Trade. I learned which French department produced "genuine Tabriz" rugs (Bouches-du-Rhône), the difference between Moroccan art work in Fez and Meknès (Fez was best for copper work, Meknès for silver and leather), or how to make sure that profits from dope-peddling surpass occasional losses (choose a location guarded by older *brigadiers* who can't run as fast as you do).

(45)

I had become acquainted with the members of the trio who performed nightly in the street in front of the Régence Hôtel. Théophile, the drummer, was a scholarly-looking fellow with the face of a thoughtful airedale. His family lived in a respected neighborhood near the Porte d'Italie; his father, a patriotic, parochial, parsimonious *petit bourgeois,* was head bookkeeper at the Société Générale. In the daytime Théophile worked there as junior bookkeeper, but he said he wasn't interested in his daytime career. His vocation was *le jazz,* hot or cold. He was in love with Claudia, the transparent girl singer, and they were engaged to be married. It was a shock for me, for I had become infatuated with the girl's haunting voice.

Théophile's family didn't object to his nocturnal activities. He said it would never occur to them to "travel"—*voyager,* he called it—to Place Pigalle, fifteen minutes by Métro from the Porte d'Italie.

"They might as well go to Papeete, Tahiti," he said, and laughed.

"But don't you have an uncle who doesn't like music?" I asked him enviously.

He gave me a blank stare. He didn't know what I was talking about.

Théophile's burning ambition was to become a regular *chef d'orchestre* and run his own band. It would have five members, he said. Around Pigalle, the *chef d'orchestre* is supposed to supply the music, and Théophile had already built up a substantial repertory of Salabert's Music Arrangements for Small Orchestra. He owned three stands and the percussion instruments and drums on which he performed. He promised to give me a *cachet*—a temporary job—as violinist as soon as he could set up his *affaire*. A cousin of his mother owned a country inn with a garden and dance hall in Saint-Rémy-les-Chevreuse, half an hour by train from the Gare Montparnasse. The cousin, a patron of the arts, was willing to give "Théophile et Son Orchestre" a start, provided it would cost him nothing. Théophile figured out, with the help of two itinerant math teachers from North Africa, that a dancing crowd of two hundred, paying two francs a person, would enable him to pay each of us thirty francs for the afternoon, and the cost of transportation besides. The cousin would throw in supper gratis.

It sounded too good to be true, but one Sunday afternoon we actually rode out on the train from the Gare Montparnasse. There were five of us: Théophile and Claudia, a saxophone-player, a pianist, and myself. Everybody was uncomfortably silent as we entered Left Bank territory after crossing the Seine and proceeded through enemy-infested boulevards to the railroad station. Théophile carried the drums, and Claudia carried the music. She looked lovelier, more haunting than ever.

Théophile et Son Orchestre were a great success at the cousin's inn, but I wasn't. I'd been raised musically on Bach, Brahms, and Beethoven, and now I had to dish out *Strawberries and Raspberries* and *Mon Paris*. My foxtrots were too fast and my *java* sounded like a Mozart minuet. I was glad when it was all over and the orchestra was having supper in the big kitchen with the cousin and his relatives: onion soup, thick slices of garlicky *gigot rôti* with *pommes lyon-naises,* salad, cheese, a good Beaujolais. It was a great day. Everybody had too much Beaujolais and was singing. I had earned thirty francs and had been invited by a French family, a rare distinction for a foreigner in France.

A few weeks later I ran into a former classmate from my home town who had also come to Paris to round out his education at the Sorbonne. He went there every day at eight in the morning, and listened to many lectures: *"Le Consulat et l'Empire," "Les Trésors de la Renaissance," "La Poésie en 1852," "Camées et émaux."* He knew a lot about *"L'Histoire de la musique en France,"* but he had never heard of *"Théophile et Son Orchestre"* and was shocked when I told him of Saint-Rémy-les-Chevreuse. He had been to the Montparnasse Cemetery but had missed the graves of Baudelaire and Maupassant. He knew no native Parisian. He had been twice on the Eiffel Tower, and spoke an aca-demic and, to me, completely unintelligible French.

He took me to his favorite restaurant. The menu featured goulash *à la hongroise* and *Wiener Schnitzel.* An anemic girl from Scotland looked shocked when I wiped my plate clean with a piece of bread. The proprietor was from Bucha-rest and shook hands with no one. Afterward my classmate took me to the Rotonde and showed me the American ex-patriates. The evening was a total loss. At ten p.m. I sneaked away on the Nord-Sud subway. I was lonely and homesick for Montmartre.

It was good to get back to Pigalle. The racket of the hurdy-gurdies, whistles, shouting people, and tooting horns was like the ticking of an old grandfather clock in a quiet living-room. I was back where I belonged. I didn't tell my friends where I had spent the evening. I was ashamed.

I might have stayed in Montmartre indefinitely if Uncle Siegfried hadn't come to Paris one night on the late train. He had gone on business to Switzerland, to buy Lindt chocolates and Emmental cheese, and had promised my mother to look me up. He went straight to the Régence Hôtel. When I came there at two in the morning, as was my habit, I found my uncle sitting at a sidewalk table next to the all-girl orchestra of the Café Le Paradis. I noticed that Uncle Siegfried, ordinarily a strong man—he had been decorated with the Austrian Army's gold *Tapferkeitsmedaille* for bravery in the First World War—looked pale and shaken.

I sat down next to him on the terrace. That, it turned out, was a mistake. Several of my North African economics teachers came by and tried to sell my uncle genuine Tabriz rugs from the Bouches-du-Rhône department, and one, Mohammed ben Ali, sat down beside us, offered my uncle his young sister and the white stuff that looked like, but wasn't, sugar, and told me that he'd just won a three-hundred-meter race against an aging *brigadier*.

Then Théophile and Claudia dropped in. Claudia kissed me on the cheek and Théophile paid me thirty francs for last Sunday's work. My uncle wanted to know what the money was for. I told him proudly about my job with Théophile et Son Orchestre. My uncle said nothing, but his face took on the hue of moldy herring. Miss Vintage Bordeaux ambled by, stopping at our table, giving me a kiss on the cheek, and asking: *"Ça va, chéri?"* She winked at my uncle and said there was nothing she would deny a friend of a friend of mine, and then she gave *him* an affectionate kiss on the cheek and pulled up a chair.

Uncle Siegfried shouted: *"Garçon!"*, paid, and made a humiliating scene on the café terrace, in front of my friends and teachers. He shouted that I was a rotter, giving a bad name to my family, and that he was going to take me to the Left Bank *right now!* My friends and teachers listened on in horrified silence.

That very night Uncle Siegfried moved me out of the Régence Hôtel and installed me in a drab, dull pension near the Sorbonne. It belonged to a former *lycée* teacher from Grenoble who had coffee for breakfast and read the collected works of La Rochefoucauld. Visitors had to be announced at the desk. There was a bed check at midnight. The roomers were dull, rich boys from Switzerland and Indo-China who pretended to be gifted and broke. They would get up at seven-thirty in the morning, and spent all day long at the Sorbonne.

I was miserable in Montparnasse. In the evening I would sneak off for a few hours to Place Pigalle. But it wasn't the same any more. My friends and teachers began to suspect me of being a Left Bank spy. Miss Vintage Bordeaux no longer kissed my cheek, Théophile hired another violinist, and one night Mohammed ben Ali offered me his white stuff, as though I were a tourist. I was no longer welcome in Montmartre and stopped going there. A few weeks later I left Paris and went back home.

Our ration has been reduced to two and a half biscuits a day. . . .   BENJAMIN FRANKLIN, *September 20, 1762*

ENCORE

I STUDIED law in Prague, but my heart wasn't in it. Paris and Montmartre had left me with the sweet aftertaste of irresponsibility.

I was out of touch with my fellow law students, who took a dim view of Montmartre and of my extracurricular activities. They loved to plunge into the legalistic labyrinths of the *Lex Romana.* They would discuss for hours the pro and contra of an obscure lawsuit involving some water rights at the time of Tiberius Gracchus, 133 B.C. They hoped to become brilliant trial lawyers, saving sexy sex-murderesses from an all-women jury, and they talked of making a million koruny in corporation law. They asked me what I wanted to become.

"First violinist with Théophile et Son Orchestre," I said.

They thought I was crazy. I didn't tell them about Claudia. They wouldn't have understood.

🎵 I did experience a brief flurry of enthusiasm for Ecclesiastical Law, which was part of my curriculum at Prague University. Sometimes I found myself gazing wistfully at the pictures of the statuesque, majestic cardinals dressed in their magnificent purple robes who had codified the Corpus Juris Canonici. The thought crossed my mind that this would be an interesting and colorful career. But I realized that my chances of becoming a cardinal were slim. I passed my examinations, excelling in Ecclesiastical Law, and went back to Paris. This time I went without the blessings, and the money, of my family.

🎵 I didn't bother to go near the Sorbonne. I settled in Montmartre, renewed my friendship with Miss Vintage Bordeaux, the economics teachers from North Africa, and Gaston, my waiter at the Prix-Fixe. When I went there the first time, after an absence of over a year, Gaston shook hands with me, asked me: *"Ça va?"* as though I had been away for a couple of days, and then went off and, without asking for my order, brought me the *spécialité de la maison,* which he liked, *tête de veau à la vinaigrette.* I was back.

Théophile had disbanded his orchestra, married Claudia,

and was planning to set up an orchestra consisting exclusively of employees of the Société Générale. For a while I performed in dimly lit dives along the rue Pigalle, where I had the assignment to needle amorous couples in dark corners until the gentleman, if he was one, would tip the musicians and tell me to beat it. Then I had a few breaks and within a few months reached the pinnacle of success: I became a first-desk violinist at the Folies Bergère.

I had arrived. Once my name even appeared on the program, in tiny letters, when I performed a violin solo, *Ave Maria* by Bach-Gounod. The *metteur en scène* thought that an "artistic transition" was needed between the preceding number—an Oriental-style dance of three emancipated harem ladies with veiled faces and almost totally unveiled bodies—and the number that followed—a burlesque about a just-married couple trying to find a room for their wedding night. I was the artistic transition.

It was always a great moment as I started to perform my solo. A bluish spotlight fell on me, lighting up my violin and my profile. There was often scattered applause after my performance. I was all set to play an encore, the "Meditation" from *Thais,* but the applause was never strong enough to warrant my playing the encore. I told all my friends to come to the Folies and listen to me, but they thought I was joking.

"To the Folies Bergère?" they said. "To—*listen*?"

One night as I was tuning up my instrument, I saw a couple from my home town in a front row. The man, a retired mining engineer, dabbled in music criticism for a local paper. His wife ran a bridge circle and was feared for her vitriolic gossip.

If they should see me perform, there might be a lot of talk back home. Mindful of my family's honor, I decided to remain anonymous. I asked the electrician backstage to skip the spotlight for the evening. He said: *"Entendu,"* and went back to his glass of wine.

I started my solo in merciful darkness. Then—I was told later—the stage director yelled at the electrician, *espèce d'imbécile*, to light me up. In the middle of a fortissimo, a strong beam of light fell on me. No one in the large auditorium could fail to see me. I got an ovation and, for the first time, felt compelled to play my encore.

The encore was over, but the spotlight was still on me. Perhaps the switch didn't work; or the *imbécile* electrician was having another glass of wine.

The applause died down. There was a long and embarrassing silence. I was still standing there, bathed in bluish light, a forlorn figure in the Folies. Some people must have wondered whether I, not Mme Mistinguett, was the star of the revue.

The retired mining engineer and his wife went back home and spread the news. The local *Ostrauer Zeitung* became so interested that they printed my biography—I wasn't even twenty—and asked me for a picture that would show me with the emancipated harem ladies. I sent them one, but they decided they couldn't print it, after all. Years later, when I had become a contributor to the newspaper, I found the picture stuck in a corner of the mirror in the men's washroom, next to two risqué drawings.

I got tired of playing in music halls and night clubs—one bleak winter I didn't see the sun for several months, sleeping in daytime and working at night—and when I was offered a job as violinist aboard a French ocean liner, I jumped at the chance. I had always wanted to see the world. And I was told that the food aboard was wonderful, better even than at the Prix-Fixe.

The chefs aboard the ships of the Compagnie Générale Transatlantique seemed to be singularly addicted to music, especially light music. After performing for the passengers we would take our instruments to the foredeck where the cooks, cabin stewards, barmen, *femmes de chambre,* table waiters, assistant chief stewards, night stewards, bellboys, bath stewards, and other crew members had their quarters. We would play for them the nostalgic songs and peppy *javas* of the streets of Paris.

The *chef de cuisine* was an enormous man, almost as broad as he was tall, with a big, sad face. He was dedicated to heavy sauces and gloomy moods; he was homesick for Paris. When we started to play *"Paris, je t'aime,"* the chef would wipe his eyes with the end of his snow-white apron. It was his 689th crossing. We tried to cheer him up by playing *"Sur le pont d'Avignon, on-y-danse, on-y-danse."* The chef would take the arm of the doyenne of the chambermaids, a gray-haired lady who was said to be reticent before, but quite complaisant after, the third glass of Pernod. She and the chef would whirl around, and everybody would clap his hands. The next day the chef would send us a large can of *caviar frais du Golfe de Riga* before dinner, and a *soufflé Grand-Marnier* afterward.

Sometimes I would go downstairs to visit the great chef in his large, stainless-steel kitchen empire where he ruled over a hundred *toques blanches:* assistant chefs, *rôtisseurs, poissoniers, entremetteurs, potagiers, sauciers, hors-d'œuvriers, grilladiers, buffet-froid* men, pastry cooks, butchers, helpers, dishwashers. He was always near the sauce department, sticking his forefinger into sauces and tasting. When he tasted a sauce, his blue eyes took on the cold fire of a sapphire, and his forehead was wrinkled in concentration. Many a time when I came down he would be on the verge of breaking into tears.

"All day long those passengers come here asking me how I make this and what I put into that!" he would say. *"Allez, allez!* Cooking at sea isn't like cooking in a big hotel. On the Atlantic you can't send out to the market because you've forgotten something. My clients are French *and* Americans. The French love liver, tripe, *cervelle au beurre noir,* kidneys, and sweetbread. Americans may eat calf's liver, but they wouldn't touch the other things. They want grillades— steak, sirloin, *châteaubriant,* lamb chops. Their doctors have told them that grilled red meat is healthy for them. *Allez, allez!* There is more to cooking than steaks. Here we are trying our best and they complain!"

The chef looked grim. The *saucier* quickly stepped in front of his pots. It was whispered that under the angry stare of the great chef a *sauce béarnaise* would sometimes curdle.

"Yesterday," he said, "a passenger ordered braised pork loin with tomatoes, spread with tuna fish, served with macaroni." He paused a little to let the horror sink in. "He was from Ohio."

We musicians had our private dining-room and a waiter for ourselves. He was a considerate man who never offered us *crêpes Suzette,* like his colleagues in first class who would make a *Feuerzauber* production out of the *crêpes.* We were never prompted to hurry, please, because the next service was waiting. And, unlike the passengers, we had work to do, and were hungry. We appreciated the efforts of the chef and his men, and they appreciated our appreciation. The passengers would order difficult-to-make dishes and then not touch them because the wind had risen and they had become sick in the middle of their meal. We never got sick during lunch- or dinner-time, only in between meals when we were expected to perform.

The humiliating illness known to the French as *le mal de mer* knows no boundaries of class, bank account, or birth. It changes kindly people into obnoxious misanthropes. I've heard people complain that "the best meals are always prepared on stormy days when few passengers are expected to appear in the dining-room." It is agony to lie on one's deck chair while delicate aromas from the dining-room drift up.

Especially when they have *coquilles Saint-Jacques,* prepared with herbs and served in a scallop shell, or *matelote d'anguille,* eel cooked in red wine with mushrooms and onions. Oddly, fish and sea food are more repulsive to seasick people than anything else.

One night the great chef was in a particularly suicidal mood. He had arranged, by order of the *commandant,* an intimate dinner for a group of American businessmen who had been recommended by the New York office of the Compagnie Générale Transatlantique. After much thought and soul-searching he had served them caviar, *petite truite de rivière Belle Meunière, suprêmes de Bresse Île-de-France, asperges de Lauris, le steak de Charolais, Terrine de foie gras,* salad, cheese, *fruits rafraîchis.*

"A very light dinner," he said to me. "Hardly more than a snack. So what happens? They don't touch my *truite.* They say that chicken *and* steak at the same meal are too much. That my *terrine* is too rich. They hardly touch their steaks. They have no appetite and blame it on my food. It's heavy, they say. *Pensez-vous!* Why don't they blame themselves instead? Sitting in the bar all day and night, playing po-*ker.* Drinking coffee with their steaks and cock-*tail* at all other times. *Allez, allez!* Let's go to my room."

His room, a combination office and bedroom, was next to the kitchen. He took a book from the shelf. It was an old chronicle about cuisine at sea. One page was marked.

I read: ". . . and the pilgrims had to get their food ashore whenever the ship called at a port. Ships were not equipped to carry fresh food and often there was no water aboard. The only food available was dry beans seasoned with vinegar and spoiled biscuits. A wise pilgrim never set out on a trip without a larder full of ham, smoked or salted meat, hard cheese, pickled food that could be kept in good condition for a long time. . . . A typical menu consisted of a glass of Malvoisie wine, lettuce with oil as hors-d'œuvre, a dish of lamb, flour pudding, and coarse Cretan cheese. Bread was available only for a brief period after port calls; usually after the fifth day it was replaced by biscuit. . . ."

The great chef closed the book with an angry snap. It sounded like a pistol-shot.

"Turning down my *suprêmes de Bresse!*" he muttered grimly. *"Allez, allez!"*

The mess sergeant is always right

THE UNKNOWN SOLDIER

ARTIST'S DREAM

F OR a great many people 1929 was the end of Prosperity. For me it was the end of Gastronomy. I was drafted for eighteen months' service into the Czechoslovak Army.

Military experts have called the old Czechoslovak Army a good army, but I've often wondered how far the army would have got if, following Napoleon's celebrated dictum, it had had to march on its stomach.

At five in the morning—the hour when I'd gone to bed in my happier days of freedom—we had to queue up for something called, for lack of a more suitable word, *"café."*

This *"café"* came in large squares, which had the size of tombstones, the color of dehydrated mud, and the smell of asphalt. The squares were dumped into large containers of boiling water, where they dissolved instantaneously into a witches' brew. It was always lukewarm when the cooks poured it into our tin cans, though it might have been piping hot only a moment ago. *"Café"* and a piece of dry bread were the soldier's breakfast. Fifteen years later, when I was drafted into another army—the Army of the United States—there used to be much griping at breakfast-time because the eggs were not sunny-side up or the milk wasn't cold enough.

There were no such gripes in the Czechoslovak Army. There were no eggs. There was no milk. We hated the witches' brew until the winter maneuvers started. After lying outdoors all night long in snow and ice, we were overjoyed at the sight of the field kitchen arriving through the misty dawn. Something miraculous had happened to the *"café":* it was piping hot, had the color of fine Italian *espresso,* and tasted like an exquisite blend of Puerto Rican and Guatemalan coffees.

The food was prepared by the forerunners of what later, in the Second World War, became known as gremlins. They served cold potato dumplings with hot prune compote. A dish called "beef stew" consisted of potatoes and sickly-looking gravy. They cooked barley together with blueberries. But the most astonishing dish was *beton,* which is the Czech word for cement. *Beton* was an amorphous, dirty-gray mass with the consistency of Portland cement. No one ever found out what went into it. Rumors said that it contained flour, stale bread, potatoes, glue, and the skins of cows that had died of old age. The dish was classified SECRET. We were told not to describe it in letters to our families.

Soup, meat, stew, blueberries, barley, prunes, and about everything else were dumped into the soldier's tin can. You sat down on a footlocker or on the floor, trying to sort out and identify the ingredients. There were no mess halls, chairs, or tables for enlisted men.

Supper was even more informal, consisting of bread and a piece of *reklamní salám,* "publicity sausage." This was a particularly cheap sort of sausage which was used as a giveaway by the big sausage-makers. Sometimes we had *tvarušky,* molded cream cheese with the taste of six-month-old Liederkranz.

Things got worse at the Officers' Candidate School in Opava, where the food was not only bad but also insufficient. Ascetic nourishment and periods of prolonged starvation were part of the future officers' education, by order of Major Syrový, the executive officer.

Major Syrový—*syrový* means "raw"—was a rotund heavyweight, extending roughly six feet in every direction. He lectured on tactical problems and the importance of being ascetic. His appetite was fabulous. He lived in a small house near the school building, with his wife and two daughters. His womenfolk were as fat and round as he was. They looked like the "Before" pictures in the "Before—and After" reducing ads. We called them *knedlíky*—the Dumplings.

They had a pretty, winsome girl named Tonka who cleaned their house and cooked for them.

Tonka, no dumpling herself, was popular with my class-mates. We always knew what the major was having for dinner. Tonka's stories frequently taxed our credulity. But one night one of my classmates was hiding in Tonka's kitchen, for reasons known only to him and to her, and when he returned to the barracks, the next morning, he told us some incredible tales. Major Syrový had eaten a whole meter of "publicity sausage," all by himself. Tonka had to peel potatoes by the kilo. She would cook the family's food in large containers such as were used in the army kitchen. Major Syrový had topped off the sausage and a kilo of potatoes with two large plates of *Krautgulash*.

It wasn't difficult to find out what the major had had for lunch. He would come to the classroom, looking contented, his lips creamed with fat, gravy, and the remainders of his meal. He never liked me. Somehow he'd got hold of the Ostrava newspaper describing my artistic career at the Folies Bergère, and thereafter he always referred to me, with undisguised contempt, as *úmělec,* the artist. I found myself frequently restricted to quarters. I stood guard on week-ends, near the ammunition depot, while most of my classmates went home on twenty-four-hour pass. During arduous field exercises I was selected by Major Syrový for the honor of carrying the lower, heavier part of a heavy machine gun.

After lugging the heavy machine gun through the snowy

fields for six hours—for no good reason at all, as far as I could see—I would return to the barracks in a state of near collapse. Sometimes I was so tired I didn't even bother to queue up for my portion of "cement." In the afternoon Major Syrový was lecturing in the classroom. The place was overheated and everybody had trouble keeping his eyes open. I often fought against sleep, but I always lost the battle.

One afternoon I dozed off during Major Syrový's discourse on infantry tactics. In the middle of a wonderful dream I heard my name called, as if from far away. I jumped up, still half-asleep.

"Wechsberg!" the major's voice was saying. "You're asleep!"

There was no use denying it. My eyes were still partially closed. I decided to make a clean sweep of it.

"Yes, sir," I said. "I dreamed."

"You—*what*?"

"I had a dream."

The class roared with laughter. Everybody was wide awake now.

Major Syrový said ominously, "You will report to my office after class."

When I went there, he let me stand at attention for the better part of ten minutes, commenting unfavorably on my sloppy, "artistic" appearance. Then he said: "So you had a dream, did you?"

"Yes, sir."

"Sound off! Talk like a soldier, not like an artist!"

"Yes, sir!" I shouted.

"And what did you dream of, if I may ask?"

"Filets de sole Dugléré!" I shouted.

I had dreamed I was back aboard the *Île-de-France* and the great chef had made for me his delicious *filets de sole Dugléré.* I frequently had such wild, gastronomic dreams in those hungry months.

Major Syrový sat up straight in his chair as though he'd received an urgent summons from the Army's Chief of Staff. The mere thought of food gave his face a greedy complexion.

"What are *filets de sole Dugléré?*"

"Sole prepared after the classic recipe of Jean Pierre Dugléré, with white wine, mushrooms, and tomatoes," I yelled, still standing at attention.

"At ease!"

Major Syrový swallowed. His sarcasm was gone. He was on the defensive. I saw the opening and moved right in, in accordance with his tactical rules.

"We had a great chef," I said. "His *petites bouchées dites à la Béchamel* were wonderful." I made a tantalizing pause.

Major Syrový looked at me with a lamentable blend of uncontrolled rapacity and wild curiosity. A low, plaintive sound formed in his massive throat. I faced him silently. I couldn't help thinking of the cold, long Saturday nights when I'd been standing guard in front of the ammunition depot.

"What—what are they?" he asked.

"Small *vol-au-vents* filled with a *haché* of white chicken meat, ham, truffles—" I stopped. Would I be on guard again next Saturday night?

"Krucinál! (Christ!)" Major Syrový's Adam's apple bumped up and down in his throat like a strip-teaser on a burlesque stage. "Tonka must try it for dinner."

"I'll give her the recipe," I said. "It's very complicated. The *champignons* must be simmered in Béchamel sauce. I've got lots of recipes at home. If I went there on Saturday—"

"Of course you'll go. I'll give you a pass. Bring me the recipes."

I brought him one, *filet de bœuf à la casserole aux pommes sautées.* The following week I brought him another recipe. I had many at home.

I no longer stood guard on Saturday nights. I don't know what happened to the lower part of the heavy machine gun. I suppose somebody else carried it.

My classmates at the Officers' Candidate School could hardly wait for their promotion to second lieutenants. To them it meant new uniforms with gold buttons, a shiny saber, the privilege of staying out all night, and escorting the more expensive girls. To me it meant eating at the officers' mess, tables with tablecloths, each course served on a separate plate.

On the day of my promotion I went to the officers' mess.

The food was almost as bad as the enlisted men's chow. It was a disappointment. I felt cheated. Even the new saber was no compensation.

The older officers were married, lived with their families off the post, and ate at home. Only we junior officers ate at the mess. We were afraid of the mess sergeant, who would steal the best portions of meat for himself and his K.P.'s. The mess sergeant was a hardy army perennial and had served in the Czechoslovak Army even before it was officially formed. During the First World War he had fought in the Czechoslavak Legions on the side of the Allies. The legionnaires later formed the nucleus of the new army. Fellow legionnaires addressed each other by the brotherly *"ty,"* "thou," and called one another *"bratře,"* "brother." The mess sergeant was a "brother" of the colonel, a fellow legionnaire. Like most *déle-slouzící* ("longer-serving") noncoms, he hated the new crop of second lieutenants who had only recently entered the army and already outranked him.

The mess sergeant had been a Prague slaughterhouse worker in his younger days. He knew how to cut up a steer. Three times a week, we were supposed to get boiled beef. The mess sergeant would throw us a few bones and loose ends. When we complained, he would say he had once served boiled beef to President Masaryk, during an inspection of the troops.

"If it was good enough for the President and Commander-in-Chief, it's good enough for you," the mess sergeant would say with finality.

Once in a while the food became inedible and we would

decide, reluctantly, to send a deputation to the colonel, asking him "to investigate and rectify the situation."

The colonel once responded by making an "unannounced" visit at the mess hall, but somehow the brother mess sergeant had been tipped off in advance. When the colonel sat down with us at the table, the meal was excellent. The soup was soup, not the usual dishwater; there were tender, juicy hunks of boiled beef, potatoes, and two other vegetables; and for dessert we had *livance,* cakes filled with plum jam and sprinkled with cinnamon.

The colonel ate seven *livance,* wiped his mouth, fondly patted his stomach, commended the brother mess sergeant in front of us, sent him and the other enlisted men out of the mess hall, and gave us hell. We were spoiled brats, he said, we didn't even know the rigors of war, our behavior was shameful, effeminate, and unbecoming to officers, and we should consider ourselves restricted to quarters over the week-end.

The colonel went home. The mess sergeant, his position stronger than ever, gave us less to eat than before. He and his K.P.'s went on eating the best pieces of meat. In those months I learned that if you want to eat well in the army—in any army—you have to be a full colonel, or a K.P.

TAFELSPITZ
FOR THE HOFRAT

IT WAS perhaps not altogether an accident that the first disappointment of my career as an officer was caused by boiled beef. Few Americans think of boiled beef as the gastronomic treat it is known for in central Europe. In Vienna there was a restaurant that was held in high esteem by local epicures for its boiled beef—twenty-four different varieties of it, to be exact.

The restaurant was Meissl & Schadn, an eating-place of international reputation, and the boiled-beef specialties of the house were called *Tafelspitz, Tafeldeckel, Rieddeckel,*

Beinfleisch, Rippenfleisch, Kavalierspitz, Kruspelspitz, Hie-ferschwanzl, Schulterschwanzl, Schulterscherzl, Mageres Meisel (or *Mäuserl*), *Fettes Meisel, Zwerchried, Mittleres Kügerl, Dünnes Kügerl, Dickes Kügerl, Bröselfleisch, Aus-gelöstes, Brustkern, Brustfleisch, Weisses Scherzl, Schwarzes Scherzl, Zapfen,* and *Ortschwanzl.*

The terminology was bound to stump anybody who had not spent the first half of his adult life within the city limits of Vienna. It was concise and ambiguous at the same time; even Viennese patriarchs did not always agree exactly where the *Weisses Scherzl* ended and the *Ortschwanzl* began. Fellow Austrians from the dark, Alpine hinterlands of Salzburg and Tyrol rarely knew the fine points of distinction between, say, *Tafelspitz, Schwarzes Scherzl,* and *Hiefer-schwanzl*—all referred to in America as brisket or plate of beef—or between the various *Kügerls*. Old-time Viennese butchers with the steady hand of distinguished brain surgeons were able to dissect the carcass of a steer into thirty-two different cuts, and four qualities, of meat. Among the first-quality cuts were not only tenderloin, porterhouse, sirloin, and prime rib of beef, as elsewhere, but also five cuts used exclusively for boiling; two *Scherzls,* two *Schwanzls,* and *Tafelspitz.* Unlike in present-day America, where a steer is cut up in a less complicated, altogether different manner, in Vienna only the very best beef was good enough to be boiled.

You had to be a butcher, a veterinarian, or a Meissl & Schadn habitué of long standing to know the exact characteristics of these *Gustostückerln*. Many Viennese had been born in the Austro-Hungarian monarchy's provinces of Upper Austria, Serbia, Slovakia, South Tyrol, Bohemia, or Moravia. (Even today certain pages of the Vienna telephone directory contain as many Czech-sounding names as the Prague directory.) These ex-provincials were eager to obliterate their un-Viennese past; they tried to veneer their *arrivisme;* they wanted to be more Viennese than the people born and brought up there. One way to show one's *Bodenständigkeit* was to display a scholarly knowledge of the technical terms for boiled beef. It was almost like the coded parlance of an exclusive club. In Vienna a person who couldn't talk learnedly about at least a dozen different cuts of boiled beef, didn't belong, no matter how much money he'd made, or whether the Kaiser had awarded him the title of *Hofrat* (court councilor) or *Kommerzialrat.*

The guests of Meissl & Schadn were thoroughly familiar with the physical build of a steer and knew the exact anatomical location of *Kügerls, Scherzls,* and *Schwanzls.* At Meissl & Schadn, precision was the keynote. You didn't merely order "boiled beef"—you wouldn't step into Tiffany's and ask for "a stone"—but made it quite clear exactly what you wanted. If you happened to be a habitué of the house, you didn't have to order, for *they* would know what you wanted. A Meissl & Schadn habitué never changed his favorite cut of boiled beef.

The restaurant was part of the famous Hotel Meissl & Schadn on Hoher Markt, which was popular with incognito potentates for its discreet, highly personalized service. The chambermaids looked like abbesses and knew the idiosyncrasies of every guest. If a man came to Meissl & Schadn who hadn't been there for ten years, he might find a small, hard pillow under his head because the abbess hadn't forgotten that he liked to sleep hard.

There were two restaurants, the *Schwemme* on the ground floor—a plebeian place with lower prices and checkered tablecloths—and the de-luxe *Restaurant* on the second floor, with high prices and snow-white damask tablecloths. The upper regions were under the command of the great Heinrich, who was already a venerable octogenarian when I first saw him in the late twenties.

He was a massive, corpulent man with the pink cheeks of a healthy baby and the wisdom of a Biblical patriarch. His hands and jowls were sagging and he had serious trouble keeping his eyes open. He never budged from his command post near the door, from where he could overlook all tables, like an admiral on the bridge of his flagship surveying the units of his fleet. Few people in Vienna had ever seen an admiral in the flesh, but everybody agreed that Heinrich looked more an admiral than many a real one. Once in a while his pulse would stop beating and his eyelids would droop, and he would remain suspended between life and death, but the *défilé* of the waiters carrying silver plates with various cuts of boiled beef never failed to revive him.

Heinrich had spent his life in the faithful service of emperors, kings, archdukes, *Hofräte,* artists, and generals, bowing to them, kissing the hands of their ladies, or wives. His bent back had taken on the curvature of the rainbow, reflecting the fine nuances of his reverence, from the impersonal half-bow, with which he would dispose of the *nouveaux riches,* to the affectionate deep-bow, which was reserved for his old habitués, impoverished court councilors, and aristocrats living from the sale of one painting to the next.

Between Heinrich and his habitués there ruled a highly civilized, strictly regulated protocol. Upon entering the restaurant the guest would be greeted by Heinrich—or, rather, by Heinrich's bent back expressing the exact degree of respect in which the guest was held. The depth of Heinrich's bow depended upon the guest's social standing, his taste for, and his knowledge of, boiled beef, and his seniority. It took a man from twenty-five to thirty years to earn the full deep-bow. Such people were greeted by *"Meine Verehrung, küss die Hand,"* which was breathed rather than whispered, and never spoken; Heinrich wasn't able to speak any more.

The guest would be taken to his table by one of Heinrich's captains. Each guest always had the same table and the same waiter. There was mutual respect between waiter and guest; when either one died, the other would go to his funeral. The waiter would hold the chair for the guest; he would wait until the guest was comfortably seated. One of Heinrich's axioms was that "a man doesn't enjoy his beef unless he sits well."

When the guest was seated, the waiter would stand in front of him, waiting for the guest's order. That was a mere formality, since the waiter knew what the guest wanted. The guest would nod to the waiter; the waiter, in turn, would nod to the *commis;* and the *commis* would depart for the kitchen.

The *commis*'s order to the cooks had the highly personal flavor that distinguished all transactions at Meissl & Schadn. It would be "The *Schulterscherzl* for General D." or "Count H. is waiting for his *Kavalierspitz.*" This implied a high degree of finickiness on the part of the habitué, who wouldn't be satisfied with so narrow a definition as the *Kavalierspitz;* his refined palate demanded that he get his private, very special part of a *Kavalierspitz.*

After a suitable interval the *commis* would bring in the meat on a massive, covered silver plate. Some people would have a consommé before the meat; clear consommé was the only preceding dish Heinrich approved of. The *commis* was followed by the *piccolo,* an eight-year-old gnome wearing a tiny tuxedo and a toy bow tie. The *piccolo*'s job was to serve the garniture: grated horseradish, prepared with vinegar (*Essigkren*), with apple sauce (*Apfelkren*), or with whipped cream (*Oberskren*); mustard, pickles, boiled potatoes, boiled cabbage, spinach, or anything else the guest wanted with the meat.

An elaborate ritual would ensue. The waiter had been standing motionless, watching his subordinates as they put the various plates on a small serving-table next to the guest's table. Now the waiter would step forward, lift the cover off the silver plate, and perform the "presentation" of the meat. This was another mere motion, since the guest's enthusiastic approval was a foregone conclusion. The waiter would serve the meat on a hot plate, place it on the table in front of the guest, make a step back, and glance at Heinrich. Then the guest, in turn, would glance at Heinrich.

There followed a minute heavy with suspense. From his command post Heinrich would review the table, with a short, sweeping glance taking in the meat, the garniture, the accessories, the setting, the position of chair and table. It was hard to understand how he managed to see anything through the narrow slit of his almost closed eyelids; but see he did. He would give a slight nod of approval to the waiter, and to the guest. Only then would a genuine habitué start to eat.

℘ Words of ordinary prose have generally been held inadequate to express the delights of boiled beef at Meissl & Schadn. Many Austrian poets were moved to rhymed praise while they regaled themselves on a well-nigh perfect *Hieferschwanzl*. But poets, especially Austrian poets, are rarely given to tenacity of purpose, and somehow the poets didn't bother to write down their poems after leaving the restaurant. Richard Strauss, an ardent devotee of the *Beinfleisch,* often considered writing a tone poem about his favorite dish, but after he finished his ballet *Schlagobers* (*Whipped Cream*), he thought that another major composition devoted to an Austrian food specialty might be misinterpreted by posterity and resented by his admirers in Germany, who, like most Germans, heartily disliked Vienna. Strauss, not unaware of his considerable German royalties, dropped the project.

"Too bad he did," a Viennese music-critic and Straussadmirer said not long ago. "A tone poem on *Beinfleisch* might have surpassed even the transcendental beauty of *Death and Transfiguration.*"

ᴄ⅏ There was a reason for the excellence of the beef served at Meissl & Schadn. The restaurant owned herds of cattle that were kept inside a large sugar refinery in a village north of Vienna. There the steers were fed on molasses and sugar-beet mash, which gave their meat its extraordinary marble texture, taste, tenderness, and juice. The animals were slaughtered just at the right time, and the meat was kept in the refrigerators from one to two weeks.

In Vienna, in those days, boiled beef was not a dish; it was a way of life. Citizens of the Danube capital, venturing into hostile, foreign lands where boiled beef was simply boiled beef, would take Viennese cookbooks along that contained the anatomical diagram of a steer, with numbered partitions and subdivisions indicating the *Gustostückerln.* This was a wise precaution. Even in German-speaking lands the technical expressions denoting various cuts of beef differ from land to land. Vienna's *Tafelspitz* (brisket), for instance, is called *Tafelstück* by the Germans and *Huft* by the German-speaking Swiss. A Viennese *Beinfleisch* is called *Zwerchried* in Germany and *plat-de-côte* among the Swiss.

ᴄ⅏ Vienna's boiled-beef-eaters are vehement chauvinists. They don't recognize the American New England dinner, the French *pot-au-feu,* or the *petite marmite.*

"The meat of the *petite marmite* is cooked in an earthenware stock-pot," a *Tafelspitz* scholar explained to me. "And the necks and wings of fowl are added. Incredible!" He shuddered slightly.

The Viennese experts take a dim view of *bœuf saignant à la ficelle,* rare beef with a string, a great French dish. A piece of fillet is tightly wrapped around with a string, roasted quickly in a very hot oven, and dipped for sixty seconds—not for fifty-eight or sixty-two, but for sixty—in boiling consommé, just before it is served. The juice is kept inside the pinkish meat by the trick of quick roasting and boiling.

But the Viennese do recognize *Tellerfleisch,* another local specialty. *Tellerfleisch* (the name means "plate meat") is eaten only *between* meals. It consists of a soup plate filled two thirds with clear beef soup, boiled carrots, split green onions, chopped parsley, with a piece of almost but not quite boiled beef and several slices of marrow, sprinkled with chopped chive.

There were two schools of cooking beef in Vienna. People who cared more about a strong soup than about the meat put the raw meat into cold water and let it cook gently, for hours, on a slow fire. They would add parsley, carrots, green onions, celery, salt, and pepper. After an hour the white foam that had formed on top was skimmed off. Sometimes half an onion, fried on the open range plate, was put in to give the soup a dark color. Others, who wanted their beef juicy and tender, put it straight into boiling water and let it simmer. This would close the pores of the meat and keep the juices inside.

The Meissl & Schadn was hit by American bombs in March 1945. A few weeks later, Red Army liberators tossed gasoline-soaked rags and gas cans into the half-destroyed building and set fire to it. The hotel burned down. But the tradition that had made Meissl & Schadn a great restaurant had come to an end long before. The restaurant was a creation of the Habsburg monarchy; its prosperity and decay reflected the greatness and decline of the Danube empire. With the help of Heinrich, it survived the hectic twenties, but when he died, the restaurant was doomed.

"People would come in and ask for 'boiled beef,' " an ex-habitué now remembers. "It was shocking."

Vienna's butchers have forgotten the fine points of cutting up a steer, and the chefs don't know how to slice a *Tafelspitz*. The small pieces at the pointed end of the triangular *Tafelspitz* are cut lengthwise, but the large, long, fibrous, upper end must be cut along its breadth.

Today most Viennese restaurants serve *Rindfleisch* or *Beinfleisch,* without any specification. The cattle are raised, and the meat is cut and cooked without the loving care that made it such a treat. It is often tough and dry, and served by ignorant waiters who recommend to their customers expensive "outside" dishes, such as Styrian pullet or imported lobster. The waiters are more interested in the size of their tips than in the contentment of the guest's palate. Restaurant-owners, operating on the get-rich-quick principle, no longer keep herds of cattle inside sugar refineries. It wouldn't be profitable, they say; besides, many refineries are located in the Soviet Zone of Austria.

Where Meissl & Schadn once stood, there is now an office building. Most of Heinrich's habitués are dead, and the few survivors have been scattered to the winds by the last war. Once in a while two of them may meet in an undistinguished Viennese restaurant whose menu offers a *Tafelspitz,* a first-quality cut of boiled beef which, the old habitués can see at a glance, is really *Kruspelspitz,* a fourth-quality cut, somewhat comparable to an American chuck or round of beef.

At such moments of gloom the old habitués are likely to remember, with a nostalgic sigh, the day in the late twenties when old, dignified Hofrat von B., one of Heinrich's favorite guests, came into the dining-room of Meissl & Schadn, exactly at twelve fifteen, as he had done almost every day in the past twenty-seven years, and was ceremoniously guided to his table. Everybody knew, of course, that the Herr Hofrat came for "his" *Tafelspitz,* the narrow part of that special cut which almost, but not quite, touches another first-quality Viennese cut, called *Hieferschwanzl.* If the Kaiser himself had come in, he wouldn't have got the Hofrat's particular piece of *Tafelspitz.* Heinrich was loyal to his habitués.

On that day, as on any other day, there was the familiar ceremonial after the Hofrat had sat down. In due time the *commis* appeared with the covered silver plate, followed by the *piccolo* who carried the *Apfelkren.* But at this point the waiter did not lift the cover off the silver plate to "present" the meat, as he'd always done. Instead he discreetly glanced at Heinrich. Then the old man himself advanced toward the Hofrat's table, slowly and cautiously, like a large ocean liner moving toward the pier. Everybody looked up at him. It had become very quiet in the dining-room.

Heinrich bent his back until his mouth almost touched the Hofrat's ear.

"I'm disconsolate, Herr Hofrat," he whispered. "A regrettable accident in the kitchen. The Hofrat's *Tafelspitz* has been cooked too long. It has—" Heinrich didn't have the strength to finish the sentence, but the tips of his fingers twitched, indicating that the meat had dissolved in the soup like snowflakes in the March sunshine. He was very pale and his jowls were sagging. He looked as though he had been dead for a while and had been resurrected by mistake.

His breath almost gave out, but with a supreme effort he continued: "I have taken the liberty to order for the Herr Hofrat the rear part of the *Hieferschwanzl,* close to, and very much like, the *Tafelspitz.*"

He made an effort to open his eyes and nearly succeeded. At his nod, the waiter lifted the cover off the plate with a flourish and presented the meat. There it was, a large, beautiful cut, tender and juicy, sprinkled with consommé, as delicate and enticing a piece of boiled beef as you could find anywhere in the world.

The Hofrat sat up stiffly. He cast one short, shocked glance at the meat. When he spoke, at last, his voice had the ring of arrogance—arrogance instilled in him by generations of boiled-beef-eating ancestors who had been around in Vienna in 1683 while the city fought off the assault of the Turks and saved—for a while, at least—Western civilization.

"My dear Heinrich," the Hofrat said, with a magnificent sweep of his hand, and accentuating every single syllable, "you might just as well have offered me a veal cutlet." A slight shiver seemed to run down his spine. He got up. "My hat and cane, please."

He strode stiffly toward the door. Heinrich made his deepest full-bow, and he remained bent down until the Hofrat had left. But people sitting near Heinrich swear that there was a smile on his face. He looked almost happy.

Not all dumplings are round.

THE AUTHOR

A DISH FOR LUCULLUS

POLITICALLY there has been antagonism for centuries between Vienna and Prague, but gastronomically the two cities complemented each other well. Vienna was the citadel of boiled beef and strudel. Prague was the stronghold of roast pork and dumplings.

To the Czechs, dumplings mean as much as rice does to the Chinese and spaghetti to the Italians. There was no meal without dumplings, and sometimes there was no single course without them. There were soup dumplings, made of ground liver, or of other ground meat, bread crumbs, marrow, greaves, ham, potatoes. There were dumplings served with the meat, instead of potatoes; these dumplings were called *houskové knedlíky,* "bread dumplings," because they contained small cubes of fried bread. And there were dessert dumplings. Czech housewives talked about *knedlíky* knowingly, at great length, and in highly technical terms—"I steam them in a napkin," a woman would say, or "I use only farinaceous potatoes." Such utterances were as unintelligible to foreigners as the mysteries of Czech grammar with its seven cases of declension.

A nation dedicated to the pursuit of dumplings could not afford to be waistline-conscious. Prague's women had great charm and vivacity, but they were rarely slim and long-stemmed. Dumplings were the national indoor amusement; to eat twenty or thirty dumplings at one sitting was considered a feat of virility.

Not all dumplings are round. The "bread dumpling" was prepared in a piece of dough, half a yard long, which had the shape of a sandwich bread. It was cooked in salt water and slit in one-inch-thick slices by a taut piece of thread. A dumpling must never be touched by the blade of a knife.

Dessert dumplings were round and "individual," but there the similarity ends. They ranged in size from a walnut to a grapefruit. They could be fluffy as a soufflé or hard as a tennis ball. They were made with or without flour; with boiled potatoes that were unpeeled and pressed; with raw potatoes that were peeled and grated; with or without yeast; with eggs or with egg yolks only; out of strudel dough or spaghetti dough; with milk; with sweet cream; with sour

(84)

cream. No one has ever recorded all the regional varieties. They were filled with whole plums—*švestkové knedlíky,* the most famous of all—or with sweet or sour cherries, strawberries, apricots, marmalade, *povidla* (plum jam), sweet cabbage, nuts, or with nothing. They were served with sugar, with brown butter, with cinnamon, with poppy seed, with almonds, with grated cheese, with practically everything else. Each hostess had her personal recipe, which she wouldn't trade for anything in the world.

My favorite dumplings, the formula for which has been evolved by my wife after long, arduous years of trial and error, are of the bantamweight variety. They are made of butter, egg yolks, dry cottage cheese, salted, with a little flour added to keep the dough from falling to pieces. My wife usually cooks a small dumpling for a test and may add more butter or flour to give the dough the needed consistency. It is almost as light as a soufflé, and much better.

Our dumplings are the size of golf balls and are served on very hot plates. You separate them in small pieces—with the fork!—and perform the ritual of sprinkling them with brown butter, sugar, and grated, dry hoop cheese, and once more with brown butter, hoop cheese, and sugar. (The second time the sugar must be on top.) You may add more layers of brown butter, sugar, and hoop cheese, ad infinitum, until the dumplings have disappeared like a northern landscape under the snow. It's a dish for Lucullus.

Bachelor's fare: bread and *vuršty* and kisses.
WITH APOLOGIES TO SWIFT

THE SAUSAGE MILLENNIUM

CZECHOSLOVAKIA's national dish is roast pork with sauer-kraut and dumplings. French gastronomes are look-ing down their noses at fresh pork, which they consider a dish of the *cuisine bourgeoise,* something you eat only at the family table. No French de-luxe restaurant puts pork dishes on its menu. In Prague, the good restaurants—and the best of them were very good—used to feature a dazzling variety of pork dishes—*carré* of pork, pork shoulder, pork tongue, pork snout, pigs' feet, pigs' ears, pork chops (breaded, grilled, fried, *à la charcutière,* with *sauce piquante,* sauté with caraway seeds, with paprika, with mustard sauce), pork goulash, pork ribs, pork schnitzel, and so on. Pork was the common denominator between all classes of the populace; the poor people ate cheap cuts of pork, and the rich ate whole suckling pig, but everybody loved pork. Some of my friends would eat pork twice a day, for lunch and dinner, hot or cold; and between meals they would fortify themselves with hot pork sausages at their favorite *uzenárna*.

Prague's *uzenárny*—the word can be translated only inadequately as "smoked-sausage shops"—were a unique institution. Some were combined with a butcher shop; sausages, hams, and smoked meats were sold in the front room, fresh meat in the back room. But the best sausage shops would not lower themselves to selling fresh pork, to say nothing of beef or veal.

In the happier prewar days when food and drink were far more important to the citizens of Prague than the speeches of their political leaders, the social standing of a man was often determined by the sausage shop he patronized and the kind of hot sausage he ate there. A sausage-eater never switched allegiance.

There were two main varieties of hot sausage: the lean ones, either short or long, called *párky,* which looked somewhat like frankfurters and wieners and always came in pairs; and the fat, short ones, called either *vuršty* (*woor*shty, after the German word *Wurst*), *klobásy,* or *taliány,* which were sold in strings, like pearls. *Taliány* ("Italians") were white and very fat, larded with pieces of bacon and garlic. *Klobásy* were somewhat bigger, fatter even, and thick-skinned.

The most popular hot sausages of all were the *vuršty*. They were juicy and less fattish, the feminine species of the hot-sausage family and were mostly eaten by men. *Vuršty* were two and three-quarters inches long; you ate them with the skin. To leave the thin skin of a *vuršta* on the plate was like putting water into vintage wine in a Burgundy wine cellar. The quality of the *vuršty* was tested by sticking in the fork. If the *vuršty* were fresh and properly made, the juice would spout into the eater's face. *Vuršty*-eaters recognized one another by the fat-stains on their ties and lapels. They wore them proudly, like campaign ribbons.

The manufacture of *vuršty* was a closely guarded secret of the sausage-makers. People would argue for hours whether the products of Chmel, Zemka, or other large factories were preferable to the ones made by the independent, small neighborhood sausage artists. The question has never been settled.

Hot sausages were eaten in the sausage shops, where they were kept steaming all day long in special containers. Sales-girls, wearing white coats like nurses, would fetch *párky* or *vuršty* with a big wooden fork out of the steaming pot and place them on a hot plate. Raw or cooked sauerkraut, potato salad, Russian, French, or Welsh salad was served with it, but orthodox sausage-eaters would order only mustard or horseradish with *vuršty,* and bread or rolls. Along the wall, across from the counter, ran a long, breast-high marble plate, for hurried customers who ate standing, and there was a back room with small tables for guests who preferred to sit down. The sausage shops were white-tiled and had stone floors. They were cool even in summertime. In winter the salesgirls would wear sweaters under their white coats.

The sausage shops opened at eight in the morning. The first customers were already waiting. They were the ones whose breakfast consisted of *vuršty* instead of coffee. By ten thirty most places were crowded with people who pretended to be in a hurry but always had time to stop in for a couple of *vuršty*.

A second rush hour started around noon, when many people stepped in for a couple of fat *vuršty* as New Yorkers step into a bar for a couple of dry Martinis. Some people came into the shops after lunch and ate sausages by way of dessert, and some came later in the afternoon. Around dinner-time the shops were crowded again. Families would have a *vuršty* dinner. A young man would take his date for *párky* before they went to the movies. Romance thrived in the sausage shops.

Some people ate hot sausages at home but for some unexplained reason they never tasted as well there as in the sausage shops. Maybe it was the steaming containers, or just plain imagination. At dinner-time, in the earlier days of our marriage, long before my wife became an accomplished lady *chef de cuisine,* she would send our maid out for hot *vuršty*. A sausage shop was on the premises, next to the entrance of our house; there was one in almost every block. Proprietors of houses with a sausage shop would often charge higher rentals on the grounds of this special "convenience," as they did for refrigerators, central heating, and elevators.

Our girl would run down and return with half a dozen steaming *vuršty*. They were delicious—but not *quite* so delicious as the ones served in the shop.

⊙⊗ I was working in a law office, having graduated, to my family's and my own surprise, from Prague University Law School. I used to spend the morning in court. Around ten o'clock the court would adjourn, and the judges, district attorney, solicitors, bailiff, and members of the jury would retire to their chambers and offices to eat *vuršty*. (About the same time, people in shops or private and government offices all over Prague would eat *vuršty* and *párky*. Work came to a stop, and fat-stains appeared on briefs, files, documents, and counters.)

A small *uzenárna* was installed on the ground floor of the court building, and an attendant would bring hot sausages up to the courtroom. Prosecutor and counsel for the defendant, plaintiff and witness would get together and enjoy their *vuršty* and *párky*. Sometimes tempers cooled off, an out-of-court settlement was reached, and everybody moved on to a near-by beer parlor for a friendly chat.

Even at night people didn't stop eating *vuršty*. I spent my evenings at the *Prager Tagblatt,* an institution of journalism referred to romantically by its enthusiastic editors as "The *Times* of Prague." Near the newspaper building were a sausage shop and an automat, which kept open all night long for the convenience of taxi-drivers, late drunks, prostitutes, newspapermen, and street-cleaners. *Vuršty* addicts went to the sausage shop, while the automat catered to the *topínky* trade. (*Topínky* were garlic-fried slices of dark bread. Around the *Tagblatt* premises they were not deemed suitable nourishment until after the second edition had been put to bed, and then the smell of garlic would mingle with the odor of printer's ink. At that time Bečvář, the gray-haired copy boy, began to carry beer glasses to the editorial offices.)

Beer went well with hot sausages. In Prague's *uzenárny* circles wine-drinkers were suspect as quaint and unreliable— potential sources of danger. All beer was tap beer; local omophagists took a dim view of bottled beer, which was inferior in quality and good only for export. The sausage shops had no license to sell beer, but almost every sausage shop was strategically located between two beer parlors; or, as the beer-drinkers would have it, a beer parlor was always in a tactical position between two sausage shops. The sausage shop would send a girl for beer—an experienced girl would manage to carry from six to eight heavy glasses in one hand —or the beer parlor would send a *piccolo* over with the beer. At certain hours of the day the streets of Prague were filled with white-coated sausage-shop girls and tuxedoed beer-parlor *piccolos* carrying beer glasses.

When Prague's sausage addicts got tired of arguing about what kind of sausage to eat, they would start to fight about what beer to drink. Outside the country the beer of Pilsen was best-known, but there were many experts in Prague who disliked its strong, bitter aftertaste and preferred other brands, such as Tomáš, Budějovské, or Velké Popovice. One of the greatest beer philosophers, the author Jaroslav Hašek, who wrote most of his book *The Good Soldier Schweik* in a beer parlor, gave his accolade to the beer of Smíchov, a suburb of Prague. Violent arguments raged over the question: "Should beer be poured gently into the slightly bent glass, or quickly from high above?" This one, too, was never settled.

Another specialty of Prague's *uzenárny* was ham. Of all good hams—Parma or Poland, York or Kentucky, Bayonne or Westphalia—Prague's hams were the finest: perfectly cured, unsalted, tasteful, and tender. They were eaten hot. (Prague hams were always steamed, never baked or roasted.) Ham was expensive; ham-eaters were in a social class all by themselves. They were bitterly resented by the *vuršty* proletariat and the *párky* sans-culottes. Around Prague's sausage shops ham was a symbol of prosperity and reaction. No wonder that hams have now disappeared from Prague's sausage shops. It may be politics; but it is more probable that the hams are being exported to the Russians who know what's good.

The Second World War raised havoc with Prague's *uzenárny*. When I went there in the final days of the war, many sausage shops were closed, some had disappeared, and the few that kept open had nothing to sell. Meat had been rationed for years; pork was obtainable only in the labyrinths of the black market. Some shops sold *vuršty,* against ration coupons, but they were filled with something that tasted like cured sawdust.

The meat shortage has never eased since. Today a generation of young people is growing up in Czechoslovakia who don't know the difference between *vuršty, párky, taliány,* and *klobásy*. Prague's wonderful hot sausages—like other, far more important things—are only a bittersweet memory of a time that seems so remote now that many people wonder whether it ever existed.

> It is difficult to make something good out of second-class materials, but it is quite easy to spoil the first-class ones.   CHARLES GUNDEL

A *BALATONI FOGAS*
TO START WITH

Some restaurants on the European continent still carry on along the lines of the highest gastronomical tradition, but practically not one of them is located in the vast, bleak area behind the Iron Curtain. No meal can be perfect if the ingredients that go into it aren't, and in the countries under Soviet domination it is impossible to obtain perfect ingredients. Often it is impossible to obtain any ingredients at all. People in Czechoslovakia, Poland, Rumania, and Hungary liked to eat well; the best restaurants in Prague, Warsaw, Bucharest, and Budapest ran a close second to the best restaurants in France. But now food is rationed in all these places. It is no longer a question of getting good food, but of getting any food at all.

Even if some of the great restaurants were still in existence, the number of potential patrons of good food would be close to zero. Europe's gourmets have always belonged to what were once the privileged classes—aristocrats, capitalists, diplomats, prosperous artists, and professional people. All of them have been "eliminated" in the Soviet orbit. As for the inevitable new rich—Communist Party leaders and black-marketeers—they don't seem to care or know anything about truly good food. Consequently, that formerly great epicurean institution, the European restaurateur who made an art of his profession, creating new dishes and inspired variations of old ones, is now almost extinct in a large part of the Continent.

Perhaps the last practicing representative of this great art in the vast, unepicurean Iron Curtain territory was Charles Gundel. A native of Budapest, Gundel—the name is pronounced "Goon-del," with the accent on the first syllable—contributed more to the fame of Hungarian cooking than any other man and is ranked by connoisseurs all over the world in a class with such restaurateurs as Escoffier and Fernand Point.

I met Gundel one evening in 1948 when I had dinner at one of the two restaurants he then operated in Budapest, in Városliget, or City Park. The restaurant occupied the ground floor of a solid two-story building surrounded by a garden that in summer was used for outdoor dining. Cream-colored curtains in the windows, plain white lights, an inconspicuous entrance, and soft music conveyed a nostalgic sense of Old World atmosphere rather than of contemporary flashiness.

As I entered, an elderly doorman with a bushy hussar mustache uttered a reverent: *"Alázatos szolgája. Jó napot kivánok"* ("Your humble servant. Good day"), which is still a familiar greeting in Budapest, Communists or no Communists. He apologized for his awkward bow, explaining that this was one of his rheumatic days, and led me to a patriarch in charge of the cloakroom. This old man was apparently too decrepit to do any work, but he had two assistants, agile boys of a mere seventy years or so, who relieved me of my hat and topcoat and wished me good appetite.

I was then taken in tow by a faultless maître d'hôtel, for whom a small army of no less faultless captains, waiters, and busboys stood aside. He guided me to a table not far from a seven-man gypsy band—two violins, a viola da gamba, a cello, a bass fiddle, a tamboura (big bass guitar), and a cimbalom (dulcimer). The *primás,* by way of tuning, expertly gave his men the D, not the A, as do the phony, Westernized gypsies in Paris and New York night clubs.

Food and music don't ordinarily mix well, I think, each being too important in its own way; but as the evening progressed I found that Gundel's gypsy band did not intrude upon my enjoyment of what was served me. The musicians played their rhapsodic songs in a hauntingly soft way, ending each piece with a sad, lingering, instrumental outcry.

It's not always easy to tell an authentic gypsy fiddler from a phony. Some impostors fool you with trills, ornamentations, rubati, and caprices in minor key that sound almost like the real thing. They play intervals less than a half tone and make sudden transitions, from C to E major or A-flat major, which are characteristic of genuine gypsies. I've often tried the gypsy tricks on my violin. It seems so easy: the constant use of the augmented second in melodic progression; a lot of improvisations; odd harmonies and sharp rhythms. But when I tried, it didn't sound exciting—just bad.

The gypsies at Gundel's were no phonies. I watched the *primás* as he put his fiddle up to his chin and started to play. He began with a deceptively simple melody, playing mostly alone. Now and then he was accompanied by the cimbalom. One by one, the others came in and the mood of the song changed. It became more primitive, violent. The structure was simple enough: they were doing variations on the leader's theme. Sometimes they would fall back, while the *primás* would perform virtuoso trills and ornamental notes, fast scales, and doubling notes. Then the orchestra would unite in a general wailing song, and the leader would play a recitative in parlando style, pleading, singing, and sobbing on his instrument.

It was an extraordinary performance. The *primás* held the bow with his whole right fist—which would have killed my old violin teacher. He played false notes and committed all major violin crimes. He would never have made the beginners' class at any music school. But he and his men were *real* and they created a genuine mood. They seemed as essential a part of Gundel's restaurant as the little busboys, the faint scent of wine and good food, the comfortably spaced tables, the mirrors and lights, the gleaming silver, and the fresh flowers on the tables.

The maître d'hôtel handed me the menu. It was printed in Hungarian and French, except for one line of English in small type along the right-hand margin. This read: "12% will be added to the amount of the bill, and 10% taxes, and in the evening 5% music."

While I was pondering this, a heavily built man appeared, bowed in a courtly, though not at all deferential, manner, introduced himself as Charles Gundel, and welcomed me to his restaurant. He looked just like the description of him given to me by some Hungarian friends of mine who are now living in New York and who become melancholy at the mere mention of his name—a massive, towering, oaklike man of great dignity, with a deeply lined face, a bald head, and an enormous double chin that half covered his black butterfly tie. He wore thick-lensed glasses, a black single-breasted suit, and an old-fashioned silver-gray waistcoat.

I introduced myself, in turn, and said that I brought him greetings from my friends, who had been faithful clients of his for many years. He smiled benevolently at this and said that he would be glad to help me choose my dinner.

My friends had warned me expressly against ordering dishes that were listed on the menu. "If you want to be re-

spected, ask for something that's not on the bill of fare,"
one of them had said.

Gundel discreetly inquired about my health, digestion,
and eating preferences, and then suggested that I start with
Balatoni fogas à la Rothermere, made after a recipe that he
had created in honor of Lord Rothermere.

"Just the filet of the fish, boiled in a *court bouillon* made
with white wine, then covered with *sauce hollandaise* and
topped off with a crayfish *pörkölt,* a ragout in a thick
paprika sauce," he said. He made a circle with thumb and
forefinger, closed his eyes, and shook his head slowly, and
for a moment there was an expression of ethereal delight on
his face.

"You can't get a better *fogas* than the one that comes from
our Lake Balaton," he went on. "This fish, called *Lucioperca
sandra,* is white and more tender than its brother in the
Danube. Life is easier for the *fogas* in the soft, calm waters
of the lake than in the swiftly flowing Danube, where he
has to fight against the strong current and overdevelops
his muscles. And the velvety sand of the lake whitens his
skin."

Gundel gave me a questioning look. I nodded, over-
whelmed by the avalanche of information.

"Afterward, how about a filet of hare?" he asked. "Larded
with bacon, grilled *à l'anglaise,* and served with *sauce béarnaise*? Or perhaps the national specialty, breaded goose
liver?"

Before I could answer, he shook his head and said: "Might
be too heavy for you, though. Let me order you a veal cutlet

done in the Pittsburgh style. We call it that because we first made it for the Mayor of Pittsburgh, when he came here some fifteen years ago. A cutlet of veal filled with a purée of *foie gras* and served with *sauce Périgueux*. A little rice to go with it, and perhaps an endive salad sprinkled with fresh, chopped chives and tarragon leaves, which I was fortunate enough to find in the market this morning."

I murmured assent to all this, at which Gundel turned to the maître d'hôtel, who had been standing respectfully a short distance behind him, and gave him the order, speaking softly in the technical jargon of his profession, like one doctor conversing with another in front of a patient, and underscoring a few fine points with gestures of his big, expressive hands. The maître d'hôtel hurried away.

"Suppose you try one of our Hungarian wines with your meal," Gundel said to me. "Egri Bikavér, perhaps—Bull's Blood, that is. It is a red, tart, mellow, aromatic wine, *genre Bordeaux,* with just the right proportion of tannin."

He wished me good appetite and said he would like to talk to me later. "I am particularly glad that you are from New York," he told me. "My oldest son is a neighbor of yours there. He is in charge of the restaurant in the Great Northern Hotel."

I asked him to sit with me while I dined, but he refused.

"Please enjoy your dinner in solitude," he said. "I'll be back."

Twice while I was enjoying my dinner Gundel came by, and both times he stopped to inquire whether everything was all right. He nodded in a matter-of-fact way when I replied that this was the best meal I had had during six months of traveling about the Continent. For dessert he suggested fresh peach compote, or pancakes filled with ground walnuts, sugar, and raisins and covered with chocolate cream. I chose the latter.

He sat down at my table while I was having a *harack* (dry apricot brandy) and *espresso* coffee, strong and black, served in a small glass. It was past ten o'clock now, and hardly a third of the tables had been occupied.

Gundel sighed deeply. "Our prices are regulated by the government, and we don't charge more than the other comparable places in town," he said, "but there just aren't enough people left here who can afford to spend the money it takes to buy a good dinner."

A complete meal at Gundel's, with a bottle of wine, would run to about a hundred forint, approximately eight and a half dollars at the official rate of exchange, or about half the weekly salary of a white-collar worker. Gundel's guests, he said, were mostly government big shots, foreign diplomats, hard-currency tourists, and local black-marketeers. Occasionally one of the former habitués of the place—an impoverished bank manager possibly, or a dismissed government minister—would sell one of his last Persian rugs and spend a good share of the money on an evening at one of Gundel's restaurants, pointing up the old Hungarian proverb: "We are poor, but we live well."

Such fleeting indulgence in high life was not without danger. An agent of the Gazdasági Rendörség, the feared

Economic Police, might happen into the restaurant, in which case he would almost surely visit the lavish spender the following morning and inquire about the source of his sudden wealth. No matter how reasonable the explanation, there was always the chance that it would be considered unsatisfactory, and, if so, serious charges would be laid against the splurger.

"It's getting so I'm always amazed when anybody comes in at all," Gundel said. "In time, I suppose, there won't be any guests, and that will be the end of it."

He gave a resigned shrug. Thirty-eight years of violent ups and downs had given him a philosophical attitude toward the vicissitudes of life. Since 1910, the year he became a full-fledged restaurateur in Budapest, Gundel had been, as he put it, "through two world wars, two inflations, two occupations, two revolutions, and one counterrevolution." In 1918 he was catering, in the grand manner, to a Habsburg archduke, and the following year he was serving the wild-eyed followers of the Communist Béla Kun.

"They would eat only the white stems of asparagus, because they considered the green tips inedible," Gundel said. "After them came Horthy and the White Terror, and we had guests who ordered roast goose and ate only the wings and legs, because they thought the breast wasn't good enough."

During the Horthy regime Gundel became what amounted to official caterer to the Hungarian government. Ten years ago he was catering to the then King Carol of Rumania, and in 1947 he catered to Ana Pauker of Rumania, who seemed much less of a connoisseur than her royal predecessor.

"I've been called a symbol of continuity through chaos," Gundel said. "Only a little over three years ago, during the three-month battle for Budapest, this place was a stable for Wehrmacht horses. Where we sit now, I saw a horse fall down and die. Practically everything I owned vanished—rugs, mirrors, curtains, linen, glassware, silverware. Shameful! I used to own enough gold plates and gold knives and forks and spoons to serve a hundred and twenty people. Where are they today? Only the chinaware was left. My great collection of rare cookbooks was burned. Some of them were five hundred years old and contained the oldest known Hungarian recipes. Also among them was a very valuable cookbook of Roman times, in an English translation by a physician of Queen Elizabeth. But the worst loss of all was the wines."

Gundel's eyes grew moist. He called a captain and asked him to bring one of the establishment's prewar wine cards. It was an eighteen-page booklet on parchment paper, arranged by categories—wines *en carafe, vins blancs du pays, vins rouges du pays,* Bordeaux wines, Burgundy wines, Rhine and Moselle wines, Tokay wines, dessert wines, Hungarian *vins mousseux,* French champagnes, cognacs, and liqueurs, as well as beers and mineral waters.

Next to the name of each of the Hungarian wines were some numerals and letters, which, Gundel explained, were for the guidance of his foreign guests. A key card with corresponding numerals and letters accompanied each wine list, and from it a customer could ascertain the precise degree of sweetness or dryness, fullness, and flavor of the wines offered. A white wine from the Badacsony district, for example, called Badacsonyi Kéknyelü, was marked "7.III.a.," meaning that it was extra dry, full-bodied, and aromatic. A white wine called Kecskeméti Edes Furmint, from the Royal Hungarian State Cellars in Budafok, bore the marking "1.III.a.b.," meaning that it, too, was full-bodied and aromatic, and, in addition, *fin,* but sweet.

I asked about the Tokay wines on the list. Gundel took off his glasses, closed his eyes and rubbed them with the palm of his hand, as if he were trying to bring back memories.

"Here we say that Tokay is the wine of kings and the king of wines," he told me gently. "It has nothing artificial in it. You drink it just as it comes from grapes grown in the volcanic soil of the Tokay district, in the northeastern part of the country—an ideal natural blend of bouquet, alcohol, and sugar. There are four principal kinds of Tokay wine. Tokay Aszu is a wine that is graded on a basis of how many butts of dried-on-the-vine grapes went into its making. The more dried grapes, the sweeter the wine, and the types are numbered from one to six. Next comes Muscatel Aszu, made of muscat grapes. Then there is Szamorodni—the name meant 'born by itself' in ancient Hungarian—a wine with a sugar content that varies according to climatic conditions. Thus there are both dry and sweet Szamorodni. Finally, there is Essence of Tokay, the rarest of them all. To make Essence, one must wait until the grapes are dry on the vine. The grapes must never be pressed. The sheer weight of them brings forth just a little juice, which in due time matures into a heavy, sweet, liqueur-like wine that makes one think of honey. It is a wine that can be kept almost forever. At the time of the war, we still had a few bottles labeled 1811, the year Napoleon Bonaparte prepared to march on Moscow." He fell silent.

"How much did a bottle cost?" I asked.

"About twenty dollars a half liter," he replied. "I recall, too, that we had some other choice vintages—1815 and 1866, and an especially fine one of 1854. That must have been one of the greatest Tokay years. Who drank those wines that were in our cellars? A lot of soldiers, I would guess, who were already intoxicated before they broke the heads off those precious bottles."

He sighed and put his glasses back on.

"I'm sorry," he said. "The memory of those old treasures always makes me sentimental. You know what Pope Benedict XIV wrote about some casks of Tokay that had been sent to him by Empress Maria Theresa? 'Blessed is the soil which produced thee, blessed is the queen who sent thee, and blessed am I who may enjoy thee.' "

Gundel turned the pages of the old wine list. "We also had some fine Bordeaux and Burgundy wines," he said. "I remember a Château Cos-d'Estournel 1928 and a great Puligny-Montrachet 1929."

Gundel and I counted up and found forty-eight liqueurs listed, among them Dreher's cherry brandy, Gessler's Altvater, Zwack's Unicum and Paprika, Fratelli Branca's Fernet Branca, Campari Bitter, Jourdes's Cordial Médoc, and Pernod's absinthe. For abstainers there were twenty-six mineral waters—Vichy, Karlsbader, Salvator, Apollinaris, Biliner, and so on.

Good food and good drink have been Gundel's chief interest in life for as long as he can remember. He was born in Budapest in 1883, and his first recollection is of hanging around the kitchen and wine cellars of the Erzherzog Stefan, a hotel that was owned by his father. In his middle teens he set out to learn the profession of hotel and restaurant management in the famous cities and resorts of western Europe. He worked in Neuchâtel, and then in Frankfurt am Main, where he met the famous Swiss hotelman César Ritz, who was impressed by his ability and took him on to Paris and then London.

"Monsieur Ritz was a great man," Gundel said feelingly. "He always used to tell me: 'Charles, be creative and inspired about new sauces and new ragouts, but remain old-fashioned about your table arrangements.' "

Two or three years later Gundel was home on a visit when his father became ill, and he felt that he ought to remain in Budapest to help out at the hotel. Its restaurant was noted for its cuisine, and with reason; Gundel, who remembers in detail the menus of distinguished dinners he has served the way Toscanini remembers scores, told me with particular enthusiasm about a luncheon party given there on his parents' wedding anniversary in 1903, when he was twenty. The meal consisted of *potage Windsor,* cold sturgeon with *sauce rémoulade,* saddle of venison with *sauce Cumberland, punch à la Romaine,* Styria *capon à la broche,* salad, compote, *parfait de noces,* patisserie, fruit, and cheese.

One of the jobs entrusted to the young Gundel was doing the daily buying at the market. There he frequently met another young hotelman, Josef Marchal, whose father, Edouard Marchal, had once been *grand chef* at the court of Napoleon III. In 1860 the elder Marchal had been sent by Napoleon as a "present" to Alexander II, Tsar of Russia; he had later made his way to Budapest, where he bought the Hotel Queen of England and settled down.

"Edouard Marchal deeply influenced a whole generation of Hungarian chefs," Gundel told me. "He taught them to use fewer spices and fewer fats, and, in general, how to make lighter dishes that would please an international clientele. When his son became manager of the new Palace Hotel in Lomnicz, a resort in the Tatra Mountains that was fashionable among Austrian aristocrats and British and American millionaires, I became his assistant. The hotel had an annex a few kilometers away, which was managed by Margaret Blassutigh, the sister of Josef Marchal's wife. Everybody assured me that she was an energetic and pretty girl, just the right wife for me. I replied that I wouldn't go near the place. I didn't like the idea of other people picking out a wife for me. Well, you know how it is. One Sunday afternoon I sneaked over, because I was so curious. I had to admit that the place was in first-class shape. I talked a little shop with Margaret, and, first thing I knew, we were engaged. We got married in 1907. Then I took the Palace Hotel over and we stayed on, running it for three years, until our third child was born."

In 1910 Gundel and his family moved to Budapest, where he bought a once well-known but by then run-down restaurant called the Wampetits. It was in this restaurant that I was dining. Gundel renamed it after himself, and hired musicians and singers, and later whole symphony orchestras and opera companies to entertain his guests. There were partitioned sections in one part of the garden for private open-air parties and a terrace for socially and otherwise prominent folk.

"People with good food and wine manners would in due time graduate to the terrace," Gundel said. He seems to look back on this era as the golden period of his life.

The end came abruptly when the First World War broke out. Gundel, after engaging a manager to help his wife run the restaurant, served forty-four months in the army, most of the time with the rank of captain and as executive officer of a battalion. He now feels that through inattention to his duties he may have contributed to the collapse of the Austro-Hungarian monarchy, for he spent most of his time in the kitchen of the officers' mess, trying to drill some sense into the cook, a stubborn Czech who before the war had been a taxidermist in Prague.

"That's the way he cooked, too," Gundel said, shuddering at the recollection.

Gundel returned to Budapest after the war and guided his restaurant through the various revolutions that swept the country. In 1926, while continuing to operate the City Park establishment, he took over the restaurant in the St. Gellért Hotel, at the foot of St. Gellért Mountain on the opposite side of the town.

The St. Gellért was a vast complex of thermal springs, parks, gardens, terraces, playgrounds, and two big swimming pools, one enlivened by artificial waves, the other by invigorating air bubbles that were forced up through the floor of the pool. The restaurant itself contained spacious banquet rooms for large gatherings, small chambers for private parties, a beer tavern, and two public dining-rooms, one with a dance orchestra and the other with a gypsy band.

Gundel called in a brother of his named François and his old friend Josef Marchal to assist him with this huge enterprise. At the St. Gellért he often had as many as twenty private parties and two or three banquets a night. A banquet might be served for as many as nine hundred people. Importers of sea food sold more of their wares to Gundel's restaurants than to all the other restaurants in Budapest combined.

Within a few years Gundel's reputation had become international. When King Victor Emmanuel of Italy visited Hungary in 1937, the government opened up the banquet hall of an old castle for him in the ancient coronation city of Székesfehérvár and asked Gundel to equip and staff it and to provide a meal there. This association with royalty made Gundel sought after by nearly all Hungarian aristocrats who could afford entertaining on a feudal scale. But Gundel emphasized that in spite of the volume of his business in those years he never lowered his standards.

"We were lucky in having first-class personnel," he told me. "Every once in a while I would send my chefs, *sous-chefs,* and maîtres d'hôtel to France to brush up a little. The French are our masters, unsurpassed."

He gravely shook his head and kept a respectful silence in honor of the French masters. After a while he said: "Our pay-roll was quite large for a place like Budapest, which, after all, has never been a very big city. Here at the City Park restaurant alone I had a steady crew of sixty-five waiters and busboys, and the basic crew in the kitchen consisted of a head cook, two butchers, two cold men, three pastry cooks, a roast man, a *saucier,* an *à-la-minute* cook, and two specialists in Hungarian dishes. We also had a few women working here, one specializing in *Wiener Schnitzel,* one in hot pastry and strudel, a vegetable woman, a cheese woman, and, during the summer months, two girls for fruit. Of course, there would always be a number of apprentice cooks and various other helpers around, too."

Gundel thought diligence, a little luck, and a continuous study of what people like are responsible for success in the restaurant business.

"The work of a competent restaurateur doesn't begin with keeping an eye on the kitchen," he said. "He must go to the market himself to get the best there is. Even then the outcome is often doubtful. It is difficult to make something good out of second-class materials, but it is quite easy to spoil first-class ones. People often appreciate a superb meal without quite realizing what makes it better than another meal of apparently much the same sort. You can't distinguish between fresh fruits and the very freshest ones unless you have eaten, let us say, wood strawberries, newly picked in a sunny glade, or tasted a ripe apricot straight from the tree. Yet it is this almost imperceptible difference between fresh and freshest that is all-important. That is why even during my most prosperous years I made it a habit to do all the marketing myself. Every morning at eight I would go to the market with a list of our needs that my chef had compiled the evening before. In addition, I would always buy whatever seemed to be exceptionally good that day—new asparagus, perhaps, or some outstandingly beautiful apples, or fresh *süllö,* as young *fogas* is called, or *kecsege,* a fish that looks something like sturgeon and is very tasty, hot or cold, and has no bones at all.

"Beef is always a problem for the one who buys. It must be aged, but it mustn't be frozen. Did you ever take meat from a freezer and watch it thaw out? The little bit of pink juice that has formed under it is now lost, and that little bit makes so much difference in the taste! We used to get beef from steers that had been fed on sugar-beet mash, but they aren't feeding cattle that way any more."

His marketing done, Gundel would proceed to the St. Gellért and busy himself in his office until noon. Then he would make the rounds of the kitchens and dining-rooms. At one thirty he would drive over to inspect his City Park place.

"Your customers should always know that you are on hand," he said to me. At three o'clock, he went on, he would sit down to lunch with his family, and then, after a short nap, spend the rest of the afternoon at a business meeting or a funeral. He has always been a zealous pallbearer.

"In the years just before the second war, it seemed to me that almost every day one of my old guests was buried," he said.

By six o'clock Gundel would be back at the St. Gellért, and later in the evening he would go to the City Park restaurant. It was a busy life, but he found time for discussions with his chefs, in the course of which many new delicacies were developed.

"Only a genius like Escoffier actually invented dishes," he said with what I gathered was excessive modesty. "You don't *invent* a dish by spreading mint sauce over a pork roast. All we did was make new variations on classical recipes."

Most people associate paprika with Hungarian cuisine, but I noticed that there were only two or three paprika dishes on Gundel's menu.

"The French influence," he said when I asked him about this. "For years now, we have been using fewer and fewer condiments. Above all, we have cut down on the use of paprika. Few Hungarians today realize that paprika, the Hungarian national spice, was hardly used at all in this country a century ago. In Hungarian cookbooks of the early nineteenth century, there is scarcely any mention of it. It isn't a native Hungarian plant, either. Columbus brought one variety of it to Spain from America. When the Turks overran Hungary, early in the sixteenth century, they brought with them another variety, some think from India. Today in our cooking we use paprikas that aren't too hot but are sweetish and piquant rather than sharp, and much milder than cayenne pepper or curry. Good paprika has a certain sugar content. It mustn't be overheated or the sugar content will turn too quickly into caramel and both the color and the flavor will be spoiled. Most foreigners call all dishes that contain paprika *gulyás*. We Hungarians divide paprika dishes into four varieties: *gulyás, pörkölt, tokány,* and *paprikás*."

He looked at me inquiringly through the thick lenses of his glasses and said: "I am not boring you?"

I assured him that I was glad to learn about paprika dishes from the greatest living authority on the subject.

He nodded absently. *"Gulyás,"* he continued, "is prepared by cooking together finely chopped onions, cubes of potatoes and meat, green peppers and tomatoes, caraway seeds, garlic, salt, and paprika, and sometimes a dough that is nipped off, bit by bit, between the forefinger and thumb. The meat used is beef, and there is plenty of gravy, almost like a soup. *Pörkölt* also contains finely chopped onions, paprika, and meat, but in bigger pieces and from fatter animals—veal, mutton, game, pork, goose, and duck. For *tokány* the meat is usually cut in lengthwise pieces. It may contain sweet or sour cream, or no cream at all, mushrooms, asparagus tips, and parsley roots. As for *paprikás*—the finest of them all, to my taste—it is made of fish, fowl, lamb, or veal, and either sour or sweet cream, or a mixture of both."

℘ Two men and a woman came in and were seated at a table near us. They were, Gundel said, Americans, and one of the men was with the United States Legation. He rose, went over to greet them, and asked what they would like.

The woman said: "Oh, a steak, I suppose, medium rare," and one of the men said: "Same for me. French fries, please, and a couple of vegetables." The other said: "Same here."

Gundel recoiled, but only slightly, and relayed the order to a captain. Then he came back to my table.

"They're fine people, generous and kind," he said. "Unfortunately, they never learned to eat. They just feed themselves. I must say, though, that I did have some American guests here occasionally, between the two wars, who appreciated good food. In fact, one of the great banquets of my career was given on June 12, 1931, in honor of a number of American businessmen, or maybe they were hotelmen. I have forgotten which, but I have not forgotten the menu."

Gundel stared up at the ceiling, like a high priest summoning divine inspiration, and said: "Cantaloupe, chicken consommé *au tokai, vol-au-vent Aurora,* saddle of venison *rôti à l'anglaise* with *sauce béarnaise,* a salad *de primeurs,* strawberries *à l'Anthéor,* hot savories, *petits fours.*"

He lowered his eyes and came back to earth. "Don't be deceived by the simple names. I've never been in the habit of giving fancy names to dishes. The chicken consommé, for instance, had nothing in common with the chicken consommés that one finds on most menus. A classic chicken consommé must have a distinctive flavor, and it takes a good chef to prepare one. The *vol-au-vent Aurora* was made with a ragout of crayfish and *sauce Cardinal*. Only a thoroughly trained chef can do it properly. And the salad *de primeurs!* Americans would probably call them fresh young garden vegetables. My son Charles sometimes sends me menu cards from New York, where, it seems, they use the word 'fresh' with everything. As if in a good place it should be considered necessary to point out that the food is fresh! Also, I am told, 'fresh' does not necessarily mean fresh in America. Here, when we say 'fresh,' we mean, of course, vegetables that are served the very same day they come out of the garden. . . . But I'm becoming garrulous. Forgive me. There are not many guests these days who are interested in the fine points of good cooking."

He gave a deep sigh. "That banquet, for instance! It was one of those memorable affairs that don't happen any more. I can only quote from Berchoux:

> *Il se mettait à table au lever de l'aurore,*
> *L'aurore en revenant l'y retrouvait encore.*"

Gundel raised his hands in a gesture of despair and said: "People are too busy in these times to care about good food. We used to spend months working over a *bonne-femme* sauce, trying to determine just the right proportions of paprika and fresh forest mushrooms to use.

"And take carp. Over in America carp isn't too popular a fish. People don't like that muddy taste. Well, I've always maintained that carp can be very good. We would put live carp taken from still lakes into screened tanks and lower them into the Danube and leave them there for two weeks. The current would wash away that muddy taste, and in the end the carp were delicious."

Gundel got up and said he would be back soon, he had to look after his guests. I sat there sipping my *barack,* listening to the gypsy musicians. The music became louder and faster now, and some of the guests began to hum and to tap the floor. The gypsies were not playing music: they were telling each other stories on their instruments, funny and sad stories, tales of love and heroism and compassion and hatred. When they stopped, I nodded to the *primás* and he came over and had a *barack* with me. He was a black-haired, mustachioed man with high cheekbones and the saddest eyes I'd seen in a long time. I asked him where he had learned his melodies.

"On our wanderings," he said. "We hear a song and play it again. It's very much like telling an anecdote. You don't always tell it the same way. You make your changes and then people hear it from you and add their own changes and exaggerations, and when the story comes back to you, you hardly recognize it. We play *lasser* (slow) or *friss* (fast), and we count either *üf* (three) or *dört* (four)." He always used Turkish words when he talked of his music. He liked to talk music all the time, but he couldn't read a single note;

none of his men could. They had never heard of triplets or diminished-seventh chords. Once they had heard Suppé's *Light Cavalry,* and in no time they rearranged the piece and played their own version of it. Everybody thought it was swell, but no one recognized it.

"We miss the right mood now," the *primás* said, sadly glancing at the almost empty dining-room. "We gypsies play best when we *feel* the music. We need dim lights, the perfume of beautiful women, the drinks and whispered voices and tears in the eyes of our listeners. To be able to excite others, we must be excited ourselves. And now—"

He didn't finish the sentence, gave me a sad nod, and returned to his orchestra. A moment later he took up one of their sad, haunting songs.

Gundel came back to my table after a while with a photograph of a group of youngsters—six boys and five girls.

"My children," he said, and there was real pride on his face. "Eleven of them, and I also have seventeen grandchildren. You must go and see my son Charles when you get back to New York. He used to help me here. He was expert at making, among other things, a delicious dessert called *rétes,* a strudel with extremely thin dough. In 1939 he went over, accompanied by a staff of four cooks and five waiters, to manage the Hungarian Pavilion at your World's Fair. I understand they did quite well, though they served a number of strange concoctions, like a drink they called a Pishta. They made it of blackberry liqueur, brandy, orange juice, lemon juice, and seltzer. And then there was something, called the Attila Cup, made out of Hungarian *mousseux,* Bull's Blood, curaçao, fruit, mint, and sugar."

Gundel reflected gloomily on these formulas, and then shook himself like a wet dog.

"When war came," he said, "Charles and his nine companions stayed on in New York. They found good jobs there, all of them. Charles later managed a restaurant called Hapsburg House and then one called the Caviar. You must go and see him at the Great Northern when you get back. Two of my other sons were not so fortunate. Franz was taken prisoner by the Russians. He did not return home until last year, and then I put him in charge of the St. Gellért restaurant. Josef, after being taken hostage by the Germans, was confined for many months in a displaced-persons camp in Germany.

"People sometimes ask me whether my children were brought up on fancy Gundel food. Naturally, they were not. They had to eat whatever came to the table, and most of the time the food was strictly middle-class. Only once in a while, on Christmas or Easter, there would be something special. It's nice to have so many children, but in times like these I worry about them."

☙ During the German occupation Gundel's City Park place was patronized almost exclusively by generals and colonels of the Wehrmacht and the S.S. at lunch and dinner, but late in the evening some of his many Jewish friends who were hiding out would sneak in through a back door for a quick meal in the kitchen. In the course of the Russian siege the St. Gellért Hotel, which had also been a favorite of Hitler's officers, was bombed and partially burned out, while the City Park restaurant underwent its conversion into a stable.

Gundel and his wife were permitted to stay on in a tiny room in the cellar of the City Park place. Gundel lost eighty pounds during the siege and came, he said, to look "almost normal." While the battle of Budapest was still going on, he began talking to contractors about yanking the horse stalls out of his City Park restaurant and making it into a dining-room again. He also set about collecting glassware, mirrors, and pots and pans wherever he could find them, and succeeded in reopening both his restaurants not long after the Red Army marched in.

Hungarian government officials immediately found Gundel's establishments highly acceptable places for the entertainment of their Russian liberators. The people of Budapest were near starvation; in the last weeks of the siege they had grown so hungry that they ate some of the animals in the Municipal Zoo.

It was impossible to get much food in the city. The peasants in the surrounding countryside didn't want to sell what little they had in return for badly inflated paper money. Gundel hired a cart and drove out to their farms to bargain. He traded the few shoes, shirts, and bits of jewelry he had left for butter, flour, eggs, and meat. His lifetime savings, two and a half million pengö, which had made him a rich man, had disappeared.

The only guests in his restaurants were Russian officers, and, later, a sprinkling of British and Americans. By February 1, 1946, a not very lavish meal at a Gundel restaurant cost over a million pengö, or what it would take a Budapest worker a month to earn. (For an American, it was only $1.66.) On the City Park restaurant menu of January 6, 1946, a cold *fogas* with *sauce tartare* was listed at 80,000 pengö; on February 3, at 130,000; on May 12, at 350,000; on July 15, at 26,000,000.

On August 1, the day the currency was stabilized and the forint was introduced as the new unit of currency, at the rate of one to 400,000,000,000,000,000,000,000,000,000,000 pengö, Gundel customers were charged twelve forint, or a dollar, for a *fogas*. Today the price has gone up to fifteen forint.

"Our bookkeeper, poor fellow, almost went crazy," Gundel told me. "Here, let me show you." He called a captain and instructed him to bring one of the ledgers that showed the firm's financial transactions during the inflation period.

Gundel opened the book at random. On June 24, 1946 the restaurant had taken in the improbable amount of 30,382,-752,000,000,000 pengö, and at that, Gundel said, he was going farther and farther into the red. The value of the pengö dropped so rapidly that frequently he lost a small fortune between eight in the morning, when he bought food at the market, and early afternoon, when he sold it. Perfidious customers would come in, enjoy a good meal, and then "discover" that they didn't have enough money with them to pay for it.

"They would pay the bill three days later, when the

amount wouldn't buy a ride on a streetcar," Gundel said. "We'd always thought the inflation was bad after the First World War, when English workers and clerks could and did come to live at the St. Gellért like millionaires on their old-age-pension checks, but during that period prices went up only twelve thousand per cent. This time it was astronomical."

Gundel closed the book and asked the waiter to bring him the guest-book. It was a bright, leather-bound volume that might well have served as the basis for a *Who Was Who* of Europe between the wars. It seemed as if every tourist, painter, banker, singer, diplomat, king, ex-king, musician, politician, and fellow restaurateur on the Continent, and many from elsewhere, had been a Gundel guest.

Gundel was most impressed by the tributes and signatures of playwrights, poets, and novelists. Like a great many other Hungarians, he liked to think of himself as something of a writer. He has written essays on Hungarian food and Tokay wines, a highly diverting cookbook, and two other books: *The Art of Entertaining* (1938), a practical guide for hostesses, and *The Profession of Entertaining* (1940), a compendium of tips for the ambitious restaurant-owner.

Perhaps the most notable of all the scribblings in Gundel's guest-book is a poem that John Galsworthy wrote one night after a dinner at Gundel's. It is called "The Prayer" * and reads:

* Reprinted from *Verses Old and New* by John Galsworthy; copyright 1926 by Charles Scribner's Sons; used by permission of the publishers.

> *If on a spring night I went by*
> *And God were standing there,*
> *What is the prayer that I would cry*
> *To him? This is the prayer.*
>
> *O Lord of Courage grave,*
> *O Master of this night of spring,*
> *Make firm in me a heart too brave*
> *To ask Thee anything!*

The gypsy musicians were playing another sad tune, and for a while Gundel said nothing, listening to the melodies of the distant past. Then a distinguished-looking elderly man in a shabby suit entered the dining-room. Gundel excused himself and hurried over to him. As the newcomer sat down at a near-by table, Gundel remarked that it seemed like ages since he'd seen him here.

The man nodded sadly, saying something about the bad times, and Gundel agreed, nodding equally sadly. Both men sighed, and then Gundel said: "And now I ask you what will be your pleasure? A pheasant *aux choux rouges*? Or a veal cutlet, as in the old days? Dipped in egg and flour, covered with mushrooms and finely shredded ham, sprinkled with . . ."

Last year, Gundel's restaurants were nationalized. Now Hungary's Communist commissars entertain their honored guests at Gundel's. The name has remained, but nothing else has. The food is bad. Gundel himself was permitted to leave. He lives in quiet retirement somewhere in Austria.

"You cannot seal in a can the shining of the sun or the blue of the sky. . . ."

HOW TO EAT IN GENOA: A GASTRONOMICAL ITINERARY

CONNOISSEURS
AND PATRIOTS

I N THE last three years when I lived in Vienna, Berlin, and other places inside or near the drab, dreary, depressing part of the world behind the Iron Curtain, I would sometimes yield to the temptation to get out and away to a country where the skies were blue and the people still knew how to laugh. I would go south—to Italy, where the soft air was filled with music and even the poor ones would enjoy life.

The approach alone was worth the journey. Northern man, forced to spend part of his life amidst snow, sleet, and slush, never ceases to marvel when he crosses an Alpine pass

(123)

on a dreary winter day and finds himself, abruptly and magically, transposed into the brilliant color scheme and the sweet scents of the southern landscape. The contrast is overwhelming in certain spots, at the Brenner Pass between Austria and Italy, or at the Mont Cenis, or the St. Gotthard. (But the ideal approach to Italy would be by helicopter, on a moonlit summer night, landing in Venice's St. Mark's Square—or, for that matter, in the middle of the Grand Canal. The colorful curses of the gondoliers will immediately create a thoroughly Italian atmosphere—the Italy of Mazzini and Garibaldi rather than that of Titian and Tintoretto.)

Metternich once said that Italy is not a country but a geographical expression. Metternich was resentful of the Italians, who caused him a lot of trouble, or perhaps he was trying to be funny; at any rate, he was wrong. Italy is a country. The unifying spiritual, historic, and artistic elements are all there. Contrasts are fused into the harmony of true beauty. There is a perfect blend of landscape, climate, people, and of the works of art they produced.

Italians never made a fetish of ultranationalism, having learned a lesson from history; they were unenthusiastic about going to war unless their nation's freedom was at stake; their sense of values is universal rather than national. But Italians can get wildly nationalistic after the "stretta" in *Il Trovatore,* or over a dish of ravioli.

Ravioli are tiny, meat-filled envelopes made of dough, so valuable they ought to be marked REGISTERED. Less known is their origin. Many an Italian city claims the distinction of having invented that supreme pleasure of the palate. Actually it was the Ligurian housewives who were the first to make it. It was in Genoa that I ate the best ravioli, in a small restaurant on the waterfront.

I went there one beautiful warm evening with the *marchese,* a medium-sized, intense man in his late fifties, but the wine and sunshine of Italy, and perhaps the noble blood of his forebears, made him look much younger. In Genoa, as elsewhere, titles have often been acquired merely by accumulating money or giving it away, but the rank of *marchese* still seems to carry some social weight there.

"My title was created in the sixteenth century by Charles V, Holy Roman Emperor and King of Spain," he told me. "Charles came to Genoa, ordered the elders of the city to assemble, and said to them: *'Estote omnes marchiones'* —'You shall all be *marcheses.'* "

I said that the way *I* had heard it, Charles had said: *"Estote omnes miniones"*—"You shall all be flunkies."

The *marchese* was not amused. "Typical low-class Communist propaganda," he said. "Not funny at all, especially coming from an American."

In Genoa, which has given birth to Christopher Columbus, Nicolò Paganini, Mazzini, and Andrea Doria, and has germinated more revolutionary movements than any other city in Italy—it was from here that on May 5, 1860, Giuseppe Garibaldi started out for his glorious conquest of Italy— patriotism is a local commodity and a way of life. The *marchese,* a man dedicated to the pleasures of the table, referred to himself as a "patriotic gourmet." He took me to his favorite restaurant, past mediaeval churches and sixteenth-century palaces with horizontally striped façades of black and white marble. The shadows were deepening and the street lights had been turned on, and the air had the scent of a Ligurian wine cellar.

The *marchese* inhaled deeply. "Just the right moment for ravioli—the true Genoese ravioli," he said.

I could hear music coming from somewhere along the street. There was the exuberant feeling in the air that always seems to hover over the filthy, picturesque back streets of Italy, with their crowds of children, dogs, cats, and peddlers —streets that are wonderful to walk through but wouldn't be a bit wonderful to live in. Cobblers, tailors, dentists, candlemakers, merchants were working under bright lights in minute caves in the building walls. The noise was strange and exhilarating. By the time we had come to the waterfront, my head felt light and airy as though I'd had half a bottle of champagne, all by myself.

The scent of the wine cellar seemed to have evaporated, and the waterfront street had the fresh, strong smell of an ocean beach at low tide. We descended a few steps into a brightly lit cellar, whose ceiling was so low that I had to duck my head. In the middle of the room was a large stove on which the food was cooked in plain view of the patrons. The *marchese* said this was the kind of place that was known only to a small group of patriotic Genoese connoisseurs. There seemed to be quite a lot of connoisseurs on hand though, waving to one another, drinking wine, and singing.

We sat down among them. The *marchese* took a booklet out of his pocket and handed it to me. It was in English and was called, *How to Eat in Genoa: A Gastronomical Itinerary*. The *marchese* informed me that it had been written by two friends of his—"extremely well-informed, patriotic gourmets." He ordered ravioli. While we were waiting for it to arrive and drinking Coronata, a local dry white wine, I looked through the guide. The introduction explained that "the Genoese people, besides of hard worker, are good eater too, and even 'gourmand,' of that honest gourmandise which will not drive a man to hell but which is, after all, one of the few pleasures that mankind can enjoy in this often sorrowful world." The authors emphasized that Genoese dishes should be eaten in Genoa or not at all. "You can export all the ingredients, and even the cook, but you cannot seal in a can the shining of the sun or the blue of the sky and the sea, and pour it into a saucepan."

A motherly-looking woman in a white apron served the ravioli. The *marchese* started a discourse on the proper manufacture of ravioli, emphasizing that the ground meat must be fresh, "not the remainders of last week's meals," and that the seasoning was all-important; but the cheerful racket of the connoisseurs in the tiny cellar was distracting, and so many friends of the *marchese*'s came over to say hello to him and be introduced to me, that I had a hard time following the thread of the story. It didn't matter, though. The ravioli, however it had been prepared, was remarkable. And the *marchese*'s friends, whatever they happened to be besides patriotic gourmets, were delightful. In Italy eating is not a serious business as it is in France, where no gourmet would break into song during a meal.

The motherly-looking woman brought another bottle of white wine, and then we had *burida,* the Genoese version of bouillabaisse. It is said that fish soup must be made of fish that is very fresh. The *burida* fulfilled this requirement. Certain ingredients seemed to be still alive and swimming around, as if to prove that they had been fished out of the sea only a short time ago. There were more dishes afterward, but I sort of lost track; I always do in an Italian restaurant. More friends and patriots came over with their glasses to shake hands, and the babble, laughter, and singing increased.

It always was that way whenever I ate in a restaurant in Italy. To enjoy Italian cooking you must be a twice-a-day devotee of *pasta.* Italy's poor are very poor; making a virtue out of necessity, they have turned their imagination toward the simple mixture of flour and water. *Pasta* is the only Italian dish reflecting regionalism. In Genoa it is known as large-formed *trenette. Pasta* also comes in wiry *spaghetti* and string-like *maccaroni* (Naples), in rectangular, flat *fettucini* (Rome), in ribbon-like *tagliatelli* and *lasagne* (Bologna), in ball-formed *gnocchi,* rolled *cannelloni,* large *pappardelle* and *recchietta,* dark-colored *bigoli,* baked *strascinati,* hatlike *cappelletti,* and thin *vermicelli,* which literally means "small worms."

There are other good things in Italy: *scampi,* superior even to Maine lobster and Louisiana shrimp, and fine cheeses— gorgonzola, parmigiano, bel paese, provoloni, stracchino, and many, many others. But the joy of discovering a small village restaurant doesn't exist; one is not served, as in

France, a simple, delicious meal no matter where one goes. And Italian sauces are long on spice and short on inspiration.

Italy never placed its wines under the government's protective custody. A fancy label is no guarantee of quality, but rather a ticket for a lottery in which few people ever win. I can think of nothing more pleasant than to drink a bottle of Chianti on a flower-bordered terrace on a sunny day, while a junior Caruso *cassata*-vender sings *Santa Lucia,* and the tables around me seem to be occupied by dark-haired, dark-eyed relatives of Lucrezia Borgia. But try the same Chianti on a cool, unfriendly day in an unheated Italian dining-room!

The popular wines are the Chianti of Tuscany, the Orvieto of Umbria, and the B's of Piedmont—Barolo, Barbero, Barbaresco, and Bardolino. There is a large selection of everything from dry red (Carema, Carmignano, Corvo, Dolcetto, Friulano, Gattinara, Grumello, Oliena, Rabosa, Sangiovese, Valpolicella) to white sweet (Albana, Cinque Terre containing eighteen per cent alcohol, Greco, Nasco, Ogliastra, Passolato, Sorriso d'Ischia), from the lightest Moscato to the heaviest Primitivo.

I am fond of Barolo, a light, red wine that is pleasant to drink, and to spill. I know. One night I dined in a small *trattoria* in the oldest part of Rome. It is frequented mostly by natives. My waiter was the enthusiastic tenor type; he would throw his arms around like Rhadamès in the Nile scene of *Aïda.* The inevitable happened: he spilled a whole liter of Barolo over a beautiful, light-gray suit I was wearing for only the second time. It always happens when you wear something new.

In any other country this would have been a major catastrophe, but this was Italy. Rhadamès led me out to the small kitchen in the rear, where two sturdy ladies didn't bat the eyes as they helped me out of my wine-drenched suit. The proprietor came with a large tablecloth, which he draped around me in toga fashion, and guided me back to my table. A new bottle of Barolo was brought and opened, and a dish with ravioli was placed before me.

The other diners in the restaurant, descendants of generations of toga-clad Romans, hardly took notice of my anachronistic costume. I went on with my meal while the sturdy ladies in the kitchen threw bucketfuls of water on my suit, rubbed it vigorously with discarded napkins, and hung it up near the stove like a salami.

By the time I had finished my gorgonzola and the next bottle of Barolo, the suit was dry. There was no charge for the spilled bottle of wine. No stains remained on my suit.

... we'll dance upon the tables,
In and out among the spoons.

THE MERRY WIDOW

THE LADIES FROM
MAXIM'S

O N MY sixth birthday my father and mother took me for
the first time to the theater, to a performance of *The
Merry Widow*. The plot and the faded beauty of the heroine
left me cold, but I've never forgotten the moment when the
dashing hero, Prince Danilo, tells his sweetheart off in great
style and announces:

> *I go off to Maxim's,*
> *Where fun and frolic beams.*
> *With all the girls I chatter,*
> *I laugh and kiss and flatter!*

Lolo, Dodo, Joujou,
Cloclo, Margot, Froufrou!
For surnames do not matter,
*I take the first to hand.**

And then the curtain went up on the second act, and there was Maxim's, the most glamorous, debauched hot spot in Paris and the world. Ladies in black stockings were swarming over the stage, singing,

> *. . . we'll dance upon the tables,*
> *In and out among the spoons. . . .*

This was Life, and right then and there I decided to grow up quickly and live at Maxim's.

As it happened, I never got there until one night thirty-six years later, when, by chance rather than design, I found myself at 3 rue Royale in Paris, in front of the brown-wood-work-and-gilt entrance that looked more like a Victorian club than a prominent Place of Sin.

It was early—half past nine—much too early for sophisticated people, and the uniformed doorman gave me a haughty look. Inside, the waiters were standing around in bored little groups. They were not noticeably cheered up by my arrival. Everything was red—the carpets, the walls, the lights, the chairs, and the banquettes, modeled after those used in the first-class waiting-rooms of small French railroad stations. In the entrance hall was a papier-mâché model of the 1900 World's Fair, with small paper figures of such

* Copyright 1907 by Chappell & Co., Ltd., London. Copyright renewed. Used here by permission.

renowned clients of Maxim's as the Prince of Wales, Tsar Nicholas II, Victor Emmanuel II of Italy, Oscar of Sweden, Alfonso XIII of Spain. On the wall was a sign: "EVERY FRIDAY: EVENING DRESS," and beneath it a Peter Arno cartoon from *The New Yorker,* showing a dissipated couple at a bar and a headwaiter who is saying: "Ah, m'sieu, I have a table for you now."

It was an encouraging start, but then I looked around and saw that the people in the cartoon were the only ones who showed any sign of dissipation. A few people were dining, but they looked extremely well-behaved and respectable.

A fat, pompous man moved slowly toward me and greeted me with arrogant aloofness. He was "Albert" Baser, Maxim's formidable maître d'hôtel, more respected in café-society circles than Albert Einstein or Albert Schweitzer. "Albert" (Baser) has been known to accept or reject kings, socialites, nabobs, and playboys, all of whom he seats without regard to their bank accounts or accumulated debts, but solely according to his own ideas of protocol. "Albert" has been called "the friend of the great of the world and of the small of the half-world," and he ranks high with members of the international smart set who derive satisfaction from being on a first-name basis with condescending maîtres d'hôtel.

"Albert" "composes" his dining-rooms as though he were orchestrating a symphony. In the old days the "omnibus," the narrow corridor leading to the bar, was *the* place to sit, and local celebrities would roost there, staring at one another, while the big room was given over to the foreign scum of the earth, Argentine beef barons, Russian grand

dukes, American millionaires, and South African sugar dad-
dies who had left wives, children and palatial homes in
search of the forbidden fruit that was symbolized by Maxim's. Today the big dining-room is the place to be seen in,
and an inner sanctum for those who would rather join the
Academy of Snobs than the Académie Française.

Paul Valéry once said that Maxim's reminded him of a
submarine that had been sunk with all its period trappings.
The baroque gilt-framed mirrors, red-plush seats and
carpets, the calla-lily lighting fixtures, the painted flowers
on the stained-glass roof, and the Chéret and Cappiello
murals of naked women may once have been the height of
extravaganza, but today they seem merely a symbol of *fin-
dè-siècle* atmosphere, noteworthy perhaps for nostalgia, but
not for beauty.

Only a few tables were occupied, by well-heeled tourists—
you have to be well-heeled to afford the prices—and by
people who had come because somebody had told them it
was the thing to do, but now that they were here, they
seemed to be wondering what they were doing here. An un-
inspired orchestra on a little platform played the *William
Tell* overture, and a thin waiter was cutting a side of beef.
He looked worried, as though he were afraid he was cutting
the slices too thick.

Several elegant figures appeared: a headwaiter, two
waiters, a wine waiter. Even the busboys looked coldly distinguished. I ordered *sole Albert de Chez Maxim's* and

poularde Maxim's, the specialties of the house. The wine waiter presented his card, which showed an undressed lady throwing away her fig leaf with cheerful abandon. I didn't blame her, after glancing through the card. It listed 338 wines and 112 varieties of champagne. Maxim's has always been best known for its cellars, formerly located on the site on which the American Embassy stands today, and now at the rue Boissy-d'Anglas. Among the 200,000-odd bottles they had a Clos Vougeot 1885, Hermitage Blanc 1899, Château Grillet 1876, Château Pichon-Longueville 1894, Château Haut-Brion 1905.

I ordered pink champagne, trying to work myself up into a state of reckless abandon. The wine waiter departed, and a short, stocky, gray-haired waiter appeared, rearranging plates, glasses, flowers, ashtrays, knives. He turned out to be Léon, the oldest of Maxim's old-timers. He has been here forty-nine years.

"The barman comes next, but he's been with the house only thirty-two years," Léon said. He was glad to talk. *"Oui, monsieur,* I have seen here *bien de choses délicates.* Of course, one doesn't talk about those things. Did you see the picture of the chasseur on the menu? That was I when I started here at the age of sixteen. I got twenty-five francs a month and food, but it seemed more than what we're getting today. Ah, the days of *la belle époque!"*

At Maxim's they now refer to the *belle époque* when they talk of the restaurant's golden age, which came after the turn of the century.

Maxim's occupies the spot where, in the gay nineties, an Italian called Imoda had a fashionable ice-cream shop specializing in "meat-juice ice cream," whatever that was. On Bastille Day 1890, Imoda put up a large German flag. The Parisians reacted, quickly and properly, by wrecking his place. In 1893 Maxime Gaillard, a waiter at the near-by Reynolds American Bar, borrowed six thousand francs, opened a restaurant, dropped the "e" from his first name, and called the place Maxim's. He hired a famous chef, Chauveau, and a famous maître d'hôtel, Cornuché, but when Gaillard died, a year later, Maxim's was almost broke and Cornuché had to borrow money. One night Irma de Montigny, a much-admired Parisian beauty, dropped in at Maxim's with some of her friends. They drank up thirty-six bottles of champagne, at the exorbitant price of ten francs a bottle. (Today a bottle costs three thousand francs.)

That night Cornuché saw the light. To make a success of Maxim's, he had to have glamorous women attached to the restaurant, who would attract generous men. It was a sure-fire formula, and it has worked for almost forty years. Cornuché bought a piano, hired a musician for five francs a night, and advertised Maxim's as "the first restaurant with music."

"Sometimes the guests would stay on until the morning," said Léon, absently polishing a well-polished fork. "At six a.m. the *arroseuses* (charwomen) would come to clean up, and the guests would offer them white wine—the best thing in the early morning. Ah, *la belle époque!*"

Cornuché did a swell job of running the place. You could order practically any dish. The famous sugar king Max Le-Baudy would drop in every night for a salad of violets. Once a guest complained loudly that he had found a beetle in his soup. While everybody looked on, Cornuché approached the soup, picked out the beetle, swallowed it bravely, and proclaimed that it was "merely a raisin."

"M'sieu Cornuché was a great maître d'hôtel," Léon said. "Even the celebrated César Ritz sang his praise."

Léon departed, and the wine waiter arrived with the bottle, filled himself a glass, tasted the champagne, approved of it, filled my glass, and, with seeming anxiety, watched the expression on my face as I drank. It was a carefully rehearsed ritual and he played his part well.

The *sole Albert* turned out to be filets of sole covered with bread crumbs on top, quickly fried in butter, and finished cooking in vermouth, which is later thickened into a sauce. The *poularde Maxim's* was cooked with mushrooms and truffles in a white cream sauce with cognac and port wine. Good dishes, though Maxim's was not an oasis of gastronomy the night I was there.

Fortunately there was Léon, still talking of the *belle époque,* and about *ces dames,* the Ladies from Maxim's who have made the place a household word the world over.

I asked him about the ladies. Had they been all demimondaines, living up to Maxim's sinful reputation? Or was it just clever promotion?

Léon coughed delicately behind the back of his hand, as

befits the citizen of a nation that gave birth to Messrs. Voltaire, Talleyrand, and Richelieu.

"If I may say so, monsieur, some of *ces dames* were quarter-mondaines even. You didn't have to introduce them to the gentlemen. They had two tables near the bar and did all right by themselves. By eight o'clock the place would be crowded. Around ten everybody would leave to dress for the theater. Many would go there to see the last act of a play. It wasn't *chic* to see the whole play. We waiters were free until eleven thirty. We would go over to a small bar in the rue Royale and play manille, a card game of the era."

Léon gave a nostalgic sigh. "At midnight everybody was back, wearing evening clothes. Around one in the morning the Ladies would arrive. Ah, monsieur, what a spectacle of *grande galanterie*! The stars among them would come in sumptuous carriages drawn by two horses. I can still see them, wasp-waisted, their bare shoulders whitened with rice powder, looking stunning in their hats and dresses and jewels. . . ."

Léon closed his eyes for a moment as he recalled the names of the Ladies of the *belle époque,* who brought infatuation to the guests, misery to their wives, and fame to Maxim's. The elegant Liane de Pougy, and the beautiful Réjane; "La Belle" Caroline Otéro, staggering under the heavy load of precious stones; Cléo de Mérode, waiting for her Belgian King; the sisters Jeanne and Anne de Lancy, twins so much alike that their suitors never knew which one they had been with last night, giving rise to a whole school of French (and Hungarian) playwrights; the gorgeous

Lina Cavalieri and the vivacious Émilienne d'Alençon; Jeanne Derval, carrying a small dog in her jeweled chastity belt; and Manon Loty, who could swear like a drill sergeant. They made spectacular entrances, while the guests applauded like an audience at the theater. Every night was a first night at Maxim's.

The spectacle of *grande galanterie* began at the entrance, where head doorman Gérard, impeccable in blue habit, blue pants, and scarlet cap and wearing a monocle, would receive the guests. Gérard divided the world's population into "goodhearts" and "choleras," the latter vastly outnumbering the former. He knew everything about everybody in Paris. He was a combination of banker, detective, promoter, and father confessor. He would slip messages into the hand of Madame while Monsieur was looking the other way.

It was Gérard who saved the reputation of the house one night when La Belle Otéro announced that her valuable diamond brooch had disappeared. Gérard had noticed that a stranger at the bar had bent over as Otéro passed by. Gérard ordered the most famous dessert of the house, a soufflé topped with a bouquet of roses, and then tripped the waiter so that the soufflé landed on the jacket of the suspected thief. When the man took off his jacket in the washroom, Gérard removed the brooch from a pocket. He returned it to Otéro in the middle of another soufflé with red roses. Such exploits now enable Gérard to live in comfortable retirement in a big house in the Pyrenees.

"Sometimes," Léon said, happily reminiscing, "we had half a dozen kings here at the same time. At the corner table over there, Edward VII was holding hands with Lily Langtry, the British actress he didn't dare see in London. King Leopold II of Belgium would be in a private dining-room upstairs with Cléo de Mérode, and King Manuel of Portugal was often here with Gaby Deslys."

Also present were the American cotton king McFadden, who once ordered for dessert, and was served, an undressed girl on a silver tray, in a pink sauce; and Rigo, king of the gypsy fiddlers, who had escaped with Princess Caraman-Charmay, the former Barbara Ward of Detroit, Michigan.

"Ah, and the Grand Dukes Vladimir, Boris, Michael, and Dimitri of Russia!" Léon continued. "Always sitting at the table next to the entrance to the omnibus. Formidable revelers, all of them. They thought nothing of celebrating four days and nights in a row. I remember one Fourteenth of July when one of the grand dukes was expected to review the French troops at Longchamps at eight o'clock in the morning with the President of the Republic. At six His Royal Highness was still lying under the table, surrounded by empty magnums of champagne. Efforts to lift him were unsuccessful. Somehow we propped him up, gave him black coffee and mineral water, and put on his uniform, making sure that all the medals and the *Grand Croix* of the Legion of Honor were in the right place. An hour later he *was* at Longchamps, looking radiant on his horse. He didn't fall off."

Léon cast a disdainful stare at the quiet, respectable people around us having their quiet dinner. "Nothing was impossible at Maxim's during the *belle époque*. I remember old Count de Seyssel, who belonged to the Gin Club that congregated here every night. At two in the morning the old Count would order two soft-boiled eggs, and then he would fall asleep at the table, and the ends of his mustache would droop into his glass of mineral water. And the Baron de Palaud would play the flute, juggle with the plates, recite the fables of La Fontaine, and bring in men carrying advertising placards for a circus. Ah, he was a great joker! Monsieur James Gor-*don* Ben-*nett* would come here often, buy a rose, and pay five golden louis for it. And there was Alphonse Cranquebille, the grocer, who arrived here with three different girls every night for three years, ordered fifteen dozens of oysters and six bottles of Chablis, and after three years went back to his wife, broke, and never came back. Many a night I served Messieurs Caruso and Chaliapin at that table over there. Monsieur Caruso would always order caviar and chicken with vegetables; Monsieur Chaliapin had borscht, a thick steak with *pommes soufflées,* and a salad with lemon. For dessert they would share a soufflé together.

"And I was here the night when a gentleman came in, ordered a big dinner, and didn't have enough money to pay the bill. Monsieur Hugo, our great maître d'hôtel, said to him: 'Don't worry, you'll pay me back when you have money.' The gentleman was Monsieur Lehár, who later wrote the song about Maxim's—"

Léon turned around to make sure he wasn't being watched, bent his head toward me, and hummed softly:

> *". . . we'll dance upon the tables,*
> *In and out among the spoons."*

For a moment I was back, thirty-six years ago, sitting between my father and my mother in a box of the Ostrava City Theater at a performance of *The Merry Widow,* watching with wide-open eyes the girls in their black stockings dancing the cancan, and getting my first taste of Life. Now, at long last, the chance had come to check up on the dreams of my childhood.

"Tell me the truth, Léon," I asked. "Did they really do it?"

Léon sniffed. He seemed on the verge of crying.

"*Mais oui, monsieur,* of course they did! It was not at all unusual to dance the cancan on the tables. The Vernon Castles once danced the cakewalk here, and later the one-step." He looked gloomily at the dance floor, where two bored, middle-aged English couples were executing their idea of a rhumba. "And there were always some gentlemen from Spain and the Argentine who would start a *bagarre.* And the ladies! *Ah, ces dames!* One night Madame Otéro arrived wearing all her jewels because she was having a feud with Liane de Pougy. Madame Otéro jingled like a Christmas tree, and when she sat down, you could almost feel the shock. A few minutes later Madame de Pougy came in, wearing a simple black robe and not a single jewel. But she was accompanied by her maid, and when the maid took off her coat, she was wearing all of Madame de Pougy's jewels. The Grand Duke Vladimir was so fascinated that he forgot to close his mouth. Naturally, Those Ladies had quite a fight afterward, and when they had a fight—" Léon preferred not to finish the sentence.

The *belle époque* came to an end abruptly one June day in 1914 when the shots at Sarajevo started the First World War. For a short while Maxim's became a playground for French officers on leave. Then came the exuberant members of the American Expeditionary Force. Within three months the management had to replace all mirrors. After the war, kingdoms tottered and princes disappeared. The only princes at Maxim's were those of the black market. It was a dark and vulgar era no one at Maxim's likes to reminisce about. The Ladies had become older and had dropped out, and the younger generation preferred to go up on Montmartre.

In 1932 Maxim's was bought by Maxim's, Limited of London, of which M. Louis Vaudable owns the majority stock. The new owners decided to break with Maxim's risqué past and make the place an island of respectability where a man would dare bring his own wife. The restaurant was redecorated in its former style, or, rather, lack of style, and air conditioning and better lighting were added. When they pushed away the red-plush seats, they exposed heaps of jewelry, gold coins, and garters that had been lost in the long wild nights. The intimate private salons on the second floor, where monarchs incognito had sought relaxation in the company of *ces dames,* were turned into two dining-rooms, one seating twenty and the other forty people. They look as debauched as the boardrooms of the Chase National Bank. Nowadays they are used by big corporations for official dinners, at which no undressed girls, with or without pink sauce, are served.

Maxim's respectability suffered a sharp setback among patriotic Frenchmen during the Second World War, when the place became the favorite hangout of Göring, Goebbels, and Field Marshal Rommel. No one at Maxim's likes to dwell on this somewhat touchy subject, beyond reminding you that the British secret service was also active inside the restaurant, and that staff meetings of the Nazi leaders in the private dining-rooms were usually reported to London a few hours later.

Things were bad all over and only in May 1949—six years late—did the management feel sufficiently fortified to celebrate the fiftieth anniversary of the restaurant with a gala dinner, which featured lobster Belle Otéro, chicken Merry Widow, and ice cream *Belle Époque,* at fifteen dollars the plate. It wasn't a bad dinner, but it was a far cry from the gala dinner that was served at Maxim's twentieth anniversary, in 1913, and which offered:

MELON GLACÉ—LOBSTER—SMOKED SALMON

TARTELETTES WITH PARMESAN

CHICKEN CONSOMMÉ

CARPE BRAISÉ À LA CHAMBORD

PORC FARCI À L'ALSACIENNE

(144)

RAGOÛT OF TRUFFLES

POULARDE MAXIM'S

SALAD

ASPARAGUS WITH SAUCE HOLLANDAISE

DESSERTS

Among the wines served were Xérès, Madeira, Pouilly-Fuissé, Château Latour 1875, half a dozen champagnes, and Chartreuse Jaune 1841.

Maxim's maître d'hôtel during the *belle époque* was the great Hugo. His little black book—kept in Maxim's safe-deposit vault—lists, alphabetically, with almost clinical detachment, the names and addresses of all the great demi-mondaines of his time, their abilities, peculiarities, special preferences, and availability. The preface, written in Hugo's schoolboyish handwriting, says: "You of today who peruse these lines do not believe that a reward of any sort whatsoever was given me for this information. I have refused many offers, and this refusal saved my honor as maître d'hôtel. Hugo."

Hugo's handwriting may be schoolboyish, but he certainly was no babe in the woods. The abbreviations alone which Hugo uses throughout his book give you the idea: *A.F.* means *à faire;* R.A.F. stands for *rien à faire* (nothing doing), sometimes softened by the promise P.L.M., *pour le moment* (for the moment); F.S.B. means *femme seule au bar* (woman alone at the bar), not exactly a compliment in those days; and E.2A. stands for *entre deux âges* (between two ages, which is a Frenchman's polite way of indicating that the lady is nearer her forties than her thirties). Finally, Hugo's supreme accolade, Y.M.C.A., *il y a moyen de coucher avec.*

Yes, those Ladies are all in Hugo's little black book, whether they like it or not. There is Mlle I. M., "young, very Parisienne, very pretty, always at all the grand galas, before A.F., but since she's become an artist, R.A.F." Mme L. B. "lives with her mother, but Mama is hard of hearing." Mme J. A. is "a beautiful blonde who doesn't like to be contradicted and maintains that when she says no, she means no." But Hugo wasn't easily fooled, for he adds: "That may be so, but I still think she will say yes." And there is Mme A. C.: "very spoiled by her mother and definitely A.F. except on Tuesdays and Fridays"; and Mlle E. D., "the little princess," "a good girl but too naïve. She will never get far because she trusts men." (How well Hugo knew his fellow men, too!) Of Mme R. de L. he writes: "*Veni, vidi, vici;* she came here for the first time, found her man, and married him. The ingrate, she never came back."

There are girls in Hugo's book who are reserved for kings and grand dukes only, and others who don't like men with mustaches. Mme D. D., a brown-haired little American, was "enticing but too loquacious. According to her, R.A.F., but I'm quite sure A.F. with a little effort." But, on the other hand, there is Mme A. Y. B., "*grande femme* of rare elegance, very much in demand, but R.A.F. since she is in love with a colonel and very faithful." At the end he adds once more, with conviction: "Absolutely R.A.F.!"

It was almost one o'clock now, the hour when, in the old days, the spectacle of *grande galanterie* had started. I looked around. Many people had gone home, the musicians sounded tired, and the place had a defeated look, like a woman who tries hard to look young and can't succeed because she doesn't *feel* young any more. I thought ruefully of the *Merry Widow* song,

> *And then the corks go pop,*
> *We dance and never stop. . . .*

Léon came over and absently wiped some nonexistent bread crumbs off the table.

"They say that La Belle Otéro lives somewhere in the south of France, in great poverty. Another one has gone to a Swiss convent. One Sunday afternoon a few weeks ago, I went to the Vel' d'Hiver to have a glass of beer and watch the bicycle riders. There I met one of the Ladies, and what do you think the poor woman was doing? Selling programs. She shook hands with me and said: 'I hear they now have wedding-anniversary celebrations and engagement parties at Maxim's?' I said yes, that was true. 'What a shame, Léon!' she said. 'The place has really gone to the dogs.'"

Léon gave a sad sigh. "Sometimes I wonder whether the *belle époque* was really as *belle* as we try to remember, monsieur? Maybe we liked it because we were all much younger."

"Yes, Léon," I said. "We were all much younger."

BLACK TRUFFLES

TRUFFLES—the luscious, piquant spots in the goose liver. Dug up by pigs. Brillat-Savarin called them the "black diamonds of the *haute cuisine*." What are they, exactly? Mushrooms? A sort of potato? Colored carrots? Or simply something the manufacturers put in *foie gras,* to make it more appealing and expensive?

I found out some of the answers on a trip through the southeast of France when I happened to pass through Périgueux, which calls itself "the truffle capital of the world." Even people coolly disposed toward this costly and hard-to-digest delicacy could find no fault with stopping over at

Périgueux, a town of genuine charm where past and present are pleasantly blended. In Puy Saint-Front, the old part of the town, you can sit in a small sidewalk café looking out on relics of prehistoric civilization and Roman walls. The *patron,* filling your Dubonnet glass to the brim without spilling a single drop, tells you, quite casually, that those hills over there were once occupied by Neolithic man and this town was later the ancient Vesunna. The town's miniature boulevards are bordered by Gothic chapels, Renaissance houses, baroque doorways, and twentieth-century chestnut trees. Truffles or no, it's a nice place.

Périgueux is the center of the region known to affluent gourmets the world over as Le Périgord, which comprises parts of the departments of Dordogne and Lot-et-Garonne. I had expected to see the local restaurants crowded with people, all of them feasting with abandon on *foie gras* and truffles, somewhat as the natives of Detroit always seem to be riding in their cars, and the inhabitants of Pilsen used to drink beer most of the time. But the only *foie gras* I saw was in cans, in the windows of the more expensive shops.

The truth is, of course, that *foie gras* and truffles are too expensive for most Périgourdins. In Périgueux, as elsewhere in France, truffles are served in bourgeois homes only on special occasions—births, christenings, graduations, weddings, and funerals—particularly after funerals when the deceased has left a nice inheritance.

Some of my friends in Paris, great connoisseurs of *foie gras truffé,* had given me a letter to M. Charles Barbier, one of Périgueux's and the world's greatest authorities on the fine stuff.

"Barbier was once a well-known chef and now spends his mellow years surrounded by truffles and *foie gras*," my friends told me. "He knows a lot about it. And he's something of a philosopher to boot."

When I found M. Barbier, he was literally surrounded by hundreds of *foie gras*. He stood in the big workroom of the canning factory of which he is the general manager—a large, rotund, placid man with rosy cheeks, a bristling mustache, a double chin, and an enormous stomach. The goose livers had been placed on long tables, one by one, and he was walking from liver to liver, giving them the sharp, merciless glance that drill sergeants have for recruits, making brief comments to a white-coated assistant who was respectfully walking behind him with a pad.

M. Barbier greeted me with enthusiasm.

"It's nice to have a visitor from America," he said. "A growing number of Americans are now beginning to appreciate the finer things in life."

He pointed at the goose livers. "If you don't mind, I'll just finish my morning parade. A shipment arrived last night and must be canned today. In this business of delicate aromas one has to work fast."

He went on grading his livers, and in between he gave me a few pointers. "A fine goose liver should be moderately fat, not too hard, not too soft. The soft ones lose too much fat during processing, and the hard ones get too dry. If they're just right, they'll show the imprint of your fingers like a piece of good, fresh butter. *Voilà!*"

He gently pressed one of the livers, applying his thumb from beneath and his four fingers on top. The fingerprint was as clear as if it had been made by J. Edgar Hoover's bright young men.

"*Extra*," said M. Barbier to his assistant, and the liver was whisked off to a special table.

The factory was not big as American enterprises go; there were perhaps fifty men and women, all looking neat in their white working coats. There are about twenty-five canning factories in Périgueux, Sarlat, Eymet, and Bergerac which process truffles and *foie gras.*

"We grade all *foie gras* into three groups," said M. Barbier. "Extra are the best ones. They go into whole blocks of *foie gras naturel,* the finest, most expensive variety. People in your country always confuse it with *Pâté de Foie Gras* and *Crème de Foie Gras,* for which we sometimes use the second-best quality, called *sur-choix.* There is also a third quality, *choix,* but we don't bother much with that." He let his hand flop down. "The best goose livers are not big; one pound and a half is the ideal weight. Ours are yellow, not white, like the ones that were imported before the war from Hungary, Czechoslovakia, and Rumania. Our peasants feed their geese with yellow maize, which accounts for the color. Personally I like the yellow ones better. Their aroma is finer, and you know why?" M. Barbier fondly graded two **extra** specimens and produced another set of fingerprints. "Because our peasants in the Dordogne, Landes, the Basses-Pyrénées, and the Haute-Savoie may have six or ten or twenty geese, but never more than thirty. No mass production, *mon cher monsieur*. Mass production is the ruin of the *grande cuisine*."

He stared gloomily into space and shrugged in a sad, resigned gesture.

"When the geese are six months old, they are put into wooden cages and the farmers begin to feed them forcibly, stuffing the maize down their throats. Not very pleasant for the poor animals, but then, monsieur, some of the nicest things in life don't start out in a pleasant way. Rough diamonds are not a pretty sight. And Madame Dubarry came out of the slums, didn't she?" He raised his hands after this aside, and continued, matter-of-factly: "After six weeks the geese get so fat they can't move any more. You have to kill them or they might suffocate. Once the merchandise gets here, we have to work fast. Unfortunately, there are never enough goose livers to satisfy the demand. We store them only six months, though *foie gras truffé* ought to remain in storage at least two or three years, until the delicate aroma of the truffles permeates the *foie gras*—"

"The truffles," I interrupted him. "What *are* truffles?"

M. Barbier's face was transfigured by an unearthly light. "Ah, *le grand mystère*," he said, closing his eyes.

He opened them again, dismissed two goose livers as *choix,* and asked me to come to his office. We entered a glass-enclosed room. On a large desk was a basket filled with what looked like black oranges. I noticed that the room was filled with a strong, piquant scent.

"*Voilà*," M. Barbier said, presenting the basket as a guide at the Louvre would present Leonardo da Vinci's *Mona Lisa*. "Truffles. Great mystery of the vegetable kingdom. Highly appreciated by epicures for their flavor and taste long before the days of the Roman emperors. Theophrastus believed them to be products of thunder. Pliny thought they were the most wonderful creations of nature, since they grow without roots. 'Truffles make the women more tender and the men more passionate,' Brillat-Savarin wrote. They grow under the ground, and are found only on the poorest soil, where nothing else will grow, and they have resisted all attempts at cultivation. Thank God," he added as an afterthought. "Otherwise they would be as commonplace and cheap as potatoes, and we would be out of business."

The truffles, M. Barbier went on explaining, come in a hundred and forty variations and in all sizes, from that of a pea to that of an orange. The best-flavored specimens have the size of an English walnut. There are white truffles in Italy and chocolate-colored ones in other parts of France, but the finest of all are black, outside *and* inside. (They are always black on the outside, but white or gray inside until they have fully matured and gained their strong flavor.) They should be firm but not hard, and they should have a marble grain.

M. Barbier broke one of the truffles in half. "See what I mean? Finely marbled; flesh of a jet-black color. Innocent-

(153)

looking fruits, but, like the roulette tables of Monte Carlo, they've ruined quite a few people. Truffles are almost as much of a gamble. No one knows exactly how they come into being. The truffle, species *melanosporum,* belongs to the genus *Tuber,* family *Tuberaceæ,* order Tuberales, class Ascomycetes. The peasants say that they are a product of soil fermentation, somewhat like mushrooms. Truffles, however, grow only in light soil, in the vicinity of trees. There are some truffles near maples, beech trees, junipers, elms, poplars, and willows, but most of them appear around a species of oak, called truffle oak, *chêne truffier.* Our peasants say: 'If you want truffles, you must sow acorns.' Unfortunately, it takes twenty years for the oaks to reach sufficient size, and even then there remains the question whether you'll find any truffles. *Ah, monsieur, la nature fait bien des choses!* I have a little property out in Ribérac where I planted oaks twenty-three years ago." He laughed silently, closing his eyes. "Well, I'm still waiting for the truffles."

Truffles have been found in other regions of France, in the departments of Vaucluse and Basses-Alpes, and also in England, but none of them compare with the truffles of Périgord (*Tuber Melanosporum*) in looks and quality. They grow in open woodland. You can't miss the formation of a *truffière*—a truffle ground—because gradually all flowers, herbs, and grass disappear.

"We say 'the truffle burns the land,' " M. Barbier said. "It's a jealous fruit that doesn't permit anything else to grow in its vicinity. Gradually the terrain begins to show cracks, especially on southern slopes where the sun easily penetrates the ground. The right climate for truffles is about the same as for wine. Wet springs, hot summers with frequent thunderstorms in July and August. Our peasants say 'August makes the truffle.' You see, old Theophrastus had something when he called them products of thunder. The autumn should be moderately cool. During harvest-time, from November to February, it must not get too cold. If the temperature drops more than a few degrees below freezing, the truffles will get brittle, fall apart, and spoil."

He sniffed at the basket, closing his eyes, and his rosy cheeks got even rosier. "If you're lucky enough to find a *truffière* on your territory, you may make *une grosse fortune* —how do you say in America? Hit the—"

"—the jackpot?"

"Exactly. I know a man who made over a million francs [$3,000] last year on truffles. Not bad, considering that there is no labor whatsoever involved, though they say a light harrowing of the soil may help. One oak tree alone netted over thirty thousand francs. Ah, but what a whim of nature! The truffles disappear as suddenly as they come. Last year you may have made a fortune, and this year you won't find a single truffle. *Hah!*"

M. Barbier puffed up his cheeks and exhaled in anger.

"We've done a lot of experimenting without solving the problem. No wonder the number of *truffières* decreases steadily. Ours is an epoch of speed and fast returns. Who wants to plant oaks today in the uncertain hope that there *may* be some truffles in twenty years? Of all the truffle people I know, there's only one who plants two thousand new trees a year. He's got four sons and *he* cares what's going to happen. The rest—*ils s'en fichent.* They say: 'In twenty years I may be dead, so why worry? Let's plant potatoes, which we can sell next fall and buy wine for the money.' What a pity! In fifty years there may be no *truffières* left at all in the Périgord." He raised his hands and clasped them in despair in front of his chest. "But when that day comes, *I* won't be here either."

That afternoon I found myself riding next to M. Barbier in his small Peugeot through the countryside, past dreamy villages, Roman water towers, prehistoric caves, and the ruins of medieval châteaux. M. Barbier was a proud and enthusiastic guide. He loved the country; he was born in the Dordogne, in Laroche-Beaucourt. His father owned a hotel in Angoulême, where young Charles started to work in the kitchen. Cooking came easy to him as, like most good cooks, he always liked to eat well.

"Father wanted me to take over the hotel, but I had the wanderlust. I went to England and worked as chef at the Savoy and Carlton in London, at the Station Hotel in Glasgow, and in various places in York and Newcastle. I had to come home to do my military service, but then I ran out again and became *chef de cuisine* aboard the ships of the P. & O.—Peninsular & Oriental line—making the Australia, China, Japan, and India run. People say the food is bad on British ships, but I assure you it wasn't bad on

the ships I was on as chef. We would make everything—
even *omelettes aux truffes.* I remember a textile manufac-
turer from Le Havre and a chap from Liverpool who would
send me a bottle of champagne once in a while, and I would
make special dishes for them, truffles *à la crème*—you peel
and slice them, fry them in butter, season with salt and pepper, add sweet cream, and stir over a hot fire until the cream
gets thick. There was another French cook on the boat who
later became chef of the Taj Mahal Hotel in Bombay. He
became so infatuated with truffles that he came to Périgueux
and took a few young oak trees to northern India, where, he
said, the climate was the same as here."

M. Barbier rubbed his nose and laughed in his silent way.
"He is still waiting for the truffles to show up, *pauvre
garçon.*"

We had arrived in front of a farm on top of a hill. Behind
the ruins of a burned house I saw a building that seemed to
have been finished recently. M. Barbier explained that the
place belonged to the *Veuve* Merlhiot, who had delivered
truffles to his factory, on and off, for twenty years.

"I used to know her husband well," said M. Barbier. "He
and their oldest son were shot by the Germans in 1944, while
his wife and their younger son were forced to look on.
Why? The Merlhiots were patriots—they loved their country."

He was silent for a moment.

"The Boches burned down the farmhouse. For three years
the Widow Merlhiot had to live in the stable. Ah, there was

a lot of suffering in this lovely country, monsieur. Each village saw its population doubled with the stream of refugees from Alsace-Lorraine. And the Maquis were hiding out in the woods. Once in a while the Boches would raid the villages and shoot people at random. Down in this small village they executed twelve peasants and seven Jews in a single night."

We walked past the stables. M. Barbier rang the bell next to the entrance door of the new house. I heard steps inside and had the uncomfortable feeling of being watched by somebody from behind a curtain. Then the door was opened and there emerged a small, sturdy, suspicious-looking woman in a black skirt and a black scarf.

"*Bonjour,* M. Barbier," she said, without much enthusiasm. She shook hands with him and gave me a sharp, searching glance.

M. Barbier seemed to have expected the lukewarm reception, for he chuckled.

"You may shake hands with my friend," he said to her. "He is not the tax-collector."

The woman shrugged. "I don't like strangers," she said, gruffly. But she gave me a nod and, somewhat reluctantly, her hand.

M. Barbier said we had come to look at a *truffière.* Would she permit us to go to her place? He looked a little worried, I thought, but the woman said: "I was just going to go there. You may come with me if you wish."

We walked over to the pigsty and the woman began to

shout in her high-pitched voice: *"Viens ici, petite, petite, viens!"*

There was a joyful grunt from inside and then a small, cheerful-looking pig came running out and jumped all over the court.

"This is Mignon." The Widow Merlhiot formally introduced the pig to us with an elegant gesture. "She's my *chercheuse*."

M. Barbier noticed my questioning glance and said: "Truffles grow anywhere from five to fifty inches below the ground. The human sense of smell isn't able to detect the peculiar flavor of the truffles, but certain animals can find them. Down in the department of Lot they're using small hounds for their truffle-hunting, and I'm told that they have trained goats in Sardinia and Italy. Here we use sows. A trained sow has a fine nose for the scent of truffles. She'll hunt a truffle as passionately as a foxhound hunts a fox. Only a few pigs, however, have that talent, and they are hard to come by. As a rule, they come from sows that have been *chercheuses* [literally, pursuers]. The peasants are always anxious to find a pig with that special instinct, and they use quite a few tricks."

He laughed and asked the *Veuve* Merlhiot: "You don't mind my telling the story?"

She shrugged, but I thought there was a smile on her face. "Well, it's no crime, is it?"

"Certainly not. When a peasant wants a *chercheuse,* he goes to the market and cautiously inquires about the prices of young pigs. Then he starts to look at them. He secretly drops a small truffle on the ground and crushes it with his heel. If one of the little pigs gets excited and smells the truffle, it will be a *chercheuse*. Naturally, the seller would now like to demand a higher price for the little pig, but he's already quoted a price and is stuck."

M. Barbier gave a chuckle. "Our peasants trust *no*body, monsieur. They keep their money in one-thousand-franc bills under the mattress. And they never tell you when they have found a lot of truffles."

"You never find a lot of them," said the *Veuve* Merlhiot, with a frown. "You thank God if you find just a few."

M. Barbier nudged my elbow and gave me a didn't-I-tell-you look. The woman had hung a white canvas bag around her shoulder. She grasped a stick. We walked toward the woodland behind the farm, followed by Mignon, the little pig, who seemed as obedient as a dog.

There was a stretch of barren land with groups of oak trees, but no flowers or grass on the ground. I noticed that the pig was getting excited. She sniffed over the ground, grunting loudly, behaving like a rabbit dog on a hot trail. Suddenly she stopped and rubbed her snout against the soil. The *Veuve* Merlhiot watched the pig for a moment, then she bent down and, with her stick, gave the animal a gentle tap on the nose. At the same time she dropped a few grains of maize behind her.

The little pig grunted happily and began to eat up the maize. Meanwhile the woman very carefully scratched the ground away with a small spoonlike utensil, until she found a truffle, as big as an apricot, that had been hidden a good

ten inches under the ground. She shook the soil off the truffle and cautiously placed it in her bag.

"*Voilà!*" said M. Barbier. "Looks easy, doesn't it? But
you've got to watch the pig or she will dig up the truffle herself and eat it up. That is why you divert the animal's attention and give her a little maize or a chestnut for consola-
tion."

"She gets a small truffle once in a while," said the Widow
Merlhiot, picking up, with Mignon's help, another couple
of truffles. One was close to the surface, the other, a 150-
gram (5-ounce) specimen, was fifteen inches down.

"Mignon's a good girl," she said. "I bought her almost
two years ago when she was six months old. She'll be good
for another three years. When they get over five, they lose
their sense of smell. *Allons,* Mignon! *Viens, petite, petite!*"

"One must be able to determine whether a truffle is ripe,"
said M. Barbier. "That's not easy, because from the outside
ours are always black. You must never touch a truffle that
you don't want to take out. If you do, it will rot. It will also
rot if you hurt the trees. The pig must be trained not to
come near the oaks."

He patted Mignon. "Good girl. Gives us so many good
things, hams and pork chops and handbags for the ladies.
And now she finds truffles for us. It's not easy. Truffles never
come in bunches. There's one here and another there,
though they're always within three yards of the tree."

He lowered his voice. "We'd better leave now. The *Veuve*
Merlhiot wouldn't like it if we stayed too long and watched
her too closely. They are *bien cachetières,* our farmers. If

Madame is lucky, she'll bring home four pounds today and make several thousand francs—more than a lot of other people here make in a week. But she won't tell you."

&ₓ We said good-by to the Widow Merlhiot, who wasn't sorry to see us go, and drove back to town. Every once in a while I would see a man or woman carrying a white canvas bag and a stick, walking with a trained pig through the woodland.

"This is the heart of the truffle district," said M. Barbier. "But go north a few miles and all of a sudden the truffle stops growing. The soil is the same, and the climate, and there are even oak trees—but not a single truffle. Why, monsieur? *Ah, la nature fait bien des choses.* However, our farmers now are smart enough to realize that one must not depend on truffles alone. So they grow grapes for wine, and grains, sell their cattle, and hope for a *truffière* in the back yard. When the *Veuve* Merlhiot comes home, she will start to clean the truffles and give them a facial, as your ladies say in America, removing imperfections. Better-looking truffles fetch better prices. Then she'll put them in baskets, the smallest on the bottom and the nicest on top. As if we didn't know! And tomorrow, first thing in the morning, she'll take them to the market."

He shook his head. "The truffle market is pretty bizarre, *mon cher monsieur.* During the harvesting season, which they call *cavage,* the farmers meet daily in their little cafés and bistros in Terrasson, Thiviers, Sorges, Brive, Cuzanne, Souillac, Sarlat, Salignac, Montignac, Thenon, and Périgueux. They arrive early in the morning and leave their baskets in the home of a friend or in a hotel under guard. *C'est fantastique*—there may be three thousand kilos of truffles on the market on a particular day, but you won't *see* a single truffle anywhere. Everything is done *'en cachette.'* The farmers wander from bistro to bistro, listening to the talk, trying to guess what the price will be. I've been here now over twenty-five years and I know the people pretty well, but if I went to one of those little dives, I couldn't buy one kilo of truffles. They just wouldn't sell them to me; they would think that something was fishy. They sell only to established buyers. Everybody has to come to the Périgord to buy truffles, even the *foie gras* manufacturers from Strasbourg, Lot, Paris, Nantes, and Bordeaux. Makes them quite bitter, especially those fellows from Strasbourg."

A slight undertone of asperity seemed to creep into M. Barbier's voice at the mention of Strasbourg, which has built up a little goose-liver reputation of its own.

"The Strasbourg people," he said, "always depended on the import of goose livers from central Europe."

He dropped the painful subject and went on to discuss the bizarre ways of the local truffle market. Seems that the buyers were also pretty shrewd traders and wouldn't commit themselves until they had gauged the supply and demand and sized up the good and bad lots. It's just like the stock market. Truffles have always been a steady commodity because they are needed by the practitioners of what the French call the *grande cuisine*.

To be a truffle-buyer you must combine the financial instinct of a Morgan with the poker-faced patience of a Talley-rand. You must watch carefully so the competitors won't snatch up the merchandise from under your eyes, and you must prod the peasants until they come out and tell you how much they will take.

Sales are made by kilos, on primitive, "Roman" scales. Once the deal is closed, the buyers are in a great hurry, for the truffles must reach the factories quickly and a lot of time has already been lost in bargaining.

The big season is just before Christmas, when every restaurant in Paris and many butchers and grocers need truffles, which adorn the roast duck that is the *pièce de résistance* of the traditional Christmas or New Year's Eve dinner.

"If I had been smart," M. Barbier said regretfully, "I would have bought lots of truffles twenty years ago, put them in cans, and stored them away. What an investment they would have made!"

Before 1914 a kilo of truffles cost ten francs. During the First World War, when the people of France were occupied with less pleasant matters than the *grande cuisine,* prices fell to an all-time low of three francs per kilo. Scores of farmers in the Périgord region went broke. They chopped down the oak trees, plowed under the *truffières,* and grew wine and potatoes. Many truffle grounds disappeared in those days; production sank sharply and has never completely recovered.

M. Barbier explained dolefully that, like everybody else, he had omitted to stock up on truffles and instead had lost his savings in foolish investments. Now he has to go out and spend a lot of money when he wants to regale guests with his own truffle recipes.

"My wife and I have a cook," he said, "but on special occasions I like to put on my *toque* and chef's outfit and prepare some of the classical truffle dishes. An *omelette aux truffes,* or scrambled eggs with small slices of truffles, which will turn a simple dish into a rare delicacy! Or *truffes fourrées,* stuffed, surrounded by a light, fine crust, baked and served with sauce Madeira; or truffles *sous la cendre,* broiled slowly over charcoals on an iron brazier. And did you ever try *truffes au champagne*? Easy to prepare, really. You put the truffles in a casserole, cover them with dry champagne, and let them simmer for twenty minutes. At the end there should be no more liquid than a teaspoonful for each truffle. Cover with a light pastry dough and bake in a hot oven for twenty minutes."

M. Barbier closed his eyes in supreme delight. The car almost went into a ditch. I managed to get hold of the wheel just in time, but he didn't seem to notice it.

"Ah!" he exclaimed. "What a dish, what a dish! Truly a feast for Lucullus!"

I observed that it was mainly a feast for extremely solvent gourmets, the prices of truffles and champagne being what they are. M. Barbier chose to treat this remark with lofty indifference. He was now gaining the full measure of epicurean enthusiasm.

"Perhaps the best truffle dish of all is *truffes en timbale.* Fill a *vol-au-vent* (puff paste) or a *bouchée* with peeled truffles that have been cut in slices or quarters and treated for two or three hours in a marinade of cognac or Madeira. Add salt and pepper, put a slice of ham on top, and bake for two hours in a moderately hot oven. Be sure to make a hole in the middle and gradually pour in the marinade. Serve very hot, with a fine old red wine."

His eyes grew misty.

"To appreciate this dish, one must be a truffle merchant from the Périgord. Nowhere in France do people, by and large, eat as well as in our region. It has been said that the Périgourdins were always great fighters and that they stopped warring only to sit down at the table. Think of the many recipes of *la grande cuisine* which Périgueux has given to the world. *Sauce Périgueux,* that wonderful concoction of *sauce Espagnole,* Madeira wine, and chopped truffles which goes so well with a *filet Mignon;* or *tournedos Rossini,* which we here prepare with slices of *foie gras* and *sauce Périgueux.* I read somewhere that *pâté de foie gras* was 'invented' by the celebrated chef Clausse, who worked for Marshal Contades, the Governor of Alsace; and that General Daumesnil, the one-legged defender of Vincennes against the Allies in 1814, a native of Périgueux, 'improved' the recipe. Rubbish! Back in the sixteenth century the farmers of the Périgord prepared solid blocks of *foie gras,* embedded in a *pâté de foie gras.* They were the first to put in the truffles, having noticed that the aroma of the truffle will accentuate the flavor of *foie gras,* just as a good cheese will bring out the bouquet of a fine old Bordeaux. Here in town no self-respecting housewife would buy canned *foie gras.*

She'll go and buy raw goose livers and truffles on the market and put up her own truffled *foie gras,* just as women elsewhere can fruits and vegetables. People here use truffles to stuff geese and ducks, and to prepare their fish. If you ever ate a sole *bonne femme,* with a white-wine sauce, thickened with butter and the yolks of eggs, in which there are not only chopped shallots and sliced mushrooms, but a few slices of truffles, you won't forget it. Not to mention the many kinds of cold *pâtés,* of sausage, and ragouts that are vastly improved by adding a small piece of that fine, black, delicious fruit."

M. Barbier's culinary reveries were interrupted by our arrival at the factory, where everybody seemed to be in a state of feverish activity. Truffles were being washed in tubs filled with cold water, cleaned of all soil with fine brushes, and carefully dried. Then the best specimens were selected by skilled workers, and a group of women peeled them carefully, cutting off paper-thin slices of the skin with sharp knives. Since no part of the truffle, no matter how small, is wasted, even the skins are put in special cans. They are cheaper and can be used for omelets or stuffings.

The truffles were placed in cans of different sizes, either with salt water or in cognac or Madeira, which increase the special aroma of the truffle as time goes on. Finally the cans were sterilized in vast vats under steam pressure—a regrettable but necessary process, during which the truffles shrink and lose as much as thirty per cent of weight.

M. Barbier took me into another hall where this morning's load of *foie gras* was being canned.

"This is far more difficult than the canning of truffles," he said. "Did you ever open a can of *foie gras* and discover that there was more *gras* (fat) in it than *foie* (liver)? *Bien sûr,* it happens to everybody, and people get mad because they've paid a lot of money for the can. Ah, but what can one do? The livers must be pre-cooked a little before they are canned. If you cook them too long, they may lose a lot of fat, but they may also get dry. If you undercook them— or if you choose second-rate merchandise that contains too much fat—there will be lots of fat in the can. We have been trying to find a happy medium. The livers are cut in half, one half is placed on the bottom of the can, a truffle is put on it, then the other half goes on top. Before the can is sealed, it is baked in the oven for five minutes at less than 200 degrees Centigrade (392° F.). Now the cans are taken out of the oven and checked for their fat content. The ones that contain too much fat are used for *pâté*. We take all precautions, but with *foie gras* one is never too sure. We often compare the livers of two animals that were raised by the same farmer under the same conditions, fed the same amount of corn—yet one may be perfect while the other contains as much as fifty per cent of fat. *Ah, la nature fait bien des choses!* After the livers are cooked, the cans are sealed and sterilized for one hour and a half at 108 degrees Centigrade (226° F.). During that time they lose more fat. You just keep your fingers crossed."

M. Barbier crossed his fingers and looked at the sterilization vats in which a new load of cans was being placed.

"No one knows exactly what he's going to find in those cans a few months or years from now. And there are minor problems. You put in a bigger truffle and right away people will say: 'Aha! Truffles were less expensive last year, so they put in a lot of the stuff!' "

M. Barbier uncrossed his fingers. "There are good and bad years in *foie gras,* depending on the climate and the quality of the corn. It's almost like vintages of wine. The customer gets what he paid for. All *foie gras* products are graded by government-approved standards. If you see the label FOIE GRAS AU NATUREL TRUFFÉ on any product of the Périgord, you are sure to get a block of whole natural goose liver which is 100 per cent truffled *foie gras* (goose or duck), with nothing else added. Next comes PÂTÉ DE FOIE GRAS, containing at least a block of 75 per cent of whole *foie gras;* the rest is minced. CRÈME DE FOIE GRAS is a hash containing at least 75 per cent of minced *foie gras,* and other ingredients. The two least expensive varieties are CRÈME DE FOIE D'OIE and CRÈME AU FOIE, containing 55 and 30 per cent *foie gras* respectively. The rest is made up of minced meat, calf's liver, and other ingredients that you would put into a homemade *pâté.*"

The people of Périgueux are great connoisseurs of homemade *pâté.* During the *foie-gras*-less season, from February to October, they prepare their own *pâtés,* which they call *ballotine, galantine, terrine, pâté maison,* or *pâté de campagne.* Almost every housewife and every restaurant has a favorite recipe. They use ground meat (beef, veal, pork, chicken) or diced calf's liver, which has been browned in butter, adding chopped, sauté onions, all kinds of seasonings, and possibly a dash of cognac or Madeira, and then they cook it. If you like a rough-textured *pâté,* you don't even have to pass it through a sieve.

"If you put in good ingredients and season to taste, you can't fail to make a good *pâté,*" M. Barbier said. "The trouble starts when people put in stuff that, they say, 'is good for no other purpose than *pâté.*' If you use ingredients that are not fine, how can you expect to create a fine *pâté*?"

It was getting late and M. Barbier took me to his office, where a table had been set up with plates and glasses, a bottle of Château Margaux, and a small block of *foie gras truffé.*

M. Barbier eyed the display fondly and carefully filled the wineglasses.

"After a hard day's work there's nothing like a slice of properly chilled *foie gras* with a glass of fine Bordeaux before dinner. Too often people serve *foie gras* at the end of a rich meal when the stomach is tired and the palate doesn't appreciate its fine aroma. And never serve salad with it! Nothing but a full-bodied, flavory, round, velvety, vintage claret deserves to be its companion. A Château Margaux 1899 or a Léoville-LasCases 1920 will do wonders for fine *foie gras*—and vice versa."

He began to cut the block with a sharp knife, which he dipped in warm water after cutting each slice.

"There are people who drink beer or ice water with *foie*

gras truffé. No wonder they get stomach trouble! Then the doctors tell you that *foie gras* and truffles are bad for you. Don't you believe them!"

M. Barbier fondly patted his stomach.

"I've been eating the good things all my life and I will be sixty-nine next May. Do I look like a man who suffers from indigestion?"

Fine wine must be treated like a lovely
woman in bed.   BORDEAUX PROVERB

ONE MOMENT IN HEAVEN

Between Périgueux and Bordeaux, in the southeastern
corner of France, there stretch seventy-five miles of
good living, an area rich in regional specialties. In the
northern part are the Duchesse and Marguerite chocolates
of Angoulême, dearly familiar to French kids, the oysters of
Marennes, the sturgeon and caviar of the coast. Farther
south is Gascony, with its trout, salmon, *cèpes,* woodcock,
garbure (cabbage soup), *confits,* and with its Roquefort and
Armagnac; Toulouse and its *cassoulet,* a fine goose stew
with white beans; Béarn, home of hot peppers and bitter

chocolate, which gave the world a great sauce; and the ham and *piperade* (omelet with red peppers) of Bayonne. Above all, there is the wine of Bordeaux, which, according to M. Landèche, is no mere beverage.

"Wine," said M. Landèche, "is a living thing. It lives, breathes, is moody and sensitive, may take sick and die. Here in Bordeaux we say: 'Fine wine must be treated like a lovely woman in bed.' "

M. Landèche was the *régisseur* (manager) of Château Lafite-Rothschild, one of the most celebrated wine châteaux in the Bordeaux region, which happens to be one of the most celebrated wine-producing areas in the world. When M. Landèche talked of wine, he would close his eyes and draw a deep breath, as though he were inhaling the bouquet of an old claret—or perhaps the fragrance of a lovely woman.

I had come to the château after an exhilarating drive through the vineyards of the region: Sauternes and Barsac in the south, with their sweet, liqueurish wines; the dry or slightly sweet wines of the Graves district; Saint-Émilion and Pomerol, where they make full-bodied, heavier wines; the less famous but often delicious wines on the right bank of the Garonne, called Premières Côtes de Bordeaux, Entre-Deux-Mers, Blaye, and Bourg; and the Médoc, where the finest red Bordeaux wines are produced, including those of Château Lafite-Rothschild. There I had met M. Landèche.

He was a robust, gray-haired man in his late sixties, with twinkling eyes and a roughly chiseled face that had the healthy color of the grapes that grow on sixty-five hectares (about 160 acres) of "his" place. He had been christened with wine, as is the local habit, had lived and grown up among the vineyards, had worked there all his life until he reached the top of his profession, and had become *régisseur* of a great château.

He breathed, talked, dreamed, and lived wine. The world began and ended in Bordeaux or, rather, at Château Lafite; the people outside of it existed only as far as they were customers for Lafite wines. Nothing else mattered.

"Lots of people have tried to cash in on the great names of our châteaux," he said angrily. "They put dishonest wines into bottles and label them with a great name that owes its fame to centuries of tradition, experience, and hard work. Fortunately we now have the Institut National des Appellations d'Origine, which set up strict rules for the use of names. It is backed by French laws."

Only the finest wines of the region, not more than ten per cent of the whole crop, are bottled and sold under the name of a château. The next best wine bears the name of certain districts and townships, such as Pauillac, Saint-Julien, Saint-Estèphe, Margaux, Saint-Saveur, Cantenac. Wines that do not qualify for the district names may be called "Médoc," provided "they come from the area bordered in the east by the Gironde and Garonne rivers and in the west by the Atlantic, contain at least ten degrees of alcohol, and are made from certain vines called Cabernet, Carmenère, Malbec, Merlot, and Petit Verdot." Médoc wines that do not fulfill these requirements may be sold only under the names "Bordeaux Rouge" or "Rouge Ordinaire."

To sell one's wines under a higher classification means better prices, and certain winegrowers have tried about everything short of murder to have their wines promoted. Their frantic and unsuccessful efforts often amused M. Landèche, who sat on top of the hierarchy and could afford to chuckle benevolently at the antics of the wine proletariat.

In his happier moments M. Landèche had a recurrent, pleasant daydream. He fancied himself as a member of the jury that, back in 1854, had set out to classify the growths of several hundred châteaux in the Bordeaux region. He saw himself sitting next to Messrs. Duffour-Dubergier, Ferrière, Blondeaux *fils,* and Nathanael Johnston, and they were tasting the finest wines on earth, from light, elegant to aromatic, full-bodied reds, from flint-dry to lush-sweet whites. When he and the other members of the jury finally arrived at their classification—which is still valid—they had merely confirmed the centuries-old opinions of earlier experts. Of the many hundred red-wine châteaux, they had selected the sixty-six best, and classified them in five growths, or *crus.* Only four of them were awarded the proud title of *Premier Cru*—and leading the four was Château Lafite-Rothschild, M. Landèche's private empire.

At that point M. Landèche would wake up from his dream, look around, and see that his dream had come true: he *was* at Château Lafite, surrounded by tens of thousands of bottles of fine wine. He had a sense of exhilaration. He would walk through his vineyards until he reached the boundary of his estate. Across the line are the vineyards of the neighboring Château Mouton-Rothschild, which has been classified as the first château among the second growth, though there is nothing second-class about its wines.

In fact, there are many people who claim the wines of Château Mouton-Rothschild to be as good as some of the first growth. There are also some people, in the Médoc, who call the wine *"le vin Hollywood."* The château has elegant banquet rooms with impressive coats of arms and the cellars are lit up by reflectors. There is a healthy spirit of free enterprise and competition in the Médoc.

⁂ M. Landèche told me that occasionally the *régisseur* is called upon to advise the owner of the château on weighty decisions—decisions that might affect the reputation of the wine.

"If, God forbid, the year's output isn't up to our standard, it must not be sold under the name of the château," he said. "In 1927 our whole crop had been paid for in advance. (We always could sell much more wine than we produce.) Well, when the time for delivery came, I had to call the buyers and give them back their money. We had decided that the wine wasn't good enough to be sold under our label. Did you notice that there exists no Château Lafite 1936? We sold the '36 wine in 1939 to the French Army, at four francs a bottle, as 'Rouge Ordinaire.' Normally a good bottle of our wine will cost 750 francs. I have often wondered whether some of the poilus inside the Maginot Line knew that they were drinking wine from Château Lafite with their *soissons* (white beans)."

M. Landèche covered his eyes at the memory of this disaster and lapsed into an abyss of gloom.

"Up at Château d'Yquem," he said later, "large portions of the crops of 1925, 1930, 1932, 1935, 1936, and 1941 were excluded by the order of the Marquis de Lur Saluces, the proprietor. Sold as anonymous 'Bordeaux Blanc.' You'd say there is nothing more beautiful than to own a wine château, but what a gamble, what a gamble! You work like a dog all year round, and then one thunderstorm at the time of the harvest puts water in your grapes, and the crop is ruined. If the weather is bad at the approach of the harvest, we have to gather the grapes early, when they are lacking in grape sugar. Such wine is too low in alcohol content. And there are other pitfalls. We try our best to keep up the high standards of quality we ourselves have set, and what happens?"

His face darkened. I feared that another outburst was imminent.

"Down in Argentina certain *types* put something called 'Sauternes' into bottles that are labeled with pictures of Château Lafite-Rothschild. Imagine! And in Chile they produce a liquid that here in Bordeaux couldn't even be sold as vinegar. Over there they call it 'Château Lafite'!"

He wrung his hands in despair.

"In California they sell a wine marked 'California Bordeaux Rouge.' *Ah, ça alors!* How would the Americans in Detroit like it if our automobile-manufacturers should sell their cars as 'French Cadillac'?"

He turned away. We crossed the large terrace of Château Lafite. Down below I saw the network of old, Roman-built canals. Behind them were the vineyards and the Gironde River. They say here that the best vines are those which "see the river." M. Landèche remarked pointedly that almost all vines of Château Lafite see the river.

We went into the château, a patina-covered old building with dark doorways and high windows. Its origins are lost in the dark Middle Ages. One of its owners was Philippe de Ségur, who once raised 150,000 louis d'or and joined Lafayette. Time means little in this region of old civilization. One of the near-by châteaux—La Tour-Carnet in Saint-Laurent fetched good prices for its wines as early as 1354.

M. Landèche preceded me down a stairway that led into the cellar. He opened a massive iron door. I felt a cool, acid draft and the smell of earth and dust. M. Landèche turned a switch. A row of dim bulbs lit up, spreading a ghostly light. After a while, when my eyes became used to the dimness, I saw that all along the walls were shelves of bottles. Some had disappeared under layers of dust and cobwebs. On each shelf was a label showing the year of a vintage.

M. Landèche walked toward a corner in the rear where, he said, the proprietor of the château kept his own collection of rare bottles—the *bibliothèque*. Silently, but with visible emotion, he pointed at a label saying "1797." Only a few bottles were lying on the shelf.

"This is the oldest red Bordeaux on earth," he said, in a whisper. His head was slightly bent in deference. If he'd worn a beret, he would have taken it off.

"Fine wines were made here even earlier," he said. "But they couldn't be stored. The glass bottle was invented only at the end of the eighteenth century. Until then the wines were kept in chinaware containers, which preserved neither taste nor color."

I asked him whether he'd ever tasted the 1797.

"No. I don't think one could drink it. Really fine wine gets better with old age, but beyond a hundred years most wines lose their taste. We still have some wonderful bottles of our 1875. But the old bottles are quite a headache. Even the best corks shrink with the passage of time and have to be exchanged. The wines shrink too, just as old people do when they get wrinkled. Every twenty-five years or so we have to open the bottles, fill them with wine of the same vintage, and insert new corks that have been soaking in wine for weeks. It's a delicate operation and must be performed by our *maître de chai* (cellar-master). Always costs us a few bottles of irreplaceable wine, but what can one do? . . . Ah, here he is," he said, and turned around.

A strong, sturdy man came toward us through the dimness. M. Landèche pumped his hand and introduced the *maître de chai*.

"To be *maître de chai* is not a profession," he said. "*Ah, quel bel et noble rôle que celui d'un maître de chai!* He is the one who talks to the wine and understands its motions and emotions. The wine, not the proprietor of the château, is his boss. Correct, *mon vieux*?"

"*Oui*," said *mon vieux*.

"He's in constant conversation with the wine," said M. Landèche. "Young wine is like a nervous child. Two or three days before a heavy thunderstorm the young wine in the barrels gets restless and starts to move. *Ça c'est fantastique!*"

"Hah!" said *mon vieux*.

"But our worries start much earlier," M. Landèche said. "They begin in May, when the vines are still tender. Ah, the vines are like a *grande dame*—they must be treated with devotion. We worry a lot about the right timing. What day, for instance, is the best to start the harvest? The book says you should harvest the grapes one hundred days after the flower appears on the vines; but will the day be right? Yet so much depends on it. After the harvest, when the grapes have been brought into the vats, we start to worry again. Will the new wine have sap and flavor and equilibrium?"

"Oh, la, la!" said *mon vieux*.

"You never stop worrying. Three times a year, for the first three years, the new wine must be worked. That means the dregs must be eliminated, some alcohol evaporates, and the wine becomes 'rounder.' After three years of constant observation the wine is bottled and stored in our cellars. Believe me, no baby is cared for better. And then people from all over the world come here and ask me whether we 'put something in' our wine to make it so good. Imagine!"

"Mince!" said *mon vieux*.

M. Landèche nodded emphatically, appalled by such ignorance. "You can form wine, like a child, by giving it a good education. But you can never change its basic character. Wine is a synthesis of grapes, soil, and climate. Just below our estate are vines that produce only an inferior wine. Why? Perhaps one of the elements is missing. You can't change the laws of nature. You must try to understand them."

Mon vieux spat out and said: *"Évidemment!"* He turned around and went out. Perhaps he felt that he'd already said too much.

We left the cellar. M. Landèche invited me to his house for a glass of wine. He lived in the near-by town of Pauillac, a sleepy little place of great charm. It was a warm, lazy day. The shades of the houses were drawn, and the streets were deserted as only French small-town streets can be on a hot day in summer, when everybody is inside, having *la sieste*.

M. Landèche lived in an old, cool house filled with Roman statues and dark, old paintings in heavy gold frames. His pride was a Murillo and a Paolo Veronese which his grandfather, an earlier *régisseur* at Château Lafite, had been given by Pope Pius IX.

"Grandfather used to send every year a few bottles of wine to Rome. The Holy Father surely knew what was good. Let us sit down outside in the patio."

The patio was a jumble of old stones, stone benches, and rose bushes. M. Landèche fetched an old bottle and two glasses. He filled them less than half, held his glass toward the light, admiring its *robe,* and watching the glycerine tears running down its walls. He sniffed at the glass, inhaled its aroma, swirled it around, took a swallow, and closed his eyes. An expression of supreme bliss appeared on his face. He seemed beatified. When he opened his eyes again, I knew that for one short moment he'd been in heaven.

"Our great 1924," he said at last. "Not quite as spectacular, though, as the 1875, which was the finest vintage ever made in the Médoc. Of course, 1899 and 1900 were also exceptional. Our 1899 was a full, round wine with a splendid bouquet, and a flavor that has been compared to the perfume of cedarwood."

I took a swallow. Yes, it was a fine wine.

"Fine?" M. Landèche looked hurt. "My friend, it's full of life, light, elegant, flavory. It excites and warms you. It stimulates the healthy man and is a tonic for the sick one. Rossini used to say: 'When I drink it, all my senses rejoice: my taste, my smell, my eyes, and even my ears, listening to the clear sound of the glass!' The great Montesquieu, who wrote his essays at the Château de La Brède, not far from here, used to say: 'The air, the grapes, and the wines of Bordeaux are excellent remedies against all diseases.' And Montaigne, as Mayor of Bordeaux, always took a few bottles along to Paris when he went there to get a loan for the city of Bordeaux. 'I have more faith in the eloquence of our wine than in that of my tongue to move the hearts of those gentlemen in the Louvre,' he would say. How right he was!"

No man is born a connoisseur, but with patience and talent you may become one.

MONSIEUR K., SR.

AFTERNOON AT CHÂTEAU D'YQUEM

Monsieur K. lived in a fine old house across from an old park. There was the smell of marble and wood, and the fragrance of wine that seems to hover over the old houses of Bordeaux, whose owners have wisely invested their wealth in fine wines.

Monsieur K. was sitting in the salon as I came in. His armchair was covered with blue velvet, and his head rested on a needlepoint lace, like a gem in the jeweler's case. He was a fragile, white-haired man with a finely shaped head, delicate features, and the hands of an artist. His art was the wine of Bordeaux. In this city, where fake experts don't last long, Monsieur K. has been respected for decades as one of the great artists of wine. I'd known him for years. He told me how pleased he was to see me again.

"Sit down, sit down," he said, pointing vaguely into space with no chair in it to sit on. "I've been trying to decide about the wines that we are going to have with our lunch."

In the adjoining dining-room the table was set up in bourgeois style. Long sticks of white bread, hors-d'œuvres, and olives were already prepared. Several decanters and wine bottles were standing on the buffet.

"Sometimes my wife can't make up her mind what to cook, and naturally I can't make up my mind before she's made up hers. People make much fuss about great vintages and fine *crus* but they pay too little attention to the relationship of food and wines. They commit the heresy of serving older, full-bodied wines before younger, elegant ones. They serve the liqueurish wines of Sauternes, Barzac, Monbazillac, Anjou, and Vouvray at the beginning of the meal. Afterward, of course, all other wines appear dull and as mild as milk. People waste fine wines by serving them with salad, the enemy of wine. The only liquid that goes with salad is a glass of mineral water."

Monsieur K. shook his head in resignation. *Rien à faire,* he said, the world was going to the dogs. People would enjoy wines much more if they would follow the simple rules—rules that have been set by the palate, not by wine growers or professional gourmets. With fish, oysters, other sea food, and hors-d'œuvres, serve Chablis, Pouilly-Fuissé,

Puligny-Montrachet, Chassagne-Montrachet, Sancerre-Sauvignon, Vouvray *sec,* Graves *sec,* Tavel, Hermitage *blanc,* Montrachet, Alsace. With white meat and fowl, serve red Bordeaux from the Médoc or Graves region; Beaujolais and light red Burgundies; Chinon, Arbois, Bourgeuil. With red meat, game, *foie gras* and cheese, serve Pomerol, Saint-Émilion, Néac; Beaune, Pommard, Volnay, Corton, Nuits-Saint-Georges, Clos Vougeot, Musigny, Romanée, Chambertin; Moulin-à-Vent, Morgon, Juliénas; Hermitage *rouge,* Côte Rôtie, Châteauneuf-du-Pape.

"People serve white wines ice-cold when they ought to be moderately chilled," said Monsieur K. "Cold wine never offers its full taste. Even here in Bordeaux some people don't know that red wines need time and warmth to release their flavors. They bring their bottles up from the cellars ten minutes before the meal. Sometimes they place them near the stove. *Ah, mais ça se casse!* The sediments fall down, the wine breaks. A few weeks ago a dinner was given here for some ships' captains. I was asked to select the wines. The following day no one called to commend me on my choice—which was unusual. So I investigated. The stewards had put the bottles into a bathtub filled with warm water to bring them up to room temperature. *Right here in Bordeaux!*"

Monsieur K. put the tips of his fingers together and gave the ceiling a contemplative stare. "People treat wine as if it were a soulless liquid. But wine is a living organism. Its cells act like the cells of a human being. Wine lives even when it seems to be dead in the bottle. Believe me, I've

stopped going out to restaurants. I just can't stand the sight of
a *type* called *sommelier* who wears around his neck a chain
that ought to be tied to his leg. He's a criminal, a murderer!
He swings a fine old bottle as though it were a soft-ball. He's
never heard of the sediments, a sign of maturity and age,
which develop over years of careful storing and must not
be disturbed. He doesn't know that the cork must be drawn
slowly and steadily, without haste or jerking. He forgets to
clean the inside lip of the bottle with a white cloth and to
sniff at the cork. Perhaps he knows that wine bottles are
stored horizontally, and Cognacs and Armagnacs are not,
because they would burn the cork. But does he know what
a wine cellar should be like—clean, dark, well aired, but
without drafts, and in a place that has no street trepidations.
Ah, it is all very, very sad."

He got up, and returned with a file containing charts and
statistics.

"My little treasure chest. Charts for every year since 1847,
giving the exact number of rainy days, the summary of medium temperatures for each month of the year, and the
hours of sunshine. There seems to be a sort of recurrent
parallelism between certain vintages, every thirty or fifty
years. Either they cross one another or they meet in pairs.
The cycles would be almost perfect if the war years
hadn't created disturbances that were not to be expected.
Take, for instance, 1895 and 1945. Both vintages have the
same characteristics. The red wines were full-bodied and
"roasted," as we call it, having been produced from overripe grapes. The wines were sweet, oily, round, and full of

sap. The white wines were sweet, flavory, *savoureux*. Similar analogies exist between 1896 and 1946. Both years produced wines that were harmonious, elegant, deep-colored."

Mme K. came in, a white-haired woman of great dignity, dressed in black. She said lunch was ready. Her husband didn't look up from his charts.

"The wines of 1868 and 1869 are similar to those of 1898 and 1899, exactly thirty years later, and again to those of 1928 and 1929. Always an outstanding year followed by a great one. The years of 1869, 1899, and 1929 have produced wines that are almost strikingly similar: round and oily, soft, yet with lots of life, near-perfect wines. Note too that the 1898 and 1928 are still growing in quality, while the 1899 and 1929 are either at their height or declining. *Ça c'est vraiment curieux!* The charts don't lie, my friend. With the help of those charts my father would be able to forecast the quality of the future harvest as early as June. He made a fortune that way. He made only one mistake, in 1858, when he didn't know that mildew can ruin a harvest. Almost broke him."

Monsieur K. gazed fondly at a framed portrait on the wall. It showed a sumptuously bearded gentleman radiating the confidence that comes from having remade one's fortune after being broke. Mme K. took advantage of the momentary lull in her husband's monologue to point at the table, with the desperate urgency of the hostess who knows that the roast in the oven is getting drier every moment. As we walked into the dining-room, Monsieur K. was reminiscing about his father.

"He used to say: 'No man is born a connoisseur, but with patience and talent you may become one.' But it takes years, many years. When I was four years old, my father let me taste some wine and asked me how I liked it. There never was a meal in our house when wine wasn't discussed at great length. You can't help learning that way."

Lunch was good and the wines were superb. There was a Margaux 1900 which Monsieur K. had decanted a few hours earlier, holding the neck of the bottle against a candle to see when the sediments started to come and it was time to stop pouring. The Margaux was served with a Roquefort that was not too strong in flavor.

Monsieur K. gazed thoughtfully at the robe of the wine, holding his glass against the light. "This Margaux gives me great satisfaction. Back in 1901, when I was a young man, my father and a friend of his went out to the vineyards of Margaux to buy some of the young wines. I was permitted to go along. They tasted this wine, which was then only a few months old. Must have been quite hard on the tongue. My father's friend said: '*Il est bon mais trop gentil.*' My father shook his head. 'This wine will be great in fifty years,' he said. How right he was! Papa was a genius."

The wines of Margaux have always been my favorites for their delicacy, aroma, and beautiful color, and this Margaux seemed to combine all their virtues. It was round and flavory, soft and elegant, truly a great wine.

"I gave a little dinner a few months ago for twelve friends," Monsieur K. said. "All of them are lovers of fine wine. I served them a Château Guiraud 1875, without showing them the label. They were to guess the origin and the year. All came pretty close. Some voted for the Pontet-Canet 1875, and some thought it was a Léoville-LasCases 1871. Everybody agreed that the 1875 was *une exquise jeune fille.* Still, these days some people make much too much fuss about vintages. After all, there have been only four unforgettable vintages in the past hundred years: 1847, 1875, 1900, and 1929."

Mme K., who, in the tradition of long-suffering French wives, had not spoken up while her husband was holding forth, asked me to take another piece of the *tarte aux fraises.* Her husband poured the wine, a liqueurish Château d'Yquem 1899.

"No matter what some people may say about Bordeaux wines, they can't say anything about Yquem," he said, with some asperity. "Yquem is perfection. I chose this wine forty-five years ago. It was the month before we got married."

"That was the Armagnac," said Mme K.

"Oh, yes. I'm sorry, *ma chère.* It was the Armagnac. We will have it later. It is pure perfume—all the sharpness and fire have gone." He gently placed his hand on the arm of his wife. "Forty-five years isn't so long in Bordeaux. At a banquet at Château d'Yquem, a few months ago, they had twenty couples, each of them older than eighty years. . . ." He looked at me and said: "Why don't we drive out to Yquem? The afternoon is pleasant."

An hour later we arrived at the gravel-covered court-yard of Château d'Yquem, a large, medieval stone structure with walls a yard thick and a round watchtower overlooking the gentle slopes of the Sauternes district. A heavy-set, elderly man with a blue beret and heavy bedroom slippers welcomed us. He seemed to be a friend of Monsieur K., who introduced M. Henriot, the *régisseur.* It must be true, as they say in Bordeaux, that people take on the color of the wine that they "work" and drink. M. Landèche's face had had the reddish color of the grapes of Château Lafite-Rothschild. And M. Henriot's hue reflected the golden glow of the wines of Château d'Yquem.

We walked past the administration buildings inside the courtyard. A white-haired patriarch in bedroom slippers came out and vigorously shook hands with Monsieur K. He was the château's bookkeeper and had been employed here fifty-nine years.

"I came in 1893," he said, and rubbed his hands. He seemed none the worse for wear. "It was a golden age. A bottle of Château Yquem cost fifty sous."

"Fifty *gold* sous," Monsieur K. explained.

"Yes," said the bookkeeper. "How easy it was to keep books! Today one needs so much space to write down all the large figures. Did the gentlemen taste our new wine, Léopold?"

"I was just going to take them there," said M. Henriot. "Why don't you come along?"

We walked over a graveled path. In front of a small house a parchment-faced, toothless woman was knitting.

"She was ninety-three last Easter," said the bookkeeper. "Last year, at the dance that Monsieur le Marquis gives at the end of the harvest, she was dancing with me and the other young men. She has her glass of Yquem every night after dinner."

"Maybe a couple of glasses," said M. Henriot. The young men smiled and Monsieur K. clucked his tongue appreciatively.

Presently we were in the cellar. I saw rows of barrels of wine forming straight lines, like soldiers at a parade. M. Henriot, moving about silently in his heavy slippers, brought us samples. The one-year-old wine was still somewhat dry and rough-cornered, but the two-year-old was sweet and luscious, and already had the peculiar flavor of Yquem. I took a swallow, and then I drank up my glass.

M. Henriot chuckled. *"Doucement, doucement,"* he said. "This wine is made of overripe grapes. *La pourriture noble,* we call it. It contains more alcohol than any of the red wines in the Médoc. Ah, our wonderful, wonderful Sauternes!"

His face was brightened up by the supreme bliss that I had noticed earlier on M. Landèche's and Monsieur K.'s faces when they tasted *their* wines. "Isn't it a ray of sunshine, caught in the glass—a bowl of liquid gold?"

We moved to another barrel, and then to the one behind, sampling more wines. A mood of contentment seemed to settle down over the cellar, and us. The old bookkeeper talked of the Cardinal de Sourdis, an archbishop of Bordeaux in the seventeenth century, who had greeted a bottle of Sauternes with the words: *"Je te salue, oh, roi des vins,"* and Monsieur K. sat on a barrel, dangling his thin legs, quoting Baudelaire,

J'allumerai les yeux de ta femme ravie,
A ton fils je rendrai sa force et ses couleurs. . . .

From the château's chapel came the sound of the Angelus bell. Through the open door of the cellar I saw the sun go down behind the softly rounded slopes of Sauternes with their rows of Semillon and Sauvignon vines. The sky took on the golden glow of the liquid in my glass, and the air had a mellow fragrance. M. Henriot shuffled around in his slippers, refilling our glasses with the liquid gold of Yquem.

Di Baus farien ma capitado ...   MISTRAL

PROVENCE WITHOUT
GARLIC

I HAVE my doubts about newly discovered, "sensational" restaurants. Too often the place turns out to be sensational only because of the overdose of garlic the chef has put into something whimsically called *Provençal,* or because the lights are turned off, or on—I don't remember which—while *crêpes Suzette* are being served.

I was more doubtful than ever when a friend from Boston told me of a "wonderful" restaurant in Les-Baux-en-Provence, France, called L'Oustau de Baumanière. Epicureanism is not a prominent Bostonian virtue. I wrote the address in my book and gave no further thought to it.

A few months later, one morning in spring, I happened to be in the Provence, aboard the northbound Marseille-Paris express, after a long, arduous, and gastronomically unrewarding trip through Africa. I began to think wistfully of a good French table. Then I remembered the address my Bostonian friend had given to me.

I asked the train conductor where to get off for Les Baux.

He didn't know, and suggested I get off at the next station, in Tarascon. "Nothing is far from Tarascon," he said with Gallic serenity.

At the railroad station of Tarascon the tracks cross in triangular design. By sheer luck, the Marseille express did not run into the Paris *Rapide*. Tarascon is a sleepy Roman town with withered ruins and gray, sun-filled squares. At the Syndicat d'Initiative, the official travel bureau, a sign said: "Open every morning from ten to twelve unless prevented."

A rheumatic old gentleman was delighted to talk to me. He said he was killing time. He didn't know how to get to Les Baux and suggested that I take *le petit train,* a branch line leaving from a tiny station near by.

"The train goes almost everywhere," he said vaguely. "They'll tell you where to get off. Unfortunately today's train has left, and you must wait until tomorrow. Better ask at the station. The train doesn't always leave at the same time."

A gendarme came in to kill time. He listened for a while and then said: "Why don't you walk to Les Baux? It's only four or five hours."

Obviously, I needed more authoritative advice. I decided to call up the restaurant. I went into the tiny post office, where a young monk was mailing dozens of packages, and put a call through to No. 7 in Les Baux, La Baumanière. After waiting for half an hour, the phone rang and I found myself connected, at the same time, with a *notaire* in Arles, with the *chef de gare* in Avignon, and with a temperamental lady who kept calling me *mon choux.* At last I got on to La Baumanière. M. Thuilier, the *patron,* came to the phone. He would pick me up in half an hour, he said. No bother, no bother at all. He was going to Tarascon anyway to look at a saddle of lamb.

Half an hour later a Talbot stopped in front of the *Syndicat d'Initiative.* M. Raymond Thuilier was a jovial, mustachioed Frenchman who looked as if he'd just heard some good news about himself. He would have been fat for a middleweight champion, but he was rather trim for a chef. He wore a topcoat over his white chef's outfit and explained apologetically that he'd been about to prepare *déjeuner* and that there had been no time to dress. M. Thuilier, it seemed, was that *rara avis,* the owner of a well-known restaurant who actually did the cooking himself.

As soon as we left the old ramparts of Tarascon behind us, M. Thuilier stepped down on the gas. Soon we were going at eighty-five miles an hour.

"I used to drive much faster," M. Thuilier said apologetically. "But I'm getting old."

We traversed the Provence at suicidal speed. I love the

Provençal landscape with its soft colors and deep shadows, the permanent, silky glow in the air, and the omniscient memory of bold warriors and romantic troubadours, but there was no time for thoughtful appreciation. We stopped briefly in the small village of Maillane, where Frédéric Mistral, last of the great troubadours, lived and is buried.

"Pablo Casals came here last year to play Bach at Mistral's grave," said M. Thuilier. "It was Mistral's poetry that made me come here. I'm from Chambéry, in the Savoie, where my parents and my grandparents were hotel-keepers."

The road began to ascend and the lovely countryside became rocky and wild. Presently the rocks grew into rocky hills and the hills became jagged mountains with grotesque patterns, like the eerie moonscapes in Arizona and New Mexico.

"Lots of fennel and thyme here," M. Thuilier said. "The air is too dry to keep our Camembert. They bring it up all *mûr* and within twenty-four hours it's as dry as bread crust."

We reached the pass. The mountains were called Les Alpilles—"the little Alps"—and below us were the bizarre formations of Val d'Enfer, the Valley of Hell, where, according to legend, Dante had found the inspiration for his *Inferno.* Way up on the hilltop, built into the rocks so that it was hard to distinguish the houses from the rocks, was the centuries-old village of Les Baux. *Baux* is a Ligurian word that means "steep"; the mineral later called Bauxite was first found here in 1822.

Back in the thirteenth century the township of Les Baux

had boasted of three thousand six hundred people, but now there were only fifty-six. All that has remained of the glory of the lords and knights of Les Baux is their coat of arms, which shows in the upper shield a cavalier with his bare sword and in the lower a star with sixteen silver rays.

M. Thuilier turned the car off the road. Suddenly, as if the scenery had been switched on a revolving stage, I found myself back in the twentieth century, with its more advanced comforts. There was a swimming pool, a stately stone house, a *patio fleuri* and a wide terrace with comfortable chairs, from where you could look out over the mysterious Camargue country, the plains of the Provence in the rear, and the bluish haze indicating the far-away Mediterranean.

"I fell in love with the place," M. Thuilier said, with the quiet satisfaction of an artist showing his life's work. "There wasn't much here when I came up in '46. A dilapidated, abandoned farmhouse. We had to rebuild the whole thing, but we stuck to the Provençal style and to the old name. *Oustau* means 'house' in Provençal. We are not sure about the origin of the word *Baumanière*. It may be the name of the family that built the house, in 1634. Or it may mean the House of the Black Cave, or the House near the Rock with Easy Access. There was a mill here and a sheep farm. The family of Mistral lived here for some time. Mistral wrote: '*Di Baus farien ma capitado*—in Baux I'll make my capital.'"

An affectionate young police dog rushed up to M. Thuilier and was introduced as Ajax. "When we bought the place with Monsieur Moscoloni, my partner," said M. Thuilier, "we had trouble finding water. We drilled, and after a few months we found enough to fill the pool."

A few people were sitting in the patio and on the terrace, and from the kitchen came the nervous sounds that always mount before mealtime like the tide. M. Thuilier said there was no hurry; he didn't like to hurry; first he was going to show me the house.

There are only ten guest rooms, but M. Thuilier knows the importance of showers, bathrooms, fireplaces, telephones, good beds, and rough towels. There were even screens on the windows. The floor had Renaissance tiles, and above the entrance was a sun clock with an inscription:

A la Teulisso lou Teule
Au Toulissaire lou Souleu.

The vaulted dining-room was comfortable with its big fireplace, Gobelin-covered chairs, and flowers everywhere. Most people were eating outside, but I thought I would rather have lunch here.

M. Thuilier agreed. "It's all right to have a picnic on the terrace—cold meat and cheese and salad—but you can't really appreciate the food outside, with the wind blowing dust on your plate and blossoms falling into your wineglass. I'm going to prepare your lunch. What do you like?"

I never tell a good chef what I like to eat; I eat what he likes to make for me. M. Thuilier was delighted. "So many people come here and order," he said. "They don't give me a chance to show what I can do."

Rodolphe, the headwaiter, was a relaxed young fellow who had worked in Paris and London and wanted to go to America. Did I think it was difficult to get to America and find a job if you knew your métier?

As we talked, a couple sat down at the table next to me, and Rodolphe turned toward them. The man was stiff and unsmiling and wore a small Swiss flag in his lapel. His wife was heavy-set and needed a shampoo. Rodolphe made suggestions. They have a printed menu but rarely bother to show it. There are three or four specialties at the most—not a long list of seventeen dishes, all as impersonal as so many cans of peaches.

"How about some warm hors-d'œuvres to start with?" said Rodolphe. "Perhaps *cervelas truffé en brioche* or a *parfait de foie gras en croûte*?" Afterward he would recommend either the *gratin de langoustes* or the *filets de sole*, both specialties of the house. Then perhaps a *poulet* or an *entrecôte*?

The fat woman started to swallow in happy anticipation. "*Filets de soles* for me and an *entrecôte*," she said. You could almost hear her mouth watering.

"Wait!" her husband commanded. "Waiter, how much are the *soles*?"

Rodolphe kept smiling. "Five hundred and fifty francs, monsieur. A very fine dish, served with *sauce crevettes* and *quenelles* that have been *flambées à l'Armagnac*."

"Too much. We'll have an *entrecôte* only."

"Very well, monsieur. A nice *entrecôte*, with a *béarnaise* . . ." Rodolphe knew his métier.

Three red-faced, hungry-looking Dutchmen came in, shook hands with Rodolphe and with René, the *sommelier,* and ordered even before they sat down. They ordered everything that Rodolphe suggested and would have ordered more.

René brought a flat-bellied bottle, uncorked it with a quick turn of his wrist, and filled their glasses. He is a blond, easy-going fellow—everybody seems to be relaxed at the Baumanière—and told me that he was half Alsatian, half Savoyard. René judged his clients by their faces. If he liked a client, he would do everything for him.

"Monsieur Thuilier is going to make you his *soles,*" he said, with amiable authority. "I want you to try this *Muscat blanc des Alpilles.*"

He brought the bottle, tasted a little in his silver cup, and filled my glass, looking at me expectantly. The wine was light, agreeable, aromatic, like the air above the soil from which the wine came.

Réne laughed. "*Amusant, hein?* One wouldn't think that such a wine could come from this countryside. You must try our red Gigondas later. It comes from a place a few kilometers east of the Châteauneuf-du-Pape. A little lighter and less *brûlant.*"

It was a fine lunch. The *filets de soles* were poached in dry Cinzano and served with a *sauce crevettes.* Any cookbook tells you how to make shrimp butter, which is the important ingredient of *sauce crevettes*—"pound shrimp remains, add their weight of butter, strain through a fine sieve"—but no book could possibly explain how M. Thuilier made his sauce.

Afterward I had a *pintadeau au porto,* with a sauce that was made of the juice of the guinea cock, with port wine and Madeira added. The mixture had been simmering on a low flame for hours. It was delicious.

M. Thuilier had his lunch at my table, a little cold meat and salad. He said he rarely ate a big meal; sometimes he didn't eat all day long. After tasting every dish in the kitchen he wasn't hungry.

"I have a small staff," he said, "an assistant, a *commis,* a *charcutier* who prepares the cold hors-d'œuvres, and a *pâtissier.* Good boys, all of them, but the trouble with the help is that they remember the difficult things and are apt to forget the simple ones. I keep telling the boys that they must never roast a chicken in a very hot oven, and only in its *own* fat. So first thing they turn on the fire and cover the *poulet* with butter. Wrong. The skin gets blisters and even the finest *poulet* from Bresse dries out inside. I put the chicken in, sprinkle it with its own juice, and when it gets gold-brown, I put a little butter on the legs. Thus the juice is kept inside and gently bloats up the chicken."

M. Thuilier asked the waiter for a bottle of Vichy water and said: "A cook shows how good he is when something goes wrong and he's got to show presence of mind. One of my friends in Morocco has a good Arab cook who can copy anything from a recipe but is not able to think for himself. He will lose his head when his *sauce béarnaise* curdles. Silly, what? Easiest thing in the world to make a good *béarnaise*."

Sure, I said. As easy as it is for Jascha Heifetz to perform the Walton Concerto.

"He added hot water to the warm sauce. Of course, it got even worse." M. Thuilier laughed, genuinely amused about such ignorance. "The trick is to add tepid water when the *béarnaise* is cold, and to add cold water when the sauce is tepid. A simple chemical reaction. Did you know that if you serve *fonds d'artichaut* you have to peel the vegetable before you cook it?"

He had another glass of Vichy water. He drinks little wine, not more than half a bottle of champagne a month, and never hard liquor. He never smokes.

"Can't afford to hurt my palate. A chef is good only as long as his palate is reliable."

Being isolated in the mountains, M. Thuilier has problems of logistics and supply. Everything has to be ordered and brought up. The chicken comes from Bresse, the *langouste* from Cap Finistère, the fish from the Mediterranean and from Lake of Annecy in the Haute-Savoie.

"The train leaves there at eight p.m. and gets here at eight in the morning," said M. Thuilier. "Of course, you've got to trust your fishmonger. I buy only the best and I must be sure that I get what I want. I had an argument last week. The fellow knows that I don't want my *rouget* (red mullet) larger than 180 or 200 grams. No *rouget* is worth anything when it's over 300 grams, *hein?*"

I couldn't help wondering what my "gourmet" friends

would say to *that*. They always talk about spices and dressings and sauces and soufflés and forget the basic things—the size of the red mullet, for instance.

"I had the mullets packed in ice and sent them back," said M. Thuilier. "The next time I'll throw them away and look for another dealer. You can't compromise on quality."

M. Thuilier prepares the mullets *en papillottes*. "You put them on vegetable parchment that is well soaked with olive oil. You place a laurel leaf on one side of the fish and a slice of slightly cured pork across the other. You close the paper at the ends like a paper bag and cook the fish in olive oil, for eighteen minutes. You open the paper bag only when you serve the fish. It is served with a sauce that is made like a *hollandaise,* except that you mash *filets d'anchois* into the butter before you let the butter melt."

A petite brunette and a man came to our table and M. Thuilier introduced me to Mme and M. Moscoloni, his partners.

"Léon is from Lyon," said M. Thuilier. "Oh, la la, the Lyonnais! They board the train at Lyon-Perrache station in great dignity, carrying that conservative paper *Le Novelliste,* but as soon as the train has passed the tunnel, they take out *La Vie parisienne,* which they had kept hidden under their coat."

Mme Moscolini said the refrigerator would be out of order for four days. They were enlarging the kitchen for the second time since the end of the war. The Baumanière serves sixty luncheons and thirty-five dinners on week-days; on

Sundays there are as many as a hundred and twenty people. During the winter most guests are French, but in summertime there is a higher percentage of foreigners—British, Dutch, Swiss, Spaniards, and many Americans.

"Americans are beginning to know a great deal about good food," M. Thuilier said. "I hope in due time they will learn that the best dishes are simple dishes. My mother used to say: *'Il faut manger simplement et sainement,'* simple food is healthy food. But simple dishes are often the most difficult to prepare. Take *purée de pommes de terre* (mashed potatoes). The slightest mistake shows up. The potatoes must be steamed, not boiled. The purée must not be too liquid and not too firm. And it must not be allowed to wait. One of the most difficult feats of the *grande cuisine* is a good omelet. But the clients would stop coming here if we served them omelets. They want things that *sound* complicated, *rougets en papillottes au beurre d'anchois* or *caneton à l'orange,* a dish that has never been my favorite. In cooking, as in music, there should be harmony, and duck just doesn't harmonize with oranges. Sometimes we have to remake a dish three or four times until it is just right. Last week one of my assistants prepared a *gratin des langoustes*. The sauce was 'short,' too thick and not clear enough. The client might have been satisfied. I wasn't. I made him remake it three times. You cut down on your profits, but you can't run a good restaurant by keeping an eye on the cash register. Above all, you must never hurry. A few weeks ago a client told me he was in a hurry, could I serve him in twenty minutes? I said to him: 'Of course I realize that

you're in a hurry, monsieur, and I will serve you—a sandwich.' "

"We work too hard here," said M. Moscolini, who had
been listening in gloomy silence. "We should close one day
of the week."

"Difficult," said M. Thuilier. "Restaurants like Pic in Va-
lence and Point in Vienne can afford to close once a week.
There is always some other place near Route 7. But people
make a detour to come up here and they would be stuck.
Have you been at Point's Pyramide in Vienne lately? Ah,
the great Fernand Point! We are old friends. We come from
the same region and were both born in the same year, 1897.
Last year we both got the Légion d'Honneur and Point gave
a special dinner. Served us a whole pheasant, with head and
feathers, but the body was made of *pâté de faisan*. Ah!"

There was a minute of reverent silence. Then we
walked over to the cave to look at some vintages of Château
Lafite, Château Gruaud-Larose, a 1928 Chambolle-Musigny,
a 1929 Charmes-Chambertin. The small cellar has a fine
assortment of Côtes du Rhône wines, Hermitage La Cha-
pelle, and a '29 Châteauneuf-du-Pape. We started to talk
about wines. M. Thuilier compared the Bordeaux to a
grande dame, and the Burgundy to an "exciting mistress."
René, the *sommelier,* remembered a Clos Vougeot '29
which—

I tiptoed away. The sun was setting. I walked up to the
high plateau past a Roman chapel where, an old man told
me, "even the unbelieving feel the urge to kneel down." I

saw a dead city of broken walls, scattered rocks, and trog-
lodyte dwellings, and the tenth-century castle, which Louis
XIII had demolished in 1632, two years before the Baumanière was built.

When I came back, the lights were burning in the patio
and there were candles on the dining-room tables. M. Thuilier was working again. I had a "simple" dinner, a marvelous
gratin de langoustes ("nothing to it," said M. Thuilier,
"once you have the feel of the sauce") and a steak that M.
Thuilier rubs with butter lightly before broiling it over a
hot fire, and butters once more later so the juice will stay in.

Later that night, when I walked up to my room, the moon
was bright and the rocks seemed to be strangely alive. I
thought I was hearing the old Provençal battle cry of the
lords of Les Baux: "*A l'hasard Bauthésard!*" but it was only
the voice of René, downstairs in the patio, telling a guest of
the wonderful bottle of Moët & Chandon 1906 which had
been in perfect condition when he opened it forty-six years
later.

This bouillabaisse a noble dish is—
A sort of soup, or broth, or brew,
Or hotchpotch of all sorts of fishes
That Greenwich never could outdo.

THACKERAY

THE MYSTERIOUS
FISH SOUP

MISTRAL caught the poetry of the Provence, Cézanne caught its colors, and the bouillabaisse caught its taste.

According to the *Larousse gastronomique,* bouillabaisse is "a Provençal dish, made of various kinds of fish cooked in water or white wine, with oil, tomatoes, garlic, saffron, pepper, laurel (bay), and other spices added." This is a lofty definition, wide open to interpretation. The bouillabaisse has become widely known beyond the boundaries of the Provence. As with other regional dishes that have achieved world-wide acclaim, fame has brought no improvement to the original recipe.

The best bouillabaisse of my experience was not served in one of the restaurants along the Riviera, where this fish soup is a time-honored tradition on the daily bill of fare (of late they double the price when lobster is added); or in the swank places, such as Prunier in Paris, Isnard in Marseille, or La Mère Terrats in La Napoule. I had my best bouillabaisse on the fo'c'sle deck of the *Azay-le-Rideau,* in the middle of the Mediterranean. It was made by my friend Étienne-Marcel, a nonprofessional cook.

As a rule, Étienne-Marcel, the parchment-faced carpenter aboard the *Azay-le-Rideau,* was as loquacious as a lobster. But he could get awfully explosive when passengers came to his quarters, where they had no business. They would stare suspiciously at his saucepan, which contained specimens of the entire fauna of the Mediterranean, and ask him what he was cooking there, *pour l'amour de Dieu.*

Étienne-Marcel would stare right back at them and say: "Not that it is any of your damn business, but let me tell you—I would not mind eating my own grandmother, God bless her, if she were properly cooked in white wine and seasoned with garlic, fennel, and saffron." It was his version of a Provençal proverb and silenced even the most persistent kibitzers.

Fishing from a luxury liner is not encouraged by the steamship companies. The only vessel on which I ever saw crew members take their dinner straight out of the ocean was the *Azay-le-Rideau,* a dilapidated Messageries Maritimes boat that had only one funnel and no serviceable lifeboats to speak of. I worked aboard as a musician.

The *Azay-le-Rideau* steamed morosely between Marseille and the French possessions in the Far East, such as Pondicherry, India, and Hanoi, Indo-China. The crew was an odd assortment of misanthropes who would have made a fine cast for a remake of *Mutiny on the Bounty.* At one time or another most of us had served aboard the Messageries Maritimes' floating palaces, *Mariette Pacha* and *Champollion,* but we had misbehaved. We had insulted passengers, both male and female, or been insubordinate to our officers, or—worst of all—damaged company property—mirrors and chairs. So we had been transferred to the *Azay-le-Rideau,* the company's mobile Devil's Island.

The ship's machinery frequently broke down at the most inopportune place and moment—in the Red Sea in July, or in the Indian Ocean during a monsoon. While the engineers struggled with the tired turbines, the deck crew started fishing.

One night in July 1930 we had an unscheduled halt in the middle of the Mediterranean, somewhere between northern Corsica and Saint-Tropez. Étienne-Marcel threw out his net and came up with a catch that would have made a fine collection for a course in ichthyology.

He built a fire in the *mécanicien's* shop, sent for saucepans, soup plates, and various ingredients, and then and there cooked the best bouillabaisse I have ever eaten. It was a glorious meal, made even more memorable by a few bottles of Chablis which two resourceful stewards had been able to procure.

I asked Étienne-Marcel for his recipe.

Shrugging, he said: "Remember just two things about bouillabaisse, *mon petit*. First, never make it for less than a dozen people. Second, never use fish that is merely fresh. Only the *very freshest* is good enough. The secret of bouillabaisse is to blend the different *parfums propres* of all kinds of fish while they still have the wonderful aroma of salt water, algæ, and seaweed."

After that, I ate bouillabaisse several times with Étienne-Marcel in Marseille, where he and his wife lived in a small house overlooking the Bassin de la Joliette. He had his fishing boat in the Vieux-Port and often invited his friends to go fishing with him, after which he cooked his bouillabaisse.

There were a few drawbacks, however. Étienne-Marcel insisted on going out at two in the morning—too early for musicians, who traditionally sleep late. And he expected you to consume vast amounts of wine out there in his boat. At dawn you would come back, cold and tired and hangoverish, and then you had to scale the fish and wash it in sea water. Personally, I should have preferred a pot of coffee, but Étienne-Marcel was contemptuous of what he called "the bad Anglo-Saxon habit" of drinking tea or coffee in the morning.

"The only way to start a new day is with fish and wine," he would say.

We carried the cleaned fish on large wooden plates to his house, where his wife, a big, friendly woman, was already encouraging a brisk fire in the coal stove. It was only a few minutes' walk, but it was much too long for Étienne-Marcel.

"Let's hurry, *mon petit*," he would say. "We want the *very freshest* fish." He was obsessed by the idea and would often tell us how to distinguish "freshest" fish from merely fresh ones.

"Look right into the fish's eyes. They must be clear and round and they ought to stare straight at you. If the fish's eyes are sunken and clouded, don't touch it. The flesh should be firm, the skin shiny, and the odor that of the tide coming *in*. Don't think that absence of odor means freshness. After being washed a few times and iced, most fish give out little odor, but that does not mean that they are fresh. And watch the gills. They ought to be reddish. There are some fish-mongers around the Vieux-Port who are not ashamed to inject the blood of some animal into the gill covers so they will look fresh."

There are as many recipes for the *bonne soupe* as there are varieties of fish that ought to go into it. Étienne-Marcel started by separating the firm-fleshed fish—gurnet, conger eel, *chapon*, dory, *rascasse*, as the French call the hogfish, bass, weever, *boudreuil*, lobster, crabs—from the tender-fleshed varieties such as whiting, *roucaou*, and *saint-pierre*, and that supreme delicacy called *loup de mer* (sea perch), which, according to Étienne-Marcel, is the finest sea fish of all, devoid of all muddy aftertaste. (The finest fish of all is brook trout, fished a few minutes before out of a crystal-clear, glacier-cold mountain brook in the Alps, cooked a few minutes in a boiling court-bouillon with plenty of vinegar, served with melted butter and boiled potatoes.)

Étienne-Marcel would explain why you couldn't cook all fish together. "If you do, either the firm-fleshed fish will be half-cooked, or the tender-fleshed varieties will dissolve."

He cut the larger fish into slices two inches wide, eliminating heads and tails. The small fish he left whole. Then he took one of those deep saucepans that the French call casseroles and put into it three finely minced onions, four crushed cloves of garlic, two peeled, crushed tomatoes, a sprig of thyme, savory, a laurel (bay) leaf, some orange peel, fennel, and parsley. He placed the firm-fleshed fish on top and added half a pint of olive oil and enough boiling water to cover the fish. He spiced the whole with salt, pepper, and half a tablespoonful of powdered saffron, and cooked it over a brisk fire. He removed a stove lid and set the casserole so that the flames licked its sides. This, *too,* was important, said Étienne-Marcel.

After five minutes—no more—he put in the tender-fleshed fish and let everything cook together four or five minutes longer. Meanwhile he prepared one-inch-thick slices of toast with a few drops of oil on each to keep them from getting soggy, and placed them on hot soup plates.

When the soup was finished—the whole preparation lasted no longer than nine or ten minutes—he strained the broth over the toast. Then he arranged the fish on a big warm plate so each of us might choose whatever kind of fish he liked to put into his soup, and sprinkled it with chopped parsley.

On one occasion he wrapped the heads and tails in linen, cooked them five minutes in boiling water, and used this liquor, instead of boiling water, for the preparation of the bouillabaisse.

"Nothing to it," he would say when we complimented him on his masterpiece. "Just be sure to separate the various kinds of fish, and to cook everything on a very hot fire— otherwise, oil and water won't mix."

Speed is imperative. *Bouillabaisse* means "boil-stop."

Bouillabaisse has a lot in common with a Stradivarius violin: everybody has heard of it but no one seems to know what makes it so good. One of the difficulties of arriving at a basic recipe is the mystery of Provençal nomenclature. The same kind of fish may have three or four different names along the thirty-five miles of coast between Marseille and Toulon. Even French ichthyophagists are not too sure about them. Bouillabaisse is called *bouiabaisso* by the Provençals.

French *bouillabaissiers* will argue for days on end about whether lobster or *langouste* should go into a classic bouillabaisse or not (I'm all for it); whether it is permissible to use wine instead of water (yes); whether mussels should be thrown in, as they do in Nice (no comment). And in Paris there are restaurants where the fish is cooked in a mixture of water *and* wine. There used to be places where they put absinthe into the soup to impress the innocent gastronomes from abroad.

Thrifty Provençal housewives cook an eccentric soup called bouillabaisse *borgne* (in Provençal, *Aïgo-saou*) which contains no fish. Here is the recipe: place the chopped white of a leek and a minced onion in a saucepan, fry in olive oil; add a crushed tomato, three minced cloves of garlic, fennel, and orange peel; add one quart of cold water, spice with pepper, salt, and half a tablespoonful of saffron. Add one pound of potatoes, peeled and cut in round slices not thicker than a third of an inch. Cook on a brisk fire until the potatoes are tender, but don't let them fall apart. While the potatoes are cooking, poach five eggs in the liquid that covers them. Strain the liquid over pieces of toast; take out all herbs and spices, arrange the potatoes on a warm plate, and put the poached eggs on top of them. Sprinkle with chopped parsley and serve.

Almost every coastal region of France has its own fish soup. Along the Atlantic Ocean they make bouillabaisse *à la Coran d'Ys,* with white wine *and* Pernod, served over toasted garlic bread. In Normandy they don't use saffron in their fish soup but put in plenty of noodles for consistency. Speaking of consistency, I should, perhaps, mention the *Schifferin-Suppe,* or Sailor-Woman's Soup of the Germans along the North Sea coast, which is prepared with sherry and white wine, and with loads of spaghetti to take the place of toasted bread crusts. And if you ever travel through Bretagne ("the only part of France from where you really see the ocean," as Jean Richepin said), be sure to go to the coast of Cornouaille, or to Pont-Aven, or Concarneau, and order that delicious Breton fish soup called *cotriade*. It is made with potatoes and shallots, and, of course, with all the fish teeming along the coast, and eating it is quite a ritual. You take a bite of boiled fish dipped in vinegar, then a bite of potato, then a swallow of cider. The bouillon is eaten afterward.

Practically everything about the bouillabaisse is problematic—even its origin. Some bouillabaisse historians state that the Carthaginians, across from Marseille on the coast of North Africa, were the original inventors. The good people of Marseille violently reject this theory. The bouillabaisse, they say, was created in Marseille by devout connoisseurs who used to eat it every Friday, and they quote;

> *Pour le vendredi maîgre*
> *Un jour, une certaine abbesse*
> *D'un couvent Marseillais*
> *Créa la bouillabaisse.*

There are stars and stars.   GUIDE MICHELIN

"WORTH A SPECIAL JOURNEY"

Every year the *Guide Michelin*—not exactly a guidebook but a fifty-two-year-old institution highly respected even by skeptical Frenchmen who have little esteem for anything on earth but a pair of pretty legs, a *bifteck,* and a bottle of *pinard*—selects a number of French restaurants and awards them one, two, or three "stars." This selection is no mean achievement. There must be several thousand eating-places—hotels, restaurants, cafés, *auberges, rôtisseries, brasseries, relais, buffets, reserves, terminus, tavernes,* bars, and what not—all over France; no one knows exactly how many there are, since the French take a dim view of cold, committing statistics. France is the only country on earth where you eat well even in small villages and back-road buffets.

("Almost everywhere in France, hotels and restaurants serve good meals and good wines," the *Guide Michelin* states. "Nevertheless, some establishments deserve to be brought specially to your notice. . . .")

To bring the "deserving establishments" to your notice, the *Michelin*'s staff members, agents, and *inspecteurs* travel all year round, strictly incognito from one end of France to the other, eating, drinking, checking up on quality, cleanliness, and prices. These inspectors are full-time, salaried professionals who consider themselves the patriotic guardians of France's gastronomic tradition. By the time they get their coffee and check (no free meals are ever accepted) they start making notes. Every evening they write copious reports, which they mail to Paris.

For its 1951 edition the *Michelin*'s editors picked 675 one-star *bonnes tables* ("a good meal for the district"), 51 two-star *tables excellentes* ("worth a detour"); and—for the first time since the end of the war—they awarded again three stars, to 7 restaurants ("one of the best tables in France; *vaut le voyage,* worth a special journey"). In a three-star restaurant, you may expect, in the words of the *Guide Michelin,* "Memorable meals, redounding to the glory of French cooking, fine bottles. . . . In these restaurants, price has no meaning. . . ."

Three of the three-star restaurants were in Paris, and four in the provinces. They were, in *alphabetic* order, the

Hôtel de la Côte-d'Or (Saulieu, Burgundy), Lapérouse (Paris), La Mère Brazier (Col de la Luère, near Lyon), Café de Paris (Paris), the Auberge du Père Bise (Talloires, Savoie), the Restaurant de la Pyramide (Vienne, Isère), La Tour d'Argent (Paris).

Ordinarily, my itinerary is not mapped out by guidebooks or travel agencies. I go where *I* like to go. Besides, any classification of restaurants is a highly arbitrary matter of the palate. *De gustibus non est disputandum.* And there are other intangibles. You visit a restaurant on a beautiful day with a *ravissante femme* and get a wonderful meal. You recommend it to a friend who goes there with a bore the next week. The weather is bad, he has a hangover and bad news from the office, and it's the chef's day out. Everything is terrible and your friend never forgives you for recommending the place.

But the *Guide Michelin* is the exception to my no-guidebook rule. No other guidebook published in France or elsewhere approaches the *Michelin's* competence, reliability, inside information, and incorruptibility. The *Guide Michelin* people have never been bribed by influence, advertising, or Christmas gifts. The guidebook is offered practically as a public service by the Manufacture Française des Pneumatiques Michelin (manufacturers of tires), which loses thousands of dollars, and gains thousands of customers, every year on the venture.

The *Michelin's* editors know that stars, to remain valuable, must not be handed out as indiscriminately as medals are awarded in certain military circles. Every year the editors and *inspecteurs* deliberate for a full month before making their three-star awards. Even after they bestow stars, they continue a rigorous check on the recipients. They know that there is nothing like publicity to ruin a good restaurant. One star or two may spell the difference between failure and prosperity, since all French motorists and many foreigners in France consult the *Guide Michelin*. If a "deserving establishment" slips, its star goes out in next year's edition, or the place is demoted to a lower stratum. (This happened to one of the three-star places a few months after we'd been there.)

The *Michelin* doesn't pretend to be infallible. "Don't compare the stars in a district with fat living with those in an area less rich in culinary resources. Don't compare the stars of an expensive de-luxe restaurant with those of a little inn where the proprietor serves a well-prepared meal at reasonable prices."

Being French, the guidebook brings up the sordid subject of money once more when it declares: "For the same standard of cooking and comfort (in the same district), the star is attributed to the establishment offering the lowest price."

This is good advice. Any competent chef can prepare a good meal for 3,000 francs; but it takes more than competence to produce one for 700 francs. High prices are no guarantee of high quality. I've eaten lousy meals in some very expensive Paris restaurants.

The *Michelin* winds up with a final plea,

DEAR READER, We do not claim to have listed all the establishments providing outstanding cuisine, nor all those in particularly pleasant surroundings. Our conclusions are the result of mature reflection, following many tests and inquiries by our inspectors. They are, in addition, weighted by the mass of comment we receive from all over the world . . . Despite all our precautions, you may have the misfortune to be served a mediocre meal in an establishment recommended by a star. Please don't hold us responsible. Perhaps you arrived on an off day . . . Don't fail to tell us if such a misfortune should befall you. Your views and suggestions will be welcome; they will add to our information and, if necessary, help us to alter our opinion. . . .

It was a memorable journey. My wife and I shall wistfully remember those glorious meals whenever financial necessities, rationing, war, restrictions, bad cooks, doctors' orders, or dietetic considerations affect our table. By and large, we agree that the *Michelin's* conclusions are "the result of mature reflection." One of the three-star restaurants, Fernand Point's Pyramide in Vienne, deserves at least six stars, in relation to the others, or should be classified *"hors concours,"* as has been done by several French gastronomic juries. And two of them, by the same measure, we found below three-star standard. (A fine French restaurant must have excellent food and wines, pleasant atmosphere, good though unobtrusive service; and it must be *French*. The two restaurants fulfilled some but not all of these requirements.)

We started our gastronomic pilgrimage in Paris, late in September. The air had an edge of sharpness to it, and the smiles of the waiters had the radiance of genuine friendliness. Everybody was fingering the dollar bills and travelers' checks that the Americans had left behind, and everybody was glad that they had gone back to America.

All spring and summer long the Paris edition of the *New York Herald Tribune* had assured its readers, every few days, that "Nearly 4400 Arrive on Three Liners" or "Thousands More Reach Le Havre on *America* and *Île-de-France*." The *Tribune* never bothered to note the departure of thousands of other Americans, creating the impression of continuous one-way traffic toward Europe—an impression confirmed in certain quarters of Paris, Rome, Venice, Cap d'Antibes, Capri, Deauville, Salzburg, Florence, and Garmisch, where the natives are beginning to talk with an American accent, and Coca-Cola signs and facsimiles of Hamburg steak have become part of the local scene.

We like to travel in the off season when roads are uncrowded, rooms plentiful, and service is more personal. We keep away from what is referred to in smart circles as fashionable places. Fashions and places are outlived quickly, and a couple of years hence a fashionable place may again be mercifully quiet and pleasantly unfashionable.

Season or no, you never escape the game of gypping, which is played all year round. There are tens of thousands of people on the Continent whose only purpose in life is the painless extraction of cash from the pockets of the Innocents Abroad. Some Innocents are partly to blame for this by proclaiming that they will pay anything for the best. Europeans consider every American a one-man Mutual Security Agency until proved contrariwise. They are indignant when the guest adds the fifteen-per-cent tip to the bill and ignores the Parade of the Outstretched Hands. In a restaurant you are supposed to leave "something" on the plate, in addition to the fifteen per cent. We would tip for special services rendered, but we did not capitulate before sheer impertinence.

We traveled by car. Ordinarily, we would start out after a cup of black coffee in the morning, propelled by the happy anticipation of the pleasures that awaited us. We would arrive at our destination in time for lunch. In France, lunch is the meal for "serious eaters." One of the most serious of all, Curnonsky (which is the *nom de table* of Maurice Edmond Sailland, elected Prince of Gastronomes), eats a copious lunch every day, but only a boiled egg at night. This has enabled him to spend much of his long life in the pleasant company of *foie gras truffé,* salmis of pheasant, and rich, wonderful sauces.

Two of the three three-star restaurants in Paris are on the Left Bank, overlooking the Seine. Lapérouse—named after a French naval commander who fought gallantly against the British in the Channel, on July 2, 1781—actually dates from the fourteenth century, when the place stood near the poultry market and had a reputation among the finicky poultry merchants who came here for solid meals. The house was once the residence of the counts of Brouillevert, who were made Grand-Maîtres of Waters and Woods under Louis XIV. It has kept its present appearance since the early eighteenth century—a fine old building with wrought-iron balcony railings, winding stairways, the homely smell of dust and old bindings that one finds in private libraries, and with intimate, low-ceilinged *salons particuliers* for two and four people.

The *salons* are decorated with ancient wallpapers—what stories they would tell if they could talk!—and with paintings by Watteau and Boucher, red carpets, and plush drapes. The doors have no knobs. No one can get in from the outside without a key, and the only key happens to be in the possession of a discreet maître d'hôtel. There is a top-secret *salon* with a concealed door opening off the curved staircase. Once a jealous husband combed the entire restaurant while his wife and her lover were in this top-secret *salon*. He didn't find them. The reputation of Lapérouse was saved.

These unromantic, sober days, when people sit in dark rooms not to hold hands but to watch television, Lapérouse's *salons* are less popular with *amoureux* than with fish-eyed officials from the near-by Quai d'Orsay, and with businessmen who have reasons to talk in private. Concerning romance, it's quite a letdown.

Everything at Lapérouse is delightfully old-fashioned. Most waiters have gray hair or none at all. The old kitchen has no streamlined appurtenances featured in brides' magazines. The big black range is heated by coal; there is sawdust on the floor. There are no gleaming dishwashers, refrigerators, garbage-disposers. From the ceiling hang copper pans that have been darkened by the passage of time and by the fine food that was prepared in them. There are big kettles filled with white and brown stock, simmering slowly, making satisfied noises. American housewives would recoil in horror from the doorstep. But remarkable creations of French cooking have come out of this dingy kitchen in the past hundred years.

Lapérouse specializes in the kind of genuine French food that is not to be had in the fancy Paris restaurants along the caviar-lobster-woodcock circuit, where the proprietors complain that you can't make money with *tripes à la mode de Caën,* or with a *blanquette de veau.* Well, M. Roger Topolinski, the third-generation descendant of a Savoyard family that has owned Lapérouse for over a century, puts two plain, genuine, wonderful French dishes on the menu, each day, and the hell with money. We had an *étuvée de bœuf maconnaise* (beef stew cooked in heavy Burgundy) and a *civet de lièvre* (hare stew), dishes which must have delighted Thackeray and Robert Louis Stevenson when they were habitués of the house.

Everybody at Lapérouse's knows a lot about good food. M. Topolinski, a heavy-set, thoughtful, bearded man, also knows a lot about good wines, music, and poetry. He started out as cook and *pâtissier* and his children keep up the family tradition; his son is working as cook in Rouen, and his daughter attends the École Hotelière in Paris. M. Topolinski spends his evenings in a small cubbyhole just off the main corridor, where he writes out the *additions,* takes in the money, hands out the change. There is no cash register. Everything is done by hand. Many of Lapérouse's "classic" recipes were created in the days of M. Topolinski's grandfather.

"Every once in a while we try to modernize our menu," he said to me one evening. "But our habitués don't want to try new things. They come back for the same old dishes, our *rognons de veau Jamais Mieux,* the *poularde poëlée Docteur,* and our *entrecôte Lapérouse."*

M. Topolinski knows that no dish can be better than the things that go into it. He gets choice meat from suppliers who fear and appreciate him as a difficult customer, fine (unsalted) butter from the Charente region, heavy cream from Normandy. In Paris they serve no whipped cream, that fluffy, delicious sweet snow that is a trademark of Vienna. Seems that it takes over forty miles for the cream to get into Paris. French refrigeration being what it is, the cream arrives in Paris half-sweet, half-sour; and that's the way it is always served.

M. Charles Delorme, Lapérouse's *chef de cuisine,* and his staff are justly proud of their *gratin de langoustines Georgette* (*langoustines* cooked in cream and cognac, with mushrooms and tarragon, served with a red lobster sauce, sprinkled with cheese, and baked in a hot oven), and of their *œufs pochés Lapérouse,* prepared in a truffle sauce. But perhaps the outstanding dishes are *la timbale Lapérouse,* and *entrecôte Lapérouse,* "classic" recipes that have retained a very distinctive flavor:

LA TIMBALE LAPÉROUSE is composed of lobster, American style, fillets of sole poached in Chablis with minced shallots, and *quenelles de brochet* (meat of pike, or pickerel, finely minced and formed into tender, finger-shaped dumplings the texture of a soufflé.) The lobster is placed in a pastry shell in the center of a large plate and, around it, arranged like the spokes of a wheel are the fillets and the quenelles, alternately. Reduce the cooking liquor, add fresh butter and a spoonful of *hollandaise,* and finish the sauce. Sauce *américaine* is poured over the lobster, and sauce *vin blanc* over the rest.

ENTRECÔTE LAPÉROUSE is a casserole-sautéed sirloin covered with a thick sauce made with the meat juice, minced shallots fried in butter, parsley and glazed with Chablis. With it they serve *pommes à la crème,* one of Lapérouse's greatest delights: potatoes three quarter boiled in water, in their skin; after they cool off, they are peeled and thinly sliced. The slices are cooked in milk a few minutes, until tender, and at the end two tablespoons of heavy cream and a piece of fresh butter are added and well mixed with the potatoes.

The cellars of Lapérouse are located under the Rue des Grands Augustins. They are old and winding, like a mediaeval dungeon; water trickles down from the ceiling. M. René Pierron, the *chef sommelier,* is an old hand at suggesting the right wine for each dish. There is an impressive list of celebrated vintages.

Unlike other restaurants, Lapérouse never closes. They are open for lunch and dinner, every day of the year. We found it one of the less expensive and one of the finest among France's three-star restaurants.

On the menu of La Tour d'Argent is a red-lettered notice: "*La grande cuisine demande beaucoup de temps,*" "the great *cuisine* demands much time." Nothing is left to improvisation at La Tour d'Argent, which calls itself the oldest restaurant in Paris. Clouds of history hover all over the place like fumes in a wine cellar. When "The Tower of Silver" was founded in 1582, on the spot where it still stands, the gates of Paris were right here, and next to the restaurant was the monastery of the Bernardines. The restaurant was an immediate success and often jammed, but there was always a way of getting a table. A cavalier who had neglected to make his reservation would pull up his horse, walk in, challenge one of the guests to a duel, kill him with sword or lance, and take his place. It is more difficult today to find a table in certain velvet-roped restaurants in New York.

Until the days of Montaigne it was good manners to eat with the first three fingers of the right hand ("Sometimes I am so hasty that I bite myself in the finger," writes Montaigne), but around 1600 a contemporary chronicler recorded with amazement: "The table was loaded with napkins and doilies, and the napkins were changed after every course. While I ate a succulent stew, I noticed four gentlemen who not once touched their meat with their fingers. They carried forks to their mouths and bowed deeply over their plates. Having no experience, I didn't dare do so, and merely ate with my knife."

It was at La Tour d'Argent that covered dishes were used for the first time—not to keep the food from getting cold, but to keep it from getting poisoned. The early menus list such specialties as soup made of almond milk, swans roasted on the spit, and wild goose served with plum sauce, the favorite dish of Cardinal Richelieu, who dined here with his lady friends. During the Revolution the restaurant was looted by the mob, and the sign, showing a crenelated tower over a red field, was burned.

After a suitable interval the place was reopened. George Sand and Alfred de Musset would eat here; Alexandre Dumas was an habitué; Napoleon III brought Marguerite Bellanger along; and Anatole France came with Sarah Bernhardt. There is a letter from Balzac at the office of Claude Terrail, the proprietor of La Tour d'Argent, which says: *"Mon cher ami, j'accepte votre invitation de samedi. Comment m'en défendre? Des plats succulents, des crus fameux, du café qui vous transporte au Orient et du Cognac 1893— tout cela est un régal, pour le goût tandis que vos propos font un régal pour l'esprit."*

In the entrance hall a framed menu, dated June 7, 1867, commemorates a luncheon that Napoleon III of France gave to Tsar Alexander II of Russia and Kaiser Wilhelm I of Germany:

HORS D'ŒUVRE

POTAGE IMPÉRATRICE

SOUFFLÉ À LA REINE

RELEVÉS:

FILETS DE SOLE À LA VÉNITIENNE

ESCALOPE DE TURBOT AU GRATIN

SELLE DE MOUTON PURÉE BRETONNE

ENTRÉES:

POULET À LA PORTUGAISE

PÂTÉ CHAUD DE CAILLES

HOMARDS À LA PARISIENNE

SORBETS AU VIN

RÔTIES:

CANETONS À LA ROUENNAISE

ORTOLANS SUR CANAPÉ

ENTREMETS:

AUBERGINES À L'ESPAGNOLE

ASPERGES EN BRANCHES

CASSOLETTE PRINCESSE

BOMBE GLACÉE

With this Their Majesties had Madère Retour de l'Inde 1810, Xérès Retour de l'Inde 1821, Château d'Yquem 1847, Chambertin 1846, Château Margaux 1847, Château Lafite 1848, and Champagne Rœderer.

The wine cellar of La Tour d'Argent is not less impressive. Behind a wrought-iron gate, under double lock, are cobweb-covered bottles of Grande Chartreuse Blanche 1875 which was made before the owners of the cloisters were driven from their hills near Aix-les-Bains. There are ports that were shipped in casks by the British five times around the world before they were bottled. The steady, slow motion of the sailing ships and the change of temperature helped to age the wine. The oldest bottle in the "museum"— as Claude Terrail calls it—is a Vieux Cognac 1788. There are a few bottles of Fine Napoléon 1805, and of Fine Champagne 1800 and 1813.

Among the rare vintages *not* listed on the wine card are a Château Palmer 1869; Château Latour 1899, Château Coutet 1876; Château Longueville 1857; Château Léoville 1899; Cos Labory 1864; Gruaud-Larose Sarget 1869; Magnums of Château d'Yquem 1890 and Château Filhot 1876. Among the Burgundies I noted: Corton 1895 and 1898; Chambertin 1865; Clos Vougeot 1876; Romanée-Saint-Vivant 1898; Musigny 1904 and 1911; Beaune 1919; Bonnes-Mares 1911.

The dining-room is on the sixth floor. You go up in a small elevator filled with the cool air from the wine cellar and step out into the Old World elegance of a glass-enclosed penthouse. The mantelpieces, oil paintings, stained-glass doors, ornate clocks, Aubusson tapestries, Gobelin-covered chairs, bits of brass and china, and the beautiful woodwork of the Régence period convey the atmosphere of a private residence—the residence of a rich man with excellent taste— rather than the dining-room of a restaurant. It is impossible not to be thrilled by the *ambiance;* I'm sorry for those who aren't. There is no more beautiful dining-room in France.

The large windows open onto a balcony, where you feel as if you were on top of a tower. At your feet is the city of Paris, the Seine, the Île de la Cité, the Louvre and the Invalides, the obelisk of the Place de la Concorde, the Panthéon and the spires of St. Paul, St. Louis, St. Gervais, the majestic contours of Notre-Dame, and, farther behind and a little obscured by the mist, the fairytale cupolas of Sacré-Cœur. Your lunch will cost you plenty, but the view of Paris alone is worth half the check. On warm summer nights they open the large windows and you can breathe the perfume of Paris, that exciting mixture of acacias, gasoline, Pernod, and dried leaves. If it happens to be a week-end, Claude Terrail will call up the Notre-Dame people and ask them to light up the cathedral for your enjoyment.

The restaurant's best-publicized, though by no means best dish is the *canard pressé*. It was premiered in 1890 by the great chef Frédéric Delair, then the owner of La Tour d'Argent. Ever since, a number has been attached to each duck. The records show that close to a quarter million people have ordered the dish, which is a long run for any production. Oddly enough, the preparation has never been permitted to fall to the level of cheap routine. This is the merit of the restaurant's five *canardiers*—duck cooks—a unique gastronomic title. The dean of the *canardiers* was M. Alphonse Delouche, a round-faced, bald-headed man with the dignity of a medieval bishop. M. Alphonse always used the third-person singular when referring to himself.

"One has been here twenty-five years and one is just beginning to learn the correct preparation of the *canard pressé*," he would say. "One of the men has been here eight years. He's still struggling with the basic elements."

The ducks come from large duck farms in the Vendée region, near Nantes, where the soil and the climate co-operate in creating half-wild ducks ideally suited for the recipe. At the age of six weeks the ducks are smothered, to prevent loss of blood, packed in paper and crushed ice, and shipped by rail to Paris, where they arrive next morning. They are roasted twenty minutes in a very hot oven and brought, quite underdone, on a silver platter into the dining-room, where the *canardier* shows them to the clients. This "presentation" is an important part of the performance.

Old-timers still remember the great Frédéric, who made a *formidable* production for his distinguished clients as he cut up the duck. He looked like a composite photograph of Thackeray and Brahms, and he would hold the duck on a big fork in his left hand and carve it in mid-air, with a long, sharp knife. People would stop eating and look on in admiration. The waiters stood by in an attitude of humble prayer. If there was no applause, Frédéric would shout at the waiters and throw out his guests.

The carcass of the duck is put through a silver press and the blood (the "juice") is caught in a special dish. Added to it are the mashed-up raw liver of the duck, a glass of port, a little Madeira, and Fine Champagne, a few drops of lemon juice, salt, pepper, and spices. The sauce is started on a hot fire, which is slowed down after a while. It must have the thickness and color of melted chocolate. The slices of the underdone meat are cooked in the sauce, under constant stirring, for twenty-five minutes, and served very hot from the silver plate. If you don't like your duck pressed, you can have it grilled, roasted with apples or cherries, cooked with oranges or turnips, and even raw, treated in a special, secret way. But there are people who don't like it no matter how it is done, and Claude Terrail admits it.

"When I ask people: 'How was the duck?' and they say: 'I should have liked it rare,' I know they would have preferred a steak," he says.

Our lunch began with *sole Sully,* a creation of the late chef Cathelin, and one of the most elaborately prepared dishes we've eaten anywhere.

If you're audacious enough to try it, you must go to the market and buy fifty (yes, fifty) pounds of sole. You cook the sole for forty-eight hours, day and night, over a slow fire, until the mixture simmers down to one (I repeat, one) pound of a reddish, jamlike *glacé* that contains nothing but the purest essence of sole. Additional fresh fillets of sole are poached in an excellent fish fumet and served with a sauce that contains one teaspoonful of the sole *glacé,* with fresh tomato purée, Noilly-Prat, and *sauce hollandaise* added. At La Tour d'Argent they frown at such vulgar ingredients as cream or flour for sauces.

Afterward we had just a simple meat dish; the finest cut of an *entrecôte* (a rib or sirloin steak), playing a pretty color scheme from light-pink inside to dark-brown outside, served with *sauce Micheline* (pure meat juice plus a little Madeira and port wine) and mashed potatoes.

Ah, those mashed potatoes! I still dream of them when I get hungry. They were light as a soufflé and tasted of fresh butter and fresh cream. People have been impressed by the Tour d'Argent's great specialties; the *quenelles de brochet* (a fish mousse with *sauce Mornay,* with Chablis added, fine mushrooms, sprinkled with bacon, truffles, and tarragon, cooked in a paper bag to keep the juices inside). Very impressive, but personally I think it's far more difficult to make the mashed potatoes the way they make them at La Tour d'Argent. Notwithstanding the recent judgment of the *Michelin* people, La Tour d'Argent will always have three stars, as far as we are concerned.

The original recipes of La Tour d'Argent are kept in Claude Terrail's safe. During the war they were hidden in a neutral country. They are linen-bound notebooks whose pages are filled with the painstaking handwriting of people unaccustomed to much writing. Each recipe was written by the chef who created it. They are not simple, but simplicity never was nor is the *leitmotiv* at La Tour d'Argent. Here are four of them:

FILETS DE SOLE CARDINAL: Sauté four crayfish in a casserole with a glass of white wine and a spoonful of cognac, a little very fine mirepoix, a piece of fresh butter, and finely chopped parsley; season with salt and pepper. Take four fillets of sole, stuff them with a well-seasoned farce of whiting, put the fillets into the (empty) shells of the crayfish, and cook them in an aromatic fumet. Add to the cooking liquor of the crayfish a little fresh tomato sauce. Reduce and finish the sauce with crayfish butter. Place the fillets of sole on a dish and arrange the tails of the crayfish to make the fillets look like crayfish. Garnish and pour the hot sauce on top.

NOISETTES DES TOURNELLES: Cut lamb fillet steaks into small tournedos and sauté them rare in clarified butter. Garnish them with the soubise and glaze in the oven. Arrange on a plate with artichoke bottoms. Drain the butter from the pan, add a glass of Madeira, reduce, add good veal stock, reduce, add butter, season, pour over the meat. (To make the soubise, fry finely chopped onions, add fresh butter and four spoons of a thick Béchamel, season, and finish on very slow fire. Strain through a cloth and finish with two egg yolks.)

POULET DU DUC: Cut a roasting or frying chicken *à la Reine* (in pieces about the size of a quarter) for sautéing; let it repose for one hour; sauté it lightly, without browning; let it cool. Place a piece of butter the size of an egg in a casserole, let it melt, put the chicken in, add about 2 quarts of cold chicken consommé. After the chicken is cooked, take it out and place on a warm plate. Add a pint of heavy cream to the sauce, strain through a cloth, add the juice of a lemon, a piece of butter, and fresh mushrooms and let simmer. Serve very hot with croutons and asparagus tips.

POIRE WANAMAKER: Prepare slices of Genoise (a light spongecake), cover them with kirsch and pear marmalade, place them on a buttered platter, cover each slice with a few pieces of pears poached in a vanilla-flavored syrup. Set them in a timbale case, bake in a moderate oven until the mixture puffs up, top with a purée of chestnuts, serve with a *Sabayon au Kirsch* (a sauce adapted by the French from zabaglione, the Italian dessert).

The Café de Paris originally stood at the corner of the boulevard des Italiens and the rue Taitbout, next to the famous Café Anglais. Both were hangouts of Messrs. Balzac, Baudelaire, Dumas *père,* Alfred de Musset, and several monarchs who came to Paris, incognito, in search of a good time. Most monarchs are gone and the remaining ones have no time for a good time, but the Café de Paris has managed to keep its dignified cachet and is still frequented by members of the international, titled set, and by princes of the stock-market, captains of industry, and oil moguls. It is now located at 41 Avenue de l'Opéra, but in spite of the proximity of the Grands Boulevards there is no demimonde in its noble halls, which glitter with bright lights, bright mirrors, glass flowers, and crystals—a set for a high-budgeted technicolor musical.

Platoons of waiters hover around trying to guess your every whim. The cooking is good but curiously lacking in character and finesse. Everything is done as competently as on most ocean liners and in certain de luxe hotels, but there are no surprises. They make all the good things that one gets everywhere—*filets de sole bonne femme, coquilles St. Jacques au gratin,* lobster Thermidor, lamb chops *aux haricots verts,* chicken croquettes Périgueux.

The cellars of the Café de Paris contain some venerable specimens, a Château Léoville-Poyferré 1864, a Château Latour 1868, and a Château Palmer 1875, the greatest Bordeaux year of all. These bottles cost 2,800 francs, a real bargain.

At lunch-time pleasant calm reigns at the Café de Paris, but at night there is music. Until ten p.m. a five-man orchestra tries to make *Stimmung,* presenting a medley of Balkan and Viennese melodies. At ten they get hold of band instruments and, reinforced by two sturdy trumpeters, carry on a noisy battle with the customers who try to finish their dinner in peace. The customers always lose. Most of them drop in after ten p.m.; if you come as early as nine, you will be regarded a hick. It is customary to take to the dance floor between hasty bites of food. The cooks of the Café de Paris must suffer from a deep frustration, knowing that their delicately prepared dishes are cooling off while the clients execute a hot samba.

We ordered two specialties, *filets de sole Café de Paris,* and *poularde au champagne.* The Café de Paris version of sole is cooked in white wine, served with lobster, American style, and with a sauce made with port wine and truffles.

The *poularde* (capon) in champagne is a veritable production of the *haute cuisine:*

(237)

Place a white pullet of about three pounds in the oven in a covered casserole, with an onion and sliced carrots, an herb bunch, 50 grams of butter, and one glass of dry white wine or champagne. Cook for 45 minutes. Place the pullet on a hot plate. Reduce the cooking liquor, add half a liter of cream, 4 yolks, cook on slow fire. Add salt and pepper. Garnish the pullet with 8 cooked champignons, and 200 grams of cock's combs and kidneys, pour the sauce on the pullet, add 8 slices of truffles and 8 pieces of puff pastry around the pullet.

Our *poularde au champagne* was fine. The music wasn't. I was thinking wistfully of the eating club somewhere in Belgium whose members, I'd been told, were forbidden to speak during dinner so they could truly appreciate it.

We were seated between a group of Americans and a group of French. The Americans ordered dry Martinis and more Martinis; afterward they had caviar, steak with salad, and peach Melba. The French went into a huddle with the headwaiter and decided on *petite marmite*—consommé with boiled beef, chicken giblets, and a marrowbone cooked in a muslin bag. Then they sent for the chef and explained to him, slowly and circumstantially, exactly how the partridge should be prepared, glazed, garnished, and served. It took them almost longer to order their dinner than it took the Americans to eat theirs.

People come all the way from America to Paris anticipating their meal at one of the great restaurants, and when they finally get there, they behave as though they were back home at the corner chophouse. They order cocktails and ignore the maître d'hôtel who is waiting for their order. "Later," they say, and order more cocktails. Then they are indignant when they have to wait a long time for the food.

But French chefs are not used to the hurried tempo of their American customers. They will prepare anything for you but they must have plenty of time. If you want a good meal, order first and have drinks afterward, if you must have drinks. Don't get unnerved by the magnificence of the headwaiter or by the jungle trails of the menu with its violet and red detours hiding the orchids of true delicacies among run-of-the-mill dishes. The right order often makes the difference between a great meal and one that is merely mediocre. Don't hesitate to *discuss* your order with the headwaiter. In a good French restaurant he is not hired to sell you slow-moving caviar at 1,600 francs the portion. He's there to give you his honest advice.

One of the great masters of his profession told me: "We want to know why the guest came here. To take out a friend? To make a business deal? To impress a woman? To eat well? We like guests who are difficult as long as they know what they want. Our heart belongs to the difficult customers who think a long time before giving their order. One bad order may spoil a restaurant for a customer. After all, any restaurant is only as good as the worst meal a client gets there."

First ask for the *spécialité de la maison*. Every self-respecting chef has one. In many restaurants they are written or printed on the menu in red ink. In a decent French restaurant, the "house specialty" is not a dish that the chef "suggests" because if he didn't the food might perish. Rather, it's a dish that has been developed over generations of good cooking. It may owe its origin to an accident; I remember one memorable *specialité* that came into being when the chef wanted to prepare *filet de sole Orly* and had to take whiting because he'd run out of sole. Some French restaurants have built their reputation on a single dish: the bouillabaisse of the Mère Terrats in La Napoule, the ham *en croûte* of Zimmer's in Strasbourg, the *omelette maison* at Joseph's in Paris, the *tripes* at Pharamond in Paris. Many restaurant-owners in New York, Los Angeles and other American cities would be well advised to drop their phony imitations of French, Italian, Austrian and other "specialties" and stick to the great, genuine and unsurpassed specialties of American cooking—sea food, chops, steaks, Hamburger, roast beef, baked ham, good potatoes, fresh vegetables, ice-cream and pies.

From Paris we drove to Saulieu, a small town in Burgundy, by way of Fontainebleau and Auxerre, following the ancient Via Agrippina, or, as it is nowadays called, Route Nationale No. 6. An astonishing number of good restaurants is concentrated in this region: the Hôtel de Paris et de la Poste in Sens, in the Champagne; the Hostellerie de la Poste in Avallon; the Restaurant Aux Trois Faisans in Dijon; the Chapon Fin in the Beaujolais country.

We arrived in front of the Hôtel de la Côte-d'Or in

Saulieu just in time to join the impressive array of automobiles with license plates from all over Europe. People who have been here once always come back.

After the refined luxury of many Paris restaurants, the rustic simplicity of the Hôtel de la Côte-d'Or was refreshing. The hotel was an inconspicuous two-story building with a large wood-paneled hall. The walls were covered with photographs of the owner, M. Alexandre Dumaine, a plump, mustachioed, heavy-set fellow in a white chef's outfit. Next to his likenesses hung the menus he had created for some noted eaters. There was one given in honor of Curnonsky, the "Prince of Gastronomes," which read:

CRÈME DE FAISAN

SUPRÊME DE BROCHETON

FEUILLETÉ DE MORILLES

JAMBON DE SAULIEU RÔTI

GIGUE DE CHEVREUIL

FROMAGES

CRÈME CHOCOLAT

Another menu featured M. Dumaine's *pot-au-feu aux quatre services*—beef, chicken, ham, and tongue boiled *à la ficelle* (tied by a string), cooked in a bouillon in a sealed vessel. This boiled symphony was preceded by cold chicken *gelée à la Marsala,* and followed by *quenelles de brochet, salmis de bécasse,* and cheese.

One wall near the small bar was taken up by a big poster, which read:

CHER CLIENT,

The quality of the products that we use and the care that we devote to the preparation of our dishes assure you of a pleasant and classic meal whenever you are here. . . .

However, if you will notify us in advance, at least the day before, and if you don't arrive too late, you can get, in accordance with the various seasons, and according to your taste:

un feuilleté léger de queues d'écrevisses, un pâté de brochet, une matelote d'anguille, une truite au Chambertin, un bisque d'écrevisses, un crème Saint-Hubert, un jambon du pays aux quatre purées, ou un millefeuille de jambon fourré au foie gras, un ris de veau Nantua, un bœuf à la cuillère, un aspic de crêtes et rognons de coq, un pâté de canard ou de gibier, un lièvre à la royale, un porcelet rôti et farci de boudins blancs et noirs, une poularde des Ducs de Bourgogne, un coq en pâté, un dindonneau Louis XIV ou

l'Oreiller de la Belle-Aurore,

which is one of the most beautiful creations of the *grande cuisine Française.*

We went into the bright, comfortable dining-room. Trays with fruits and cheese were standing around informally. On the printed menu it said: "Give us 45 minutes for the preparation of our *poulardes de Bresse.*"

Mme Dumaine, the wife of the chef proprietor, came to take the order. She is a slim, modest, friendly woman, with the serious mien of a schoolmarm. When she talked about her husband's creations, her eyes lighted up. We ordered two specialties, a *terrine de pâté maison* and a *gratin de médaillon de langouste Cardinal,* which we shared. In a good French restaurant they don't mind if two people share several dishes; on the contrary, they consider it an expression of culinary interest.

Next we shared one of M. Dumaine's masterpieces, called *la poularde cuite à la vapeur d'un pot-au-feu,* which is M. Dumaine's version of "creamed chicken." It is neither poached, poëled, braised, roasted, cooked, nor grilled, but steamed—steamed in the aroma of a *pot-au-feu* inside a hermetically closed large earthenware vessel. The *pot-au-feu* (boiled beef with fresh vegetables) is kept simmering for three hours; then the chicken, with thin slices of truffles inserted between skin and breasts, is placed in a casserole on top of a tripod inside the vessel. For one hour it is left steaming in the aroma of the *pot-au-feu,* which slightly expands the truffled fowl. The result is miraculous, served with a cream sauce made of the fowl's liquor.

Afterward we tried another Dumaine specialty, *jambon de Saulieu à la crème gratiné:* thin slices of rosy ham, cooked in heavy cream, sprinkled with cheese, and baked. Shows you what you can do with ham, cream, and cheese, if you know how. There are other Dumaine delights. He makes *fonds d'artichaut,* with a *sauce d'écrevisses, gratiné,* which is a dream.

Dumaine, a native of Digoin, served his apprenticeship in Dijon and Vichy and at the Café de Paris, under the great chef Mourier. In the twenties he got sidetracked to North Africa, where he worked for the Compagnie Générale Transatlantique's Grands Hôtels des Circuits du Sahara, which at that time had a gastronomic reputation.

"Sometimes the supply truck wouldn't arrive and we were stuck with African mutton," Madame said. "They're still talking about the things my husband would make out of mutton."

In 1931 the Dumaines bought the Hôtel de la Côte d'Or and settled in Saulieu, where Monsieur feels securely surrounded by an abundance of supplies—fine meats and poultry, excellent cream, butter and cheese, and the wines of Burgundy. It's a chef's paradise. On the town square of Saulieu stands the monument of a cow, which, I suppose, gave only heavy cream.

M. Dumaine does all his work himself, with a few helpers in a small kitchen. He lives, talks, dreams cooking and, like all genuine artists, is never satisfied with his work.

"You must be absolutely sure of your technique," he said to us when we'd managed to get him away from his kitchen for a while. "People ask me how do I know that the steamed chicken will be right when we open the earthenware vessel. Well, it's my business to know that it will be right. It's mathematics and chemistry. You know the weight of the chicken, and the heat inside the vessel, don't you? The rest is up to you. If you open the vessel ten minutes early, the chicken will be underdone; if you wait ten minutes too long, it will fall apart."

"A few years ago he was very sick," his wife said. "We

worried a lot about him. Between attacks of delirium he would talk only of cooking. Once he said to me: 'I think I know now how to make a good *coq au vin*.' I said: 'But you've made it for the past thirty years,' and he said: 'That was just practice!' "

Among the many cheeses was an excellent Château Double-Crème, one of the finest of France's two hundred and forty varieties of cheese. The wine card of the hotel looked like a list of stockmarket quotations, liberally sprinkled with such blue chips as Richebourg '34 and '29, Chambertin Clos de Bèze '29, many fine years of Romanée-Conti, back to 1926, and Château d'Yquem 1900 and 1892, at 6,000 francs. We drank the pleasant local wines, a Pouilly-Fuissé "Le Clos" and a Morgan 1950, which cost 300 francs and blended admirably with the food. We left with a satisfied glow and the aftertaste of a pleasant meal. It was four p.m., and M. Dumaine was back in his kitchen, preparing a special dish for the Princess of Monaco who was coming through for dinner on her way to Paris.

From Saulieu we drove to Lyon, crossing the Burgundy, Mâcon, and Beaujolais regions, via Chalon-sur-Saône. It is no accident that the four three-star restaurants outside of Paris which the *Michelin* editors picked for the 1951 edition are either near Lyon or within easy driving distance from that city. Lyon, the gastronomical capital of France, is to French eaters what Detroit is to American motorists. Strategically located between the vineyards of Burgundy, Beaujolais, and the Côtes du Rhône, the fish, game, meat, sausages, and cheese treasures of the Auvergne, Dauphiné, Franche-Comté, and Savoie, and the poultry area of Bresse (where they keep the chickens in coops and force maize down their throats), Lyon—truly a "region of fat living"—has contributed to French cooking more regional specialties than any other French city. In Lyon you may order many menus composed exclusively of local specialties, from *andouilles* and *saladier lyonnais* (made of leg of mutton, chicken livers, hard-boiled eggs, and herring!) to hot *cervelas, quenelles, matelote lyonnaise* (a local fish soup, cooked in Beaujolais), *daube de bœuf lyonnaise* (a thick, seasoned beef stew), *gras-double lyonnais, le gigot de sept heures* (seven o'clock leg of lamb), *le cochon de lait lyonnais, la soubise lyonnaise* (a purée of onions), *poulet aux marrons* (broiled chicken with chestnuts), pheasant with raisins, and so on and on and on.

The restaurant called La Mère Brazier is located on the top of the Col de la Luère, a 2,000-foot hill thirteen miles west of Lyon. A narrow winding road leads up to a spacious, comfortable house, surrounded by a beautiful park. From the open and covered terraces one has a splendid view of Lyon.

Mother Brazier is a heavy-set woman of the rugged pioneer type, with voluminous forearms, the voice of a reformed foghorn, and the mood of a drill sergeant on Monday morning. She came up here in 1928. Four years ago she enlarged the restaurant, which is popular among the well-to-do, well-living bankers and silk merchants of Lyon. Mother Brazier owns a second restaurant at 12 rue Royale in Lyon, also called La Mère Brazier, which is run by her thirty-two-year-old son, features the same cooking, but was awarded only two stars by the editors of the *Michelin,* while Mamma got three. Never underestimate the power of a woman. Mother Brazier learned her art from the Mère Fillioux, another famed name in Lyonnais gastronomy, which is dominated by momism. In Lyon they also have La Mère Guy, La Mère Bigot, and Tante Alice. It's quite a town for the ladies who cook.

Mother Brazier's kitchen is a homemaker's dream: big, airy, white-tiled, streamlined, with shining copper pans hanging from the white ceiling. She showed us her new laundry room, where mountains of freshly laundered linen were stacked up. Everybody at the place seemed to be laundering, cleaning, and polishing, as in a Dutch home the week before Easter.

"We use rough linen on our tables," Mother Brazier said, adjusting her foghorn voice to the bare necessities of polite conversation. "Hell, this is no fancy place with silk and damask. Here we do everything ourselves. Until last year we received no electric current from Lyon. So what? We had a motor and made our own. Damn thing often broke down. Didn't bother us. Everybody pitches in here. The kitchen helpers double as gardeners, and my daughter is the bookkeeper and *une espèce de* maître d'hôtel. When the place gets crowded, we simply phone to the house in Lyon and they send everything up—supplies, silverware, waiters."

There are two menus, priced 1,000 and 1,500 francs. The smaller one features *quenelles au gratin,* the famous pike forcemeat, which a real Lyonnais seems to eat at least four times a week, either homemade or ready-made, plain, with *beurre d'écrevisses, à la crème, en timbale, à la Nantua,* and in many other ways; followed by *volaille demi-deuil,* cheese, and dessert. The larger menu substitutes *melon glacé* and *langouste Belle Aurore* (made with *sauce Cardinal*) for the *quenelles.* That's all. No such nonsense as ordering à la carte. If you want an omelet, or steak, or game, don't bother to come up.

Mother Brazier, whose rugged likeness appears on her menus and chinaware, cooks her chicken (Bresse chicken, to be sure) in a bouillon made with salt, carrots, and herbs, but without onions (which is unusual, onions being the trademark of Lyonnaise cooking). The chickens are larded with slices of black truffles and wrapped in white muslin bags, so they will be cooked evenly from all sides. Three or four chickens are cooked together in large earthenware vessels. Mother Brazier's *volaille "demi-deuil"* (which means "half mourning," because of the black-white effect of the black truffles under the white skin) is served on large plates with the soup, carrots, and boiled potatoes, and with salt, small pickles, and mustard on the side. It is a "simple," fine dish. Everything Mother Brazier does she does very well, but it remains doubtful whether the preparation of two or three fine specialties should put her in the company of the greatest French chefs. Maybe the *Michelin* guys fell for the feminine touch.

We were served by a frail, melancholy waiter who sniffled

and sneezed. It was raining up on the hill, and fog was settling down. The waiter said he was from Nice, where they have sunshine throughout the year and where they cook with oil.

"Here it is cold and everything is cooked with heavy cream and butter," he said. "Goodness, I won't touch boiled chicken, or chicken livers, or chicken soup as long as I live— and I hope to live to be eighty, monsieur. The chicken livers are not served to the clients, so Madame makes a *pâté* out of them for the personnel. Sometimes I think there must be more chicken livers in France than potatoes. And there's so much chicken soup that they give it away to the poor people in town, or we feed it to the pigs here, imagine!"

From Lyon we continued by way of Grenoble and Aix-les-Bains to Annecy, a pleasant, Swiss-like town on the shore of the Lake of Annecy, which is cool, dark, and peaceful like all Alpine lakes. It is highly regarded by ichthyophagists since it is the home of *omble chevalier* or char, a member of the salmon trout family that is almost as delicious as brook trout. The char is very exclusive; it lives near the bottom of the lake, comes up only in the early morning, is hard to catch and even harder to transport, and is in season only two months of the year. There are many ways to prepare it, but the best is *à la meunière,* in clarified butter, which brings out its fine flavor.

We went on to Talloires, a small (population, 239), idyllic village eight miles from Annecy. Talloires is quite a place, gastronomically speaking. Of its six restaurants that are listed in the *Guide Michelin,* one has three stars and three others have one star each—a record. There are two Bise restaurants, the Auberge du Père Bise (three stars), owned by Marius Bise, and the Cottage, owned by his brother Georges Bise (one star). To make matters even more confusing, there used to be the Restaurant Bise, which belonged to the father of the two boys and was famous for the cooking of old Mamma Bise. Both sons learned the métier at home; Georges became a good cook under his mother's guidance, and Marius, a gregarious fellow who knew good stories and good vintages, was the maître d'hôtel. Unfortunately the brothers later broke up and each opened his own place.

The Auberge du Père Bise is a charming, rustic house right on the lake. On beautiful summer days—the restaurant is open only from March to September—people eat on the terrace overlooking the lake. The place should be called Restaurant de la *Mère* Bise, as all the cooking is done by the wife of Marius. He is the maître d'hôtel, still telling good stories and recommending good vintages.

Mme Bise, a shy, modest woman, said to us: "I'm not a great chef like some of my famous colleagues. I'm a craftsman. I've learned to prepare a few things, mostly from my late mother-in-law. After you make them for years, you learn to make them well."

This, we soon discovered, was fine understatement. Mme Bise's modesty is the modesty of a humble artist. There are two menus. The smaller one offers:

PÂTÉ CHAUD FEUILLETÉ—MOUSSE DE FOIE DE VOLAILLE

TERRINE TRUFFÉE—MELON

OMBLE CHEVALIER OU TRUITE DU LAC MEUNIÈRE

OU

GRATIN DE HOMARD NANTUA

POULARDE DE BRESSE BRAISÉE À L'ESTRAGON

RIZ CRÉOLE

FROMAGES DE SAVOIE

FRAMBOISE BISE—PÂTISSERIES—FRUITS

The *pâté chaud feuilleté* (hot pastry in thin layers) is filled with sweetbread, chicken *quenelles* (minced and strained pike), sliced truffles, mushrooms. Mme Bise makes an excellent *gratin de homard;* but the pièce de résistance is her pullet, stuffed with tarragon leaves, braised, finished in a cocotte, served in a cream sauce made of the liquor with seasonings, and reduced. The Savoie is famous for cream and butter. The Bise butter, which comes in large blocks, is an hors-d'œuvre by itself; and the cream is heavy as syrup and goes especially well with fresh raspberries.

The cellar under Père Bise is up to the quality of the Mère's cooking. It's a fine restaurant, and a pleasant one.

It was a memorable journey, but it had its ups and downs. We found other restaurants throughout the length and breadth of France which made us wish that the editors of the *Michelin* would perfect their guidebook by adding a list of places Where *not* to Eat. The list would be appreciated by many Frenchmen and by all foreigners in France, particularly by Americans who don't consider their grand tour of Europe a success unless it includes a sampling of cuisine. (It's plain *food* in the States, but on the Continent it's always *cuisine*—even when it isn't.)

In the glowing accounts of returning American travelers their gastronomic experiences now run a close second to bargain-hunting and flea-marketing, outranking even their educational, sexual or cultural memories. Many return home with an acute sense of letdown and having been cheated. Much disappointment could be avoided by a guidebook that listed the country's *worst* restaurants as well as the best. As one who likes to listen to the subversive temptations of his palate but is constantly bothered by the loyalty checks of his delicate stomach, I believe that a campaign is overdue against the pitfalls of used-over fat.

The list of the worst restaurants must be compiled with no malice toward chefs and headwaiters. I recommend the sound principles of research and evaluation which have made the *Guide Michelin* the best of its kind. Its agents, *inspecteurs,* and editors are well qualified to select the country's worst restaurants, which might be marked with one, two, or three gallstones.

Three-gallstone restaurants are the Country's Worst ("must be avoided even if it takes a special detour"). Two-gallstone places serve Very Bad Meals. In one-gallstone restaurants you'd better use the bicarbonate right with your demitasse. When several restaurants compete, the gallstone awards should go to the restaurant asking the highest prices.

Three gallstones should be awarded to restaurants consistently using bad ingredients, overcharging their customers for phony regional specialties, serving suddenly deceased birds as *"coq au vin"* because otherwise they wouldn't be fit for consumption, and offering decadent fish left-overs with an extra dose of saffron as *bouillabaisse marseillaise.* In this category belong restaurants where pseudo-gypsy fiddlers surround your table before you are at the dessert; restaurants violating the medium standards of cleanliness; and several expensive restaurants in Paris which thrive on the snobbishness and ignorance of their clientele.

Two-gallstone restaurants often specialize in chlorine-treated sea food, serve the overflow of last week as *petits pâtés chauds en croûte,* and offer "exotic" grilled meats on flaming spits while the lights go out. The customer is blinded and fails to notice the third-rate quality of the meat. In two-gallstone restaurants the *sommeliers* serve a dishonest *vin du pays* in straw baskets because this makes it look more expensive. The chefs use sauces not to enhance the taste of a dish but to camouflage its sorry appearance. The *sauce béarnaise* is prepared in advance in big containers and reminds you of lubrication grease.

One-gallstone restaurants often put a smoke screen of garlic around the entire meal and serve hot entrées on lukewarm plates. The Camembert is young and the *langouste* is old. The waiters treat the guests with condescension and go around refilling their glasses right up to the brim. There is no *ambiance.* The amount of the bill is arrived at by multiplication.

(253)

Of the *Guide Michelin*'s seven three-star restaurants only one remained to be visited. From Talloires it is a few hours of pleasant driving to Vienne. All epicurean roads lead to Vienne—to Fernand Point and his Restaurant de la Pyramide.

> I always try to make every meal *une petite merveille.*
> FERNAND POINT

THE FORMIDABLE
MONSIEUR POINT

I SHALL never forget my first lunch at Fernand Point's Restaurant de la Pyramide in Vienne. That was a few years ago; the war was over, and France was slowly getting back to peacetime abnormalcy. My Parisian friends had stopped griping about the black market and rationing and were again discussing, passionately and at great length, the heady mysteries of *la grande cuisine,* which, next to women, has always been their favorite topic of conversation in times of content. My friends were "serious eaters"; they loved truly good food and scorned the snobbism of self-appointed "gourmets" and one-dish amateur cooks. They didn't consider themselves gourmets, but they would confide to each other, with the air of brokers divulging something hot in the market, the addresses of good restaurants.

The finest restaurant in France, and perhaps anywhere, it was agreed by my well-informed friends, was not in Paris. If I wanted to have the epicurean experience of my life, they assured me, I would have to go to Vienne, a town of twenty-three thousand inhabitants in the department of Isère, seventeen miles south of Lyon, at the confluence of the Rhône and Gère rivers. There I would find the Restaurant de la Pyramide and its proprietor, the great, the formidable, the one and only M. Point.

"Ah, Fernand Point!" said one of my French friends with a deep, reverent sigh. "The greatest epicures in France and Navarre sing his praises. He's been given the highest eulogies by the gastronomic guidebooks. France's most famous chefs call Point "the King." His *gratin d'écrevisses* is true perfection. And I once had a *volaille en vessie* there that . . ."

"Point's hors-d'œuvres alone are worth a trip to Vienne from anywhere in the world," someone else said. "He calls them hors-d'œuvres but they are a meal in themselves—and what a meal! There is a *pâté de lièvre chaud* . . ."

"Last year at Point's I had the best lunch I've had since Escoffier left the Ritz," a third friend told me matter-of-factly. This friend was a man of seventy-four years and three hundred and twenty pounds, and he had spent most of the former in increasing the latter with good food. "In short, you must go to Point's restaurant."

I objected mildly that I wasn't too much interested in the "show places" of *la grande cuisine*. France's restaurants are, by and large, the best in the world, I said, and I could see no reason for patronizing fancy establishments when there is such an astonishing number of small restaurants all over the country where one can get a delicious omelet, a succulent *blanquette de veau,* a fine Brie, and a bottle of honest *vin du pays* for the equivalent of a dollar and a half.

"Ah, but Point's restaurant is not a show place," my wise old friend said. "It is a temple for gastronomes who know that *la grande cuisine* must be well orchestrated, that it must be surrounded by careful details, ranging from the temperature of the dining-room to that of the wines, from the thinness of the pastry shells to that of the glasses, from the color of the fruits to that of—"

"All right," I said, "I'll go."

"But it's not a question of whether or not you will *go,*" my friend said. "The question is, will Monsieur Point let you eat in his place? He has thrown out American millionaires and French ex-ministers when he didn't feel like serving them. Only last week a friend of mine called Monsieur Point long-distance and asked him to reserve a table for the next day. That, of course, was a mistake, because Monsieur Point usually insists on being notified at least three days beforehand. My friend gave his name—a *very* important name in French politics, I assure you. Ha! Monsieur Point pretended to be totally unimpressed and kept saying: 'Would you mind repeating the name?' Before long my friend had lost his celebrated poise and could only mumble that he was being recommended by the Aga Khan. And what do you think Monsieur Point said to that? He said: 'And who is the Aga Khan, if I may ask?' "

My friend chuckled. "But I think I can help you out with an introduction. I have a British friend, Monsieur Piperno, who happened to be among the Allied troops that liberated Vienne, and I'll have him give you a letter that will open all doors to you. Any friend of Monsieur Piperno's is treated royally at Point's. But be sure to call Monsieur Point well in advance to reserve your table. And, for heaven's sake, don't think of ordering your meal! You don't order at Point's. *He* tells *you* what to eat."

A few days later I received a note from my friend enclosing an amiable letter of introduction from a Mr. T. H. Piperno, and decided to put in a person-to-person call to M. Point without delay to reserve a table for lunch some day the following week. Finally, after some misunderstandings involving Point's name, my name, and the name of a girl, Denise something, who had a lovely way of yawning and seemed to be the long-distance operator in Vienne, I got hold of a man with a high, querulous voice who said yes, he was Point, and there were no tables available for the next week—or the next two weeks, for that matter.

I quickly said that I was a friend of Mr. Piperno's.

M. Point's voice abruptly dropped several notes as he said: "Oh!" Then he precipitately told me that I might come any day I liked, absolutely, it would be a pleasure, and how about tomorrow? And in whose name should the table be reserved?

I began to spell out my name, but M. Point must have got restless, because he said not to bother with the name—there would be a table. He hung up forthwith, without a good-by.

My friends in Paris had urged me to prepare myself for my monumental lunch by eating only extremely light food, and very little of it, during the preceding twenty-four hours, and I was hungry and cross when my overnight train pulled into Vienne early the following morning. A gentle rain was misting down upon the green trees of the town's miniature boulevards and blurring the outlines of the narrow, gray streets bordered by old, grimy houses and small, dark shops. I set out for the near-by Grand Hôtel du Nord, where, again on the advice of my friends, I had engaged a room.

"You'd better plan to spend the night," they had said. "No use trying to rush away. You have to relax after a meal at Point's."

There were only a few people on the street—pale, stockingless girls who were carrying small lunch boxes, and shabbily dressed men who looked as though they surely had never lunched or dined at Point's.

The Grand Hôtel du Nord, despite its name, was an unassuming establishment that did not indulge in such extravagances as elevators, a bathroom on every floor, and warm water after nine in the morning, but my room was clean and the comforter on my bed was filled with eiderdown. I had a pleasant view of two sides of a square—on one flank the town museum, on the other the Café du Commerce et des Voyageurs and its clients, all of them, I was sure, busy in lively discussions of politics, soccer, and the high cost of living. I washed up, read a newspaper I had bought at the station (politics, soccer, and the high cost of living), and finished my interrupted sleep.

When I awoke, it was getting on toward twelve o'clock, and nearly time for me to present myself at the Restaurant de la Pyramide. As I stepped into the street, I was stopped by a young man wearing a raincoat and a beret and carrying a pipe. He smiled at me like a Fuller Brush man, asked my pardon for his presumption, and informed me that he was Jean Lecutiez, an archæologist who had been sent to Vienne by the Ministry of National Education to dig up the ruins of the houses, temples, aqueducts, baths, and assorted monuments that the Romans left there two thousand years ago.

"I happened to be visiting my friend the desk clerk of your hotel as you came in, and I saw on the registration blotter that you were a writer," M. Lecutiez said. "Right away I told myself that I would make it my business to take you around."

I tried to protest, but he said: "Oh, don't worry—no bother at all. My two colleagues will carry on with the work. There are three of us archæologists here—a very old man, *un homme mûr* (a mature man), and myself."

M. Lecutiez prodded me energetically with the stem of his pipe. "You must realize, monsieur, that Vienne, the old Vienna Allobrogum, was the capital of the Allobroges in

the first century B.C. Julius Cæsar established a colony here.
Later the Romans went up north and founded Lugdunum,
which eventually became Lyon. Naturally, the people in
Lyon don't like to hear this, but it's true—"

"I'm sorry," I said. "That's wonderfully interesting, but
I have a luncheon engagement at—"

M. Lecutiez ignored this interruption.

"Vienne, like Rome, is built around seven hills," he went
on as he grasped my arm and relentlessly walked me away.
"They are Levau, Mont Salomon, Mont Arnaud, Mont
Pipet, Sainte-Blandine, Coupe Jarret, and Mont Saint-Just.
I'll take you up on every one of them. Now, this afternoon
we're going to start with—"

"It's almost lunch-time," I said. "How about an apéritif?
Then I'll really have to run for my appointment."

"Thank you, I never drink," he said. "Would you like to
see the pyramid?"

"Ah," I said. "That's exactly where I'm going. I'm lunching at Point's."

"The restaurant, *je m'en fiche*," said M. Lecutiez. "I mean
the real pyramid, which for hundreds of years was com-
monly, and erroneously, thought to be the grave of Pontius
Pilate. There is nothing like it anywhere. Come, it's no distance at all."

As we crossed the street, a wild bicyclist almost ran us
down, but M. Lecutiez seemed not to notice.

"It was the great French architect Delorme who first
stated that the pyramid dates from the fourth century and

was the domed center of the *spina,* a longitudinal center wall, of a Roman circus, where chariot races were held. Now we turn here, and *voilà!*"

There before us, an island in the middle of the street, was the pyramid, a monument, perhaps fifty feet high, that looks like a giant metronome. Its square base is pierced by four arches. The thoroughfare it stands in is one of the drab, deserted side streets that one sees in so many small French towns.

"Excavations undertaken in 1854 by Constant Dufeu proved Delorme completely right," M. Lecutiez went on, hardly pausing for breath. "We are indeed standing in the middle of what was once a vast Roman circus. It was a big arena, fifteen hundred feet long and . . ."

On the other side of the street, set in a ten-foot wall, was a gate, and beside it a black marble plate inscribed in red letters: "F. Point, restaurateur."

". . . and the chariots must have come from over there," M. Lecutiez was saying, pointing up the street. "They would pass right where we're standing, and then—"

"It's been a very instructive talk," I broke in, "and I am most grateful to you, but I must really go."

M. Lecutiez looked at me with a hurt expression, but I walked firmly across the street toward the gate in the wall. On the left the wall connected with a decrepit three-story building that looked as if it should have been condemned long before the Renaissance; on the right it joined a house that was considerably newer but was rather inconspicuous and in need of a coat of paint.

The rain had stopped and the sun had come out, but even under these favorable conditions the exterior of M. Point's temple for gastronomes presented a modest, unprepossessing appearance. Then I walked through the gate and found myself suddenly, without any transition, in another world.

I was in a lovely garden with clean gravel paths, green lawns, beds of flowers, and a terrace shaded by old maples and chestnuts, and covered with white tables and wicker chairs still wet from the rain. The courtyard walls of the building that I had thought should have been condemned were completely cloaked with ivy, which blended admirably with the beautifully landscaped grounds. To my right was a two-story house—the one that from the front I had thought was rather inconspicuous and in need of a coat of paint. Its garden side was immaculate. The frames of its wide windows were freshly painted, and the whole building looked as clean and spruce as a Dutch sugar house.

I walked up three steps, scuffed my shoes on a mat, opened the big door, and entered the hall of what seemed to be a handsome country residence. On the wall were paintings and an old print of the pyramid bearing the caption: *"Un Monument Antique, Vulgairement Appelé le Tombeau de Pilate."*

A man in a white jacket approached from the rear of the house, greeted me cheerfully, and took my raincoat and hung it on a hanger in the hall, as is the custom in French homes. This feeling of being in a home never left me while I was at Point's. I was ushered into a small, pleasantly furnished salon. The walls were hung with paintings and mirrors, a gold pendulum clock stood on a buffet, and a large glass-topped table sat in the middle of the room. On the table were champagne glasses and a half-empty magnum of champagne, and behind it was standing a huge man.

He must have been six feet three and weighed three hundred pounds. He had a longish, sad face, a vast double chin, a high forehead, dark hair, and melancholy eyes. I couldn't help thinking that one of M. Lecutiez's sybaritic Roman emperors had come to life. He wore a comfortably large suit and a big bow tie of black silk ornamented with a flowery design, like those the eccentric citizens of Montparnasse and flamboyant Italian tenors wore in the old days.

I introduced myself and we shook hands. I gave him Mr. Piperno's letter.

M. Point read it casually and shook hands with me again.

"Sit down!" he commanded with a magnificent gesture. "For the next few hours this house will be your home. I'm delighted you came early. Gives us a chance to talk and drink champagne. Quiet, Véronique!"

On a chair beside him a precisely clipped brown poodle was making hostile noises.

"Véronique belongs to the family," he said. "We also have a daughter, Marie-Josette. *Enfin!*" He filled two of the champagne glasses and said: "*A votre santé!*"

We drank.

"I like to start off my day with a glass of champagne," M. Point said. "I like to wind it up with champagne, too. To be frank, I also like a glass or two in between. It may not be the universal medicine for every disease, as my friends the champagne people in Reims and Épernay so often tell me, but it does you less harm than any other liquid. Pierre—our *sommelier*—and Madame Point and I go to the champagne district every year to buy. And, of course, to Burgundy, too. Last week we visited a great friend, the Marquise de la Tourette, the proprietor of one of the great Hermitage vineyards."

M. Point filled the glasses again. "*Ah, quelle grande dame!* She won't sell her wines in the commercial market. You have to be her friend, and you must literally force her into selling the stuff. She is over eighty, and every day she walks from her château to the church and back. Permit me to drink the health of the Marquise de la Tourette!"

While we were solemnly drinking the health of the Marquise, a man wearing a beret and the light-blue overalls and apron that are the uniform of France's winegrowers and *sommeliers* came in. He had a shriveled face that looked as though it had been chiseled out of a piece of seasoned wood.

"Ah, Pierre," said M. Point. "Monsieur, this is Pierre Chauvon, our *sommelier* and great connoisseur of that ever new miracle, wine."

The old man scratched his head under his beret with his left hand as he gave me his right.

"*Allons, allons, chef!*" he said, embarrassed but quite pleased. "You know a lot about wines yourself, and Madame Point knows even more. I assure you, monsieur," he said to me, "Madame is *épatante*. She is *très, très forte*. When we go to the vineyards and taste the wines, the winegrowers always look at her first. She's better than I am, and I certainly know my business."

He smiled, revealing a few side teeth and almost none in the front.

"Unfortunately, Madame always gets hungry around noon, and once you've eaten, your taste and judgment aren't reliable any more. I don't eat when we're out. Mustn't make a mistake, *chef, hein?*"

"Everybody calls me *chef* here," M. Point explained to me. "Never *patron*. They just won't forget that I used to be my own chef in the kitchen. Now I merely supervise things there, and my wife takes care of the clients in the dining-room. Well, Pierre, why don't we show our friend the cellar? Nothing to be ashamed of, is it?"

M. Point led the way out into the hall, through the kitchen, around a few corners, and down a stairway into a big, brightly lighted wine cellar with earthen walls. It was cool, and the dirt floor was as clean as much sweeping could make it. All along the walls were shelves on which bottles were stacked horizontally. Tacked to the lower left-hand corner of each shelf was a small label giving the place of origin and the vintage of the wine. In the center of the room was a table covered with baskets of fresh fruit—enormous pears, Calville apples, lush peaches, and aromatic *fraises de bois,* wild strawberries.

A roster of the wines in the cellar hung on one wall. It listed two hundred and nineteen names, in four columns. I remembered an article by one of France's leading wine experts which had called Point's cellar "incontestably the first in France." Glancing at random down the second column, I saw Richebourg '42, Romanée-Conti '35, Corton-Charlemagne '38, Les Grands-Échézeaux '42, Hermitage '98, Romanée-Conti '43, La Tache '43, Hermitage la Cour Blanche '06, Clos Vougeot '37, Vosne-Romanée '93, Corton-Charlemagne '42, La Tache '37, Romanée-Saint-Vivant '40, Pouilly '40, Montrachet '29, Richebourg '29, Chambolle-Musigny '21, Hermitage Blanc '70, Marc de Bourgogne '29, and Vire Chapitre '26. Among the Bordeaux was a Château Haut-Brion 1900, magnums of Château Lafite '69, Château Cos d'Estournel '07, and many, many others.

"What a mess!" said M. Point, waving his hands wildly at the chart. "We've always mixed them up—don't know why. Anyway, it's not a bad selection. We have all the great years of Château d'Yquem, back to 1874, and a lot of the fine years of Château Margaux and Château Lafite-Roth-schild. You can see we're crowded in here. I had to rent a place down the street for Pierre to keep his champagnes in."

He pointed to a section of the shelves at my right.

"How do you like our cognacs?" he said.

They were impressive—cobweb-covered bottles of eighty-year-old Otard and *hors-d'âge* Camus, along with batteries of gin, Scotch, apéritifs, and liqueurs.

M. Point slapped his stomach. "Before the war I refused to serve cocktails. Now they bring their own bottles if I don't serve them. My God, after a couple of those concoctions your palate can't distinguish an 1899 Château Margaux from 1949 fountain-pen ink! What's that you have, Pierre?"

The *sommelier* was examining a small bottle of the sort

in which winegrowers send samples to merchants and restaurateurs. "The new Moulin-à-Vent," he said.

"We buy many wines by the barrel—*la pièce*," M. Point said, "and Pierre 'works' the wine, draining it from one barrel into another three times a year. The dregs remain in the old barrel. Pierre knows what he's doing. He wouldn't make a *soutirage*—as the process is called—while a south wind is blowing. The wind must be from the north. Right, Pierre?"

"*Bien sûr, chef.* I make three *soutirages* a year—in January, March, and September. Each barrel of Burgundy contains two hundred and twenty-five liters, and each barrel of Beaujolais two hundred and eighteen liters. When the wine is ready, I bottle it myself in my workroom. I've always done it. Had my own *bistro* in Lyon and would go to Burgundy three times a year to buy wines. Those were nice times, before my wife—"

He stopped and scratched his chin. "Ah, why warm up those old stories? I'm happy here now. I'm sixty-seven, and I hope to stay here until I die."

"*Allons, allons,* Pierre!" M. Point cried, and his high-pitched voice almost cracked. "What kind of talk is that? Go on, tell me how the wine is."

Pierre uncorked the sample bottle and took a big mouthful of the wine. He let it roll over and under his tongue, closed his eyes, and made a gargling sound. Then he spat on the floor.

"It'll be all right in three years," he said with authority.

"Good!" M. Point took my arm. "Let's go up to the kitchen and give some thought to your lunch."

The kitchen was large and cheery, with a white-tiled floor and walls. Copper pots hung from hooks on the ceiling, and silver trays were stacked on broad white tables. The ranges and slicing machines were so highly polished that they looked brand-new. M. Point told me that coal was used to cook everything except pastry, which was baked in an electric oven. At the rear of the kitchen were four refrigerators. Through their glass doors I could see hors-d'œuvres and butter in the first, rows of dressed chickens in the second, fillets of beef and veal tenderloin in the third, and potatoes, bunches of white asparagus, and other vegetables in the fourth.

The room was a busy place. Cooks and apprentices were washing vegetables, cutting meat, mixing sauces, and doing various other chores, but there was a total absence of haste or nervousness.

An elegant gray-haired man in a spotless chef's outfit joined us and was introduced to me as M. Paul Mercier, the *chef de cuisine*.

"Do you like chicken, monsieur?" he asked me. He picked one up from a table. "All of ours come from the region of Bresse. Each is tagged with a silver label and a serial number. We store them in the refrigerator for four or five days after getting them, but we don't freeze them. They do a lot of freezing in America, don't they?"

(269)

"*Malheureux, malheureux!*" M. Point exclaimed, clasping his hands in deep unhappiness. "Of course they do a lot of freezing. It's such a hot country they have to, I am told. But you can't expect to get a good piece of chicken from a freezer. Here we keep everything just above the freezing point."

As he talked, his eyes roved over the kitchen, taking note of every bit of activity. "The main thing about cooking is to see that only the very best ingredients are used, and used as they should be. When you are interested in *la grande cuisine,* you can't think of money or you are licked from the start. Some well-known restaurants are run by men who are maîtres d'hôtel, not chefs. *Malheureux!* A maître d'hôtel wants to make money. A chef also wants to make money—but, above all, he wants to cook well. You must never be afraid of extra work. We have a man here who does nothing all day but press trout *mousse* through fine sieves—three or four times if necessary. And you have to go out yourself and get the ingredients. At six o'clock this morning Monsieur Mercier himself went to Lyon to buy the very freshest strawberries and asparagus he could find in the markets. And butter, naturally. How can anybody expect to cook well without using the finest butter? *Du beurre, du beurre, du beurre,* I keep telling my men—that's the secret of good cooking. The finest butter and lots of time."

I noticed that the bustle in the kitchen had subsided and that most of the undercooks were listening to M. Point with hushed attention.

M. Point solemnly raised his right hand and proclaimed:

"*La grande cuisine* doesn't wait for the client. It is the client who must wait for *la grande cuisine*."

He stopped and looked around the kitchen.

"*Allons, mes enfants!*" he said, clapping his hands. "Let us go back to work."

These days, M. Point said to me, he rarely does any cooking himself, but his people work as well together as the members of the Boston Symphony. M. Point would arrive at the kitchen every morning before seven. He would spend several hours there, brooding, trying, tasting, mixing, experimenting, inventing. Unlike all other good chefs in France, M. Point is not satisfied merely to reproduce or improve the classic dishes of French cuisine. He belongs to the select, small group of kitchen immortals—like the great Carême, Montagné, and Escoffier—who *created* new dishes.

"*Je cherche, je cherche toujours,*" he said to me with a sigh. "I am always searching."

He ushered me through a doorway and took me into a small courtyard. "I want to show you our aquarium," he said.

The aquarium consisted of two square tanks. In one I saw a couple of dozen brook trout swimming around, and in the other a number of crayfish. The water in each tank was kept fresh by a flowing faucet.

M. Mercier joined us. "Are we going to serve Monsieur a trout?" he asked. "*Au bleu,* perhaps?"

"I haven't decided yet," M. Point said.

He turned to me. "So often our clients ask for what they call difficult things, with long and fancy names. People don't know that the most difficult and also the best dishes are the simple ones. What did you cook for your family on your last day off, Paul?"

"A *choucroute,*" M. Mercier said.

"There you are. Here is a great chef, who can cook a chicken in champagne with truffles the like of which has never before been tasted, and what does he cook for himself at home? A *choucroute*—cabbage, delicious soft ham, Alsatian sausage, and very young potatoes—and what could be better?"

He swallowed. I found myself swallowing too. My stomach was gnawing.

"But it takes experience," he said. "What looks easier than to make a *sauce béarnaise*? Butter, egg yolks, chopped shallots—nothing to it, is there? But years of practice are needed before you can do it right. Forget to watch for a single instant and it's gone, finished, lost. Everybody thinks he can fry eggs, and I suppose anybody can, but to fry them so they are soft and mellow throughout, not burned on the bottom and raw on top—*that* is art, my friend. Isn't that right, Paul?"

"Absolutely," said M. Mercier.

"Absolutely. Now, monsieur, let us return to the salon and think seriously about your lunch."

In the hall we encountered a slim, middle-aged woman, charming and well dressed. She was carrying an order pad under her arm. M. Point introduced me to his wife, Marie-

Louise. "Our friends call her Mado," he said. "Our friends think I would be broke if it were not for Mado." His eyes were soft, and tender.

The financial operations of the House of Point have always mystified his friends, since he uses only the finest, costliest ingredients, yet charges prices lower than those of most high-class restaurants in Paris. His friends agree that Point might have gone bankrupt long ago but for his wife. "Mado" Point is one of those storybook wives—charming, elegant, efficient, always smiling, always ready to cheer up her husband. She acts as maître d'hôtel, purchasing agent, wine-taster, cashier, house physician, confidential secretary, and chronicler. Someday, she hopes, she will collect her husband's recipes and put them in a book for posterity's sake. This won't be easy. M. Point takes a dim view of the printed word and keeps "the elements" of his creations in his head, where they are no good to anyone else. Once he watched a new member of his kitchen staff for six months before he decided to confide to him the elements of an important recipe.

Mme Point smiled at me and whispered into M. Point's ear.

"Madame *who*?" he said. "No, no. Tell her we have no table. I don't want her. She smokes before dessert. The last time she was here she even smoked after the hors-d'œuvres."

He escorted me into his salon. The magnum was empty, and he called loudly for another. It was quickly brought in an ice bucket by a frightened young waiter. M. Point watched the youth sternly as he worked out the cork and stopped the flow of foam by pressing a silver spoon over the mouth of the bottle.

"A little trick," M. Point said. "Metal will stop the flow. Don't pour yet, Marcel. Always leave the bottle open in the ice bucket for a few minutes."

He gave a sad shrug and said the silly doctors objected to his drinking too much champagne.

"My legs hurt me," he said. "They claim I have water in my knees. Ignorants! How can it be water when I drink only champagne?"

M. Point was always on the lookout for fine champagne. Sometimes he would drink the private *cuvées* of the owners of the great champagne firms; but he is a discoverer at heart and enthusiastically propagates a small house that produces a good blend. Nothing would please him more than to find an airy *Cramant blanc de blancs,* so light that it seemed only bubbles and bouquet. He loves the honest *vin du pays* of the near-by Condrieu and Juliénas regions. He loves a glass of Beaujolais with his meal.

A drop of champagne had spilled on the tabletop, and the waiter, before leaving, carefully wiped it away with his napkin.

M. Point nodded in approval. "So many otherwise good restaurants in France don't teach their personnel the importance of the attention to detail that makes for flawless service," he said.

I saw Mme Point greeting four guests, and a waiter or two scurrying by in the hall. In a minute a boy in a white apron put his head in the door and said that a M. Godet was calling from Lyon about a reservation, and would M. Point—

For some reason this seemed to infuriate M. Point. He shooed the boy away, went to the door, and announced down the hall in a loud voice that he was about to have a glass of champagne and that he would be grateful if the world would leave him in peace for a few minutes. Then he shut the door, came back, and sat down.

"Too many people," he said. "Vienne is halfway between Paris and the Riviera, and everybody wants to stop over to break the monotony of the trip. Not many Vienne people come here; most of my clients are from the outside world. It's been that way ever since I opened the restaurant, twenty-nine years ago, when I was twenty-six years old."

He poured us each a glass of champagne and looked thoughtfully into his.

"I was born near here, and I always wanted to cook. My father was a chef. A very good chef. He made me start from the beginning—washing dishes, waiting on tables, peeling potatoes. It's quite important to peel them right, believe me. Then I learned to cook vegetables and make soups and things like that, and after that I went to Paris. Remember Foyot's? Ah, they had a great *saucier*! He taught me a lot. And for a long time I worked at the Hôtel Bristol. I came back home in 1923 and bought this place with my savings. It was just a shack and a few trees then. In time Father and I added the second floor and a new kitchen, the wine cellar, and the terrace. We had the garden landscaped and bought the adjoining lot. Father died a few years ago. All this time I was doing the cuisine myself, always learning, always trying to improve a little. I remember the first dish I ever made in our kitchen, *petits pois à la Française* (green peas). I burned them completely. We had a *prix-fixe* menu for five francs, and I would stick to omelets, *navarin, poulet rôti.* Then I began to experiment with new things. The old customers ran away and no new ones came in. The people of Lyon are thrifty; they thought they would have to pay for the new building and the improvements. Word must have got around, for suddenly they all came. In the thirties we would often have as many as a hundred and thirty *couverts.* People would eat outside in the garden and downstairs in the dining-room and upstairs on the terrace. Mado was my *maître d'hôtel.* She never made a mistake. Nothing was ever written down but no one's order got mixed up. I had the phone next to my working-table in the kitchen; I would hold the phone with one hand and prepare the *gratin* with the other. And all the time I would eat well. You've got to love to eat well if you want to cook well. Whenever I stop at a restaurant while traveling, I go and look at the chef. If he's a thin fellow, I don't eat there. I've learned much about cooking, but I still have far to go."

M. Point leaned back, reached into the drawer of a table behind him, and pulled out a leather-bound book with a gold inscription on its cover: "F. POINT, LIVRE D'OR."

"I started keeping this on the restaurant's tenth anniversary, in September 1933," he said. He handed it to me. On page 1 was a short note: *"Quel excellent déjeuner!"* signed by the Aga Khan.

"He knows how to eat well," M. Point said, with a note of respect.

A couple of pages on, the Fratellinis, France's most famous clowns, had written: "Today we have eaten at Lucullus's"; and Colette had written: "The trout was rosy, the wine was sparkling, the pâtisserie went straight to my heart —and I am trying to lose weight! This is definitely the last time I come here—*on ne m'y reprendra pas!*" Farther along there was an unfinished sentence by Léon Blum: *"Si j'en trouve encore la force après un tel déjeuner . . . !"* a drawing by Jean Cocteau, and an observation by Curnonsky: "Since cooking is without doubt the greatest art, I salute my dear Fernand Point as one of the greatest artists of our time!"

Nothing was entered from January 1940 until September 2, 1944. On the latter date someone had written: *"Premières Troupes Alliées—Merci 1000 Fois!"* over an excited, illegible signature. Below was the exclamation *"Vive la France!"* and the signatures of, among others, the Abbé de Pélissier, F.F.I., and Lieutenant Colonel H. C. Lodge, Jr., and Carl F. Gooding, "American jeep driver."

Several pages beyond I came upon a pasted-in letter, dated December 3, 1946, and typed on the stationery of the War Office (Room 900), Whitehall, London S.W. 1. It read: "Mr. Fernand Point: I have the honor to inform you that His

Majesty the King has approved the award to you of the
King's Medal for Courage in the Cause of Freedom, for your
good services in France. . . ."

I asked M. Point about the letter. He shrugged and took
the *livre d'or* away from me and threw it back into the
drawer.

"No time for that. Time for lunch. If you will go into
the dining-room, I'll step into the kitchen and see what can
be done. I've thought it all out."

At the entrance to the dining-room I was taken in tow
by Vincent, the cheerful headwaiter, who led me to a table.
Mme Point came up with the order pad still under her arm.
She gave me a long, speculative glance—the kind of glance
that wives so often give their husbands' drinking companions—and then she smiled and said that she hoped I would
have a nice lunch.

She went off and I looked around the dining-room. I had
the feeling of being in a comfortable home in the country.
The room wasn't so small as to give one a sense of being
cooped up with a lot of other people (there were perhaps
twenty-five or thirty other guests), and not so large as to give
a feeling of mass production. There were pretty white curtains on all the windows. There were flowers inside the windows, but none on the tables. In the center of the room stood
a long buffet covered high with stacks of big, ivory-colored
plates, piles of silver, and rows of glasses. The curtains, and
the plates, and the glasses, and the ashtrays bore the sign of
the pyramid. Against one wall was a grandfather's clock.

When I opened my white napkin of rough linen, it turned out to be almost the size of a small bedspread and exhaled the fragrance of fresh air and of the grass on which it had been dried in the sun.

A waiter placed one of the ivory-colored plates in front of me, and another waiter served me the first hors-d'œuvre, an excellent *pâté campagne en croûte*. French cooks are generally expert at baking an extremely light, buttery dough called *croûte,* but never before had I eaten *croûte* that almost dissolved in my mouth. When I had finished, the first waiter replaced my plate, fork, and knife with clean ones, and a third waiter served me a slice of *foie gras naturel truffé* embedded in a ring of *crème de foie gras.* The ritual of changing plates and silver was repeated after each hors-d'œuvre—hot sausage baked in a light pastry shell, accompanied by delicious *sauce piquante;* a *pâté* of pheasant; crackling hot cheese croissants; fresh asparagus (which M. Mercier must have bought in Lyon that morning), set off by a truly perfect *sauce hollandaise.*

A bottle of wine—an elegant, airy Montrachet—was brought in an ice bucket; the waiter filled my glass half full and gave it a gentle swirl to spread the bouquet. It was a great show and a fine wine. The last hors-d'œuvre was followed in person by M. Point, who informed me that I had now completed the "overture."

"The overture merely indicates the themes that will turn up later," he said. "A good meal must be as well constructed as a good play. As it progresses, it should gain in intensity, with the wines getting older and more full-bodied."

Having delivered himself of this pronouncement, he returned to the kitchen.

Whenever I think back to that lunch, I feel contentedly well fed; the memory of it alone seems almost enough to sustain life. The next course was *truite au porto,* which, the headwaiter told me, had been prepared by M. Point himself; brook trout boiled in water to which vinegar, pepper, salt, and bay leaf had been added, and then skinned, split in half, and filled with a ragout of truffles, mushrooms, and vegetables. With it came a sauce made of butter, cream, and port wine.

It was a masterpiece. I was by then entirely willing to take the word of my friends in Paris that Fernand Point is today France's greatest chef. The trout was followed by a breast of guinea hen with morels, in an egg sauce; a splendid Pont-l'Evêque; strawberry ice cream, made of *fraises de bois* that had been picked the same day; and an array of pâtisserie.

M. Point had chosen as a wine for the guinea hen a rich, full-bodied Château Lafite-Rothschild '24. And at the end of the meal, with my coffee, there was a Grande Fine Champagne '04, the taste of which I still remember vividly.

Later M. Point sat down at my table. The smell of good coffee and good cigars and the sound of soft, relaxed conversation drifted through the room.

M. Point acknowledged my praises with the casual air of a seasoned virtuoso who had expected nothing else.

"We always strive for near-perfection," he said.

The inevitable bottle of champagne in its ice bucket was whisked up to the table by the headwaiter, and two glasses were filled.

"Of course, I know that there is no such thing as perfection. But I always try to make every meal"—he closed his eyes, searching for the right words,—"*une petite merveille.* Now, you won't believe it, but I gave a lot of thought to your lunch. I said to myself: 'Maybe he should have a *sole aux nouilles* instead of the *truite au porto.*' I decided against it. It might have been too much, and I don't want my clients to eat too much. Only in bad restaurants is one urged to order a lot. *Enfin,* you are satisfied."

I said he could probably make a fortune if he opened a restaurant in Paris.

His face darkened as if making a fortune were the worst thing that could happen to him.

"Yes, my friends have been telling me that for years. But why should I leave? I belong here. I like my friends to come and stay with me here. My men like to work for me. We have thirteen men here in the dining-room, and eight cooks and two *pâtissiers,* under Paul Mercier, in the kitchen. Many of them have been with me for over twelve years, and some have been here a lot longer than that. They don't quit, as they do in Paris. Look at Vincent, here. He's been with me for twenty years—or is it twenty-one, Vincent?"

The gray-haired headwaiter filled the glasses again and gave the champagne bottle a twirl as he replaced it in its bucket.

"Twenty-one, *chef,*" he said, giving the chef a fond smile.

"You can't get rid of them," said M. Point. "I could throw Vincent out the door and he would come right back in through the window. No, *mon cher ami. Point ne bouge pas.* Point stays at the Pyramide."

He lifted his glass with forefinger and thumb, holding it at the base. "Let us drink to the Pyramide!"

"To the Pyramide!" I said.

Since then I've gone back to the Pyramide many times, undaunted by distances, borders, and customs guards. Each meal has been a memorable event—one of those rare moments when you know that it *couldn't* be any better. Repetition has intensified rather than dulled the delight of my first lunch at the restaurant.

Fernand Point is incontestably the greatest chef on earth. His perfection, like the perfection of Toscanini, is a blend of hard thinking, much work, and a dash of genius. At the Pyramide nothing is left to chance. M. Point isn't satisfied to use *poulet de Bresse,* the finest chicken in France. He "searches" until he finds the finest chicken in the Bresse region, which happens to be near Vienne. He has suppliers all over the fat French countryside who send him their choice products when they are "in season." I've eaten in his house the finest butter, the mildest caviar, the freshest sea fish, the tastiest sturgeon, the juiciest steak, the youngest vegetable, the daintiest woodcock, the ripest cheese, the best-flavored fruit.

Point's craving for perfection is evident at every stage of

his work. When, after years of "searching," he finally arrived at his own recipe for *mousse* of brook trout—he adds a little *mousse* of chicken livers among many other mysterious things—he wasn't satisfied with the copper sieves that his emissaries had sent him from Paris. Instead he had special, extra-fine sieves made through which the delicate trout meat is strained not once but several times. The cooks in his kitchen work with a degree of perfection I have seen nowhere else outside a Swiss watch factory. When they make a *pâté* of pheasant, they wouldn't think of serving it in a *terrine,* as elsewhere; instead, they stuff a pheasant with the *pâté.* The "presentation" is no mere stage effect, but is calculated to enhance the supreme enjoyment of the dish. At the Pyramide they bake their own bread and *brioches,* and make their own sausages, which are served among the hors-d'œuvres. Point uses few spices and almost no garlic: he maintains that one must never make things too obvious. I remember a meal at which he served a special dish. He was pleased as a kid when no one present could accurately define what it was—a *mousse* made of carp's milt.

In spite of such precautions, many of his recipes have been copied, not too successfully, by imitators. When that happens, Point loses interest in the creation and stops serving it. Instead, he comes up with something new that surprises the finicky palates of France's gastronomes. Not long ago he gave a luncheon to two of France's finest chefs and served them *la Croustade de moules sur fond d'épinards et nappée d'une sauce crémeuse.* "It was not only wonderful to taste but a symphony of color," one of the chefs remembers. The other one told me, "Next to Point we are merely apprentices."

Point sees to it that his creations are properly appreciated. When he serves a delicate dish, such as his magnificent *gratin de queues d'écrevisses,* he asks his guests not to wait until all people at the same table are served. This may be bad manners according to the etiquette experts, but in the gastronomical etiquette of Fernand Point, it would be infinitely worse to let the *gratin de queues d'écrevisses* get cold. Recently he banned flowers from his tables because their scent was distracting. He doesn't approve of ladies who wear too much perfume when they sit down at the table. And he takes a dim view of restaurants that thrive on two or three *specialités de la maison.*

"Every good cook can design five or ten different meals," he said to me once. "But to change your menu every day, and to prepare three hundred and fifty meals a year—that's difficult."

M. Point is a generous grand-seigneur in the old style, who loves the company of enthusiastic fellow eaters. His friends claim that he keeps his restaurant mainly because it gives him a chance to entertain his friends. M. Point is particularly touched by the loyalty of some friends who don't care about his food and come to the Pyramide to see *him.* One of them, a local citizen, is a heavy though not discriminating eater.

"*Il vient ici pour se nourir,*" (he comes here to feed himself), Point says, with a chuckle. That anybody should come to the Pyramide to *eat,* instead of to taste, enjoy, appreciate, dream, amuses him no end.

As you come in, you will be offered a glass of champagne. Hold it with forefinger and thumb, at the bottom, thumb up—never by the stem! Raise your glass and drink to the Pyramide. M. Point appreciates little things like that. He has mastered three words of English: "yes, sir," and "darling," and uses them as indiscriminately as a Hollywood producer.

At the Pyramide I've never been offered the same dish twice. Mme Point has an uncanny memory for menus and remembers what you ate there as long as two years ago. M. Point claims that a meal must be "composed and orchestrated" like a symphony. It should start with light dishes and proceed to heavier ones, with the accent on the specialties of the particular season—whatever best fish, fowl, game, fruit, cheese happen to be available at the moment.

Point's closest friends agree that the best day to eat at the Pyramide is Tuesday. On Tuesdays the restaurant is closed, and Point himself goes down to the kitchen to cook for his family and his friends. He makes what he calls a "simple" dish, a *blanquette de veau à l'ancienne,* or a beef stew in Chambertin (he uses vintage wines for cooking), or his inimitable *gratin dauphinois*—but it's the simplicity and delicacy of a Mozart symphony. The coffee is perfect, which is rare in France, and there are surprises even when the liqueurs arrive. Lately M. Point has been experimenting with flavors. Last spring he placed an empty glass bottle over a small pear hanging from a tree. During the summer the pear grew inside the bottle, as in a glass house. In the autumn Point took the ripe pear off the tree—by that time it had become too large to be removed from inside the bottle —and added pure alcohol. The result is the finest, strongest pear liqueur that was ever caught in a bottle. The label says: "POIRE EST CELUI QUI N'EN BOIT POINT."

One October day, when the leaves of the chestnut trees in his garden were playing the colors of a Cézanne painting, M. Point composed and orchestrated this lunch for us:

PÂTÉ CHAUD DE CANETON AU CHAMBERTIN

BRIOCHE DE FOIE GRAS

TERRINE DES GRIVES AU GENIÈVRE

MOUSSE DE TRUITES

HUÎTRES CHAUDES GRATINÉES

GRATIN DE QUEUES D'ÉCREVISSES NANTUA

PERDREAUX CASSEROLE

CHOUCROUTE, PURÉE DE POMMES

LES FROMAGES DE ST. MARCELLIN ET DE BRIE

GÂTEAU SUCCÈS MARJOLAINE

GLACES PYRAMIDE

MIGNARDISES POINT

POIRES CARDINAL

CORBEILLES DE FRUITS DE LA VALLÉE DU RHÔNE

Cramant blanc de blancs 1949

Condrieu 1950

Juliénas 1949 (en carafe)

(286)

Moulin-à-Vent 1945
La Romanée-Conti 1929
Pommery 1945 (en magnum)

I never asked M. Point to give me the recipe of one of his creations. What's the use? It would be like attempting to play the cello by watching Pablo Casals.

But I didn't finish the story of my first lunch at the Pyramide. M. Point and I had drunk a considerable number of champagne toasts—to France; to the United States; to Escoffier; to Dom Pérignon, who put the bubbles in champagne; to the memorable day when M. Point prepared his first *truite au porto;* and there were many toasts in between "to the Pyramide!" I was beginning to master the difficult trick of holding my flute-shaped glass at its base, with forefinger and thumb. It was with a delicious feeling of lightheadedness and supreme contentment that, in the late afternoon, I paid my bill, bid an affectionate farewell to M. Point, and went out into the garden.

It had rained again, but now the sun was shining. The earth had a strong smell of mushrooms and flowers. I headed back to my hotel.

At the corner of the Cours Président Wilson, I ran smack into M. Lecutiez. He was talking to an unworldly-looking, white-bearded patriarch, who I presumed was the oldest of the three archæologists, but M. Lecutiez introduced him to me as *l'homme mûr,* the mature man. He said good-by to his colleague and seized my arm with great enthusiasm.

(287)

"I've been waiting for you!" he said, waving his pipe happily. "We've got lots of things to do. We still have time to climb at least three of Vienne's seven hills."

I said that he must excuse me, because I was hardly able to make the Grand Hôtel du Nord, having just had lunch at M. Point's.

"Monsieur Point has a very interesting place," M. Lecutìez said.

"Interesting?" I said. "He has the finest restaurant this side of paradise. The Pyramide is a triumph to French civilization, like Notre-Dame or the Château of Versailles—"

"Oh, I don't mean that," M. Lecutiez broke in. "I don't give a damn about the restaurant. I care only for antiquities, you know, and Monsieur Point has plenty of them buried under his place. When they landscaped his garden ten years ago, they came across a couple of first-class Roman sculptures. I wish we could take over Monsieur Point's place and start digging in earnest. I'll bet there are any number of marvelous relics under his wine cellar."